REVISE EDEXCEL GCSE (9–1)

Biology

REVISION GUIDE

Higher

Series Consultant: Harry Smith
Authors: Pauline Lowrie and Sue Kearsey

A note from the publisher

In order to ensure that this resource offers high-quality support for the associated Pearson qualification, it has been through a review process by the awarding body. This process confirms that this resource fully covers the teaching and learning content of the specification or part of a specification at which it is aimed. It also confirms that it demonstrates an appropriate balance between the development of subject skills, knowledge and understanding, in addition to preparation for assessment.

Endorsement does not cover any guidance on assessment activities or processes (e.g. practice questions or advice on how to answer assessment questions), included in the resource nor does it prescribe any particular approach to the teaching or delivery of a related course.

While the publishers have made every attempt to ensure that advice on the qualification and its assessment is accurate, the official specification and associated assessment guidance materials are the only authoritative source of information and should always be referred to for definitive guidance.

Pearson examiners have not contributed to any sections in this resource relevant to examination papers for which they have responsibility.

Examiners will not use endorsed resources as a source of material for any assessment set by Pearson.

Endorsement of a resource does not mean that the resource is required to achieve this Pearson qualification, nor does it mean that it is the only suitable material available to support the qualification, and any resource lists produced by the awarding body shall include this and other appropriate resources.

Question difficulty

Look at this scale next to each exam-style question. It tells you how difficult the question is.

For the full range of Pearson revision titles across KS2, KS3, GCSE, Functional Skills, AS/A Level and BTEC visit:
www.pearsonschools.co.uk/revise

Contents

A small bit of small print
Edexcel publishes Sample Assessment Material and the Specification on its website. This is the official content and this book should be used in conjunction with it. The questions have been written to help you practice every topic in the book. Remember: the real exam questions may not look like this.

Plant and animal cells

Animals and plants are formed from **cells**. Animal cells and plant cells have some parts in common. These parts have particular functions in a cell.

Generalised structures

Generalised animal cell

Generalised plant cell

Cell membrane: controls what enters and leaves the cell, e.g. oxygen, carbon dioxide, glucose

Nucleus: a large structure that contains genes that control the activities of the cell

Cytoplasm: jelly-like substance that fills the cell – many reactions take place here

Mitochondria (single: mitochondrion): tiny structures where respiration takes place, releasing energy for cell processes

Ribosomes (present in the cytoplasm but not visible at this size): where proteins are made (protein synthesis)

cell wall

central vacuole

chloroplasts

Worked example

Name the three structures that are found in most plant cells but not animal cells, and describe their functions. **(4 marks)**

Chloroplasts are the structures where photosynthesis takes place to make food for the plant cell.

The cell wall is made of cellulose, and is tough so that it helps support the cell and helps it keep its shape.

The large central vacuole contains cell sap, which helps to keep the plant cell rigid.

1 mark is for naming the three structures and there is 1 mark for each function.

Watch out! The cell membrane and cell wall are different and separate structures.

Now try this

1 Muscle cells contain more mitochondria than skin cells. Suggest why. **(3 marks)**
2 Plants don't have skeletons. Explain how they stand upright. **(2 marks)**
3 Explain why not all plant cells have chloroplasts. **(2 marks)**

Different kinds of cell

Some plant and animal cells are **specialised** for different functions. Bacteria have a different kind of **cell structure** from plant and animal cells.

Bacterial cells

Bacteria have a simple cell structure. Like animal and plant cells, they have a cell membrane surrounding the cytoplasm. But they do not have a nucleus. These are called prokaryotic cells.

A single loop of **chromosomal DNA** lies free in the cytoplasm. This carries most of the bacterial genes.

cell membrane

Some bacteria have a **flagellum** to help them move.

Ribosomes are tiny structures that make proteins.

Some bacteria have extra circles of DNA called **plasmid DNA**. Plasmids contain additional genes that are not found in chromosomes.

Many bacteria have a **cell wall** for protection, but it is made of different substances to plant cell walls.

Worked example

Many cells are specialised to carry out a particular function. The diagrams show three specialised human cells. Explain how the specialisation of each cell is related to its function. **(6 marks)**

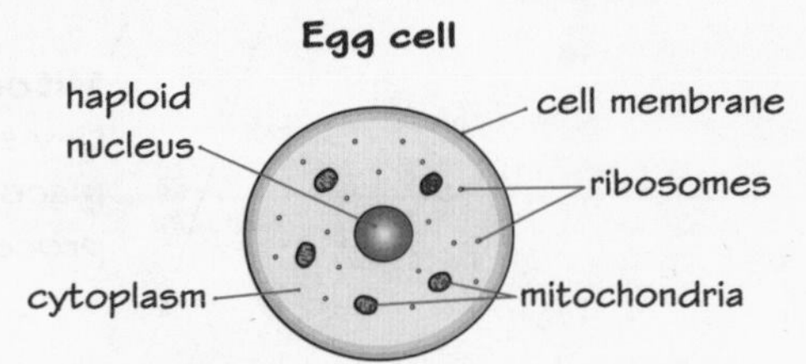

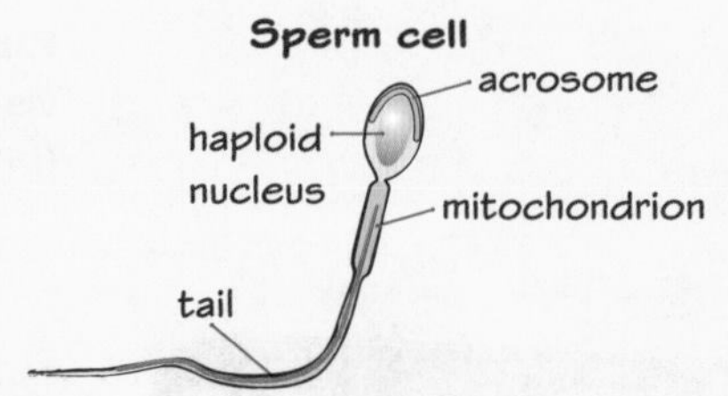

Ciliated epithelial cell

cilia; ribosomes; mitochondrion; cell membrane; cytoplasm; nucleus

An egg cell contains nutrients in the cytoplasm to supply the growing embryo. It has a haploid nucleus that can fuse with another haploid nucleus from the sperm to form a diploid zygote. After fertilisation, the membrane changes so that no more sperm cells can enter.

A sperm cell has a tail for swimming to the egg cell for fertilisation. Many mitochondria around the base of the tail release the energy needed to propel the sperm. The sperm cell has a haploid nucleus that fuses with the egg nucleus to form a diploid zygote. The acrosome contains enzymes to digest a way through the egg cell membrane.

Epithelial cells line tubes, such as the trachea. Cilia move things along the tube, such as mucus. This cell has a lot of cilia to move mucus, containing dirt and bacteria, away from the lungs.

Make sure that you can recognise an unusual feature of a cell, which may be a specialisation to allow the cell to carry out a particular function.

Now try this

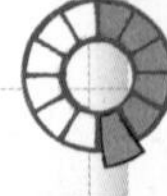

1 Give **one** similarity and **one** difference between a bacterial cell and an animal cell. **(2 marks)**

2 The diagram shows a root hair cell.
Explain how the shape of this cell is related to its function. **(2 marks)**

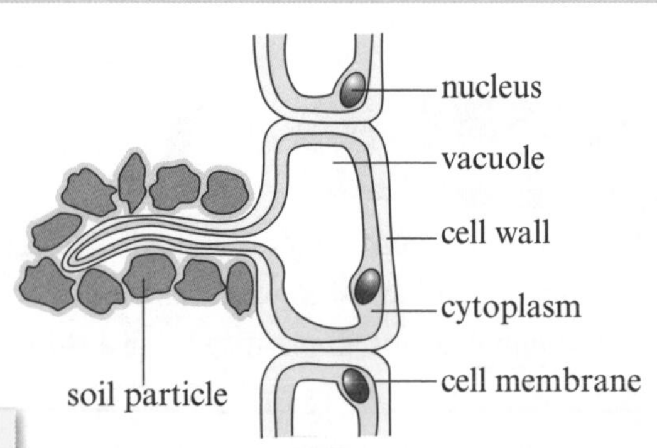

Describe how the shape of the cell is different from other cells, and then give a reason why this is an advantage.

Had a look ☐ Nearly there ☐ Nailed it! ☐

Core

Microscopes and magnification

As microscope technology has developed over time, we have been able to see more of the **structures of cells** and to know more about the **role** of sub-cellular structures.

Using microscopes

Before microscopes were invented about 350 years ago, people could not see the cells in organisms. Magnification enables you to see plant cells, animal cells and bacterial cells, and the structures inside them.

A **light microscope** uses light to magnify objects. The greatest possible magnification using a light microscope is about ×2000.

An **electron microscope** uses electrons to view an object. This makes it possible to magnify objects up to about ×10 million. You can see objects in cells more clearly and in far more detail with an electron microscope than with a light microscope.

Maths skills: Calculating magnification

$$\text{Magnification (M)} = \frac{\text{Image size (I)}}{\text{Real size (R)}}$$

- Measure image in millimetres (mm).
- Multiply by 1000 to get measurement in micrometres (μm).
- If the image has a scale bar, use that to find the answer.

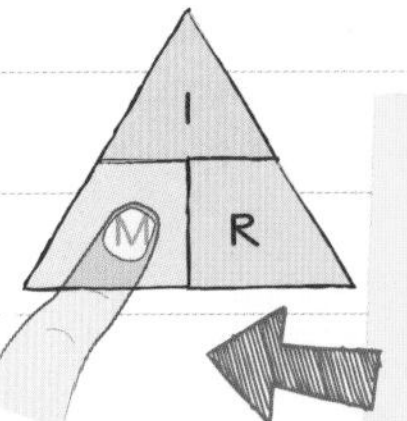

Cover up the term you are trying to find to show the expression required to calculate it.

Worked example

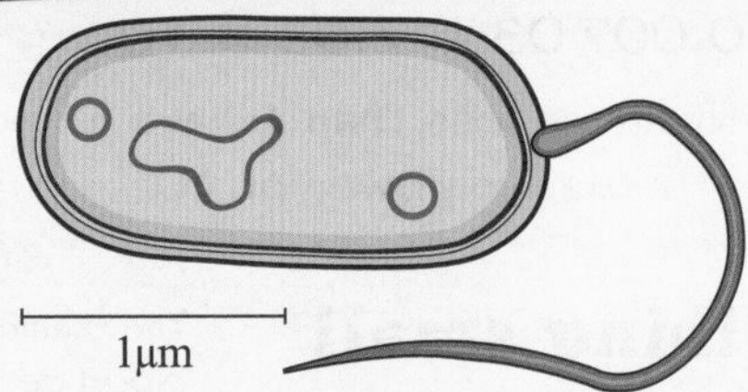

Calculate the magnification of this image. **(2 marks)**

scale bar (image size, I) = 20 mm

$20 \times 10^3 = 20\,000\,\mu m$

so I = 20 000 μm

real size (R) = 1 μm (from diagram)

magnification = I ÷ R = 20 000 ÷ 1

magnification = ×20 000

Worked example

Some cells were viewed by microscope using a ×4 eyepiece and a ×20 objective. Calculate the magnification of the cells seen through the microscope. **(1 mark)**

Magnification of object

= magnification of eyepiece × magnification of objective

= 4 × 20 = 80

The cells will be magnified 80 times by the microscope.

Always show your working in a calculation. Even if you get the answer wrong you may be able to show that you understand the method.

Now try this

A bacterium is viewed under a light microscope using a ×40 objective and a ×10 eyepiece. The image is 1.2 mm long. Calculate the actual length of the cell. **(2 marks)**

Dealing with numbers

Many structures in biology are very small so you will use very small **units of measurement.**

Standard form

Numbers in standard form have two parts.

$$7.3 \times 10^{-6}$$

This part is a number greater than or equal to 1 and less than 10

This part is a power of 10

You can use standard form to write very large or very small numbers.

$$920\,000 = 9.2 \times 10^{5}$$

Numbers greater than 10 have a positive power of 10

$$0.007\,03 = 7.03 \times 10^{-3}$$

Numbers less than 1 have a negative power of 10

Maths skills: Counting decimal places

You can count decimal places to convert between numbers in standard form and ordinary numbers.

3 jumps

$7900 = 7.9 \times 10^{3}$ — $7900 > 10$ So the power is positive

4 jumps

$0.00035 = 3.5 \times 10^{-4}$ — $0.00035 < 1$ So the power is negative

Be careful!

Don't just count zeros to work out the power.

Describing small structures

Smaller structures need smaller units:

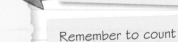

unit	milli-	micro-	nano-	pico-
	10^{-3}	10^{-6}	10^{-9}	10^{-12}

The diameter of a human red blood cell is 9×10^{-6} m

The diameter of DNA is about 4×10^{-9} m

A millimetre is one thousandth of a metre, or 10^{-3} metres

A micrometre is one millionth of a metre, or 10^{-6} metres

Worked example

(a) State how many picograms there are in 1 g. **(1 mark)**

1 000 000 000 000 or 10^{12}

(a) 'Pico' means 10^{-12}

A mitochondrion measures 0.000 002 m.

(b) (i) Write this in standard form. **(1 mark)**

2×10^{-6} m

Remember to count the number of decimal places.

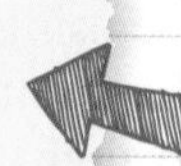

(ii) Write this in micrometres. **(1 mark)**

2 micrometres or 2 μm

Remember that 'micro' means 10^{-6}

Now try this

1 Match the structure to its correct average size.

Protein molecule	Chloroplast	Cell
2 micrometres	10 nanometres	0.1 millimetres

(2 marks)

2 A human egg is 0.000 13 m long.

(a) State the length of the egg in standard form. **(1 mark)**

(b) State the length of the egg in micrometres. **(1 mark)**

3 The bacterial cell on page 3 is 2 μm long. Use this information to estimate the width of the cell. **(1 mark)**

Had a look [ ] Nearly there [ ] Nailed it! [ ]

Using a light microscope

Practical skills You can use a **microscope** to **observe cells**. You can then produce accurate labelled diagrams from your observations (see page 6 for how to produce a labelled diagram).

Core practical

Using a light microscope safely

- Always start with the lowest **power objective** under the eyepiece.
- Clip the **slide** securely on the stage.
- Adjust the **light source (mirror)** so that light goes up through the slide.

If you use the Sun as a source of light, make sure the microscope mirror does not point directly at the Sun as this could permanently damage your eyesight.

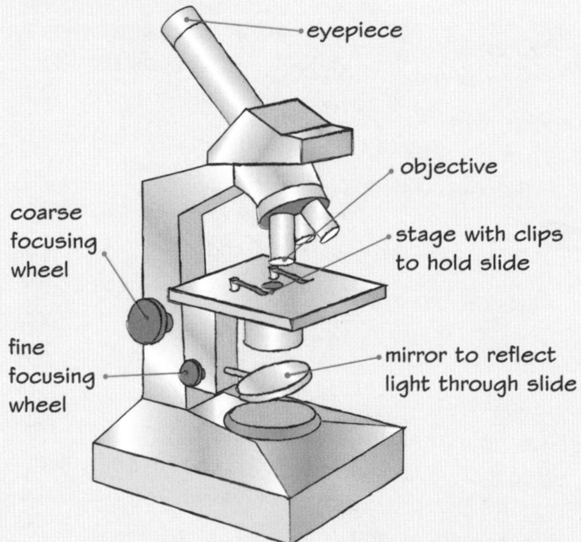

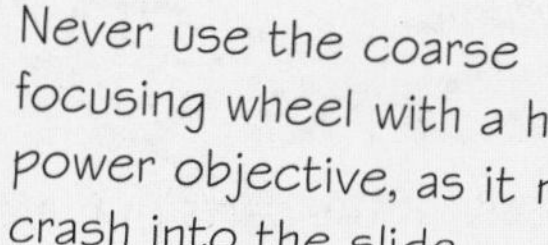

Never use the coarse focusing wheel with a higher power objective, as it may crash into the slide.

- Use the **coarse focusing wheel** to focus on the slide.
- Move the slide so that the cell you will draw is in the middle of the view.
- If needed, move a higher power objective into position above the slide.
- Use the **fine focusing wheel** to bring the cell back into focus.

If you cannot see the part of the slide you need with a higher power objective, go back to using the lower power objective to bring it back to centre view and to focus it before returning to the higher power objective.

Now try this

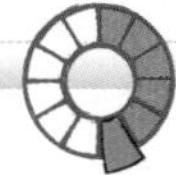

A student is given a microscope slide of a section through a leaf.

(a) Describe how the student should use a light microscope to study xylem cells in the leaf section. **(4 marks)**

(b) The lens closest to the specimen is called the

- [ ] **A** subjective
- [ ] **B** eyepiece
- [ ] **C** objective
- [ ] **D** stage

(1 mark)

Drawing labelled diagrams

Practical skills You can use a microscope to produce **accurate labelled diagrams** of cells and their structures (see page 5 for how to set up and use a light microscope).

Core practical

Aim

To produce a labelled diagram of a plant cell.

Apparatus

- light microscope
- unlined paper
- sharp HB pencil
- rubber
- ruler

Method

Focus the microscope on a single cell.

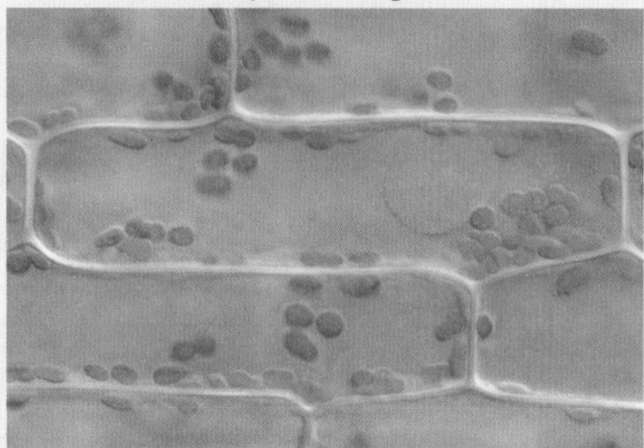

Carefully draw details of the parts that are important to your study. Other parts can be drawn just in outline.

Keep looking back at the specimen as you make the drawing, and only draw what you see, not what you think you ought to see.

Results

Pondweed cell ×650

chloroplast

cell walls of two neighbouring cells

cytoplasm and vacuole (not obvious)

nucleus

If a line is in the wrong place, rub it out cleanly before drawing it in the correct position. Your drawing should be as clear as possible.

Keep the relative sizes of structures approximately correct and label all the key parts of your drawing.

Labels should be outside the drawing and label lines must not cross.

Use a ruler to draw label lines to link labels to the correct parts of the drawing.

Never use shading.

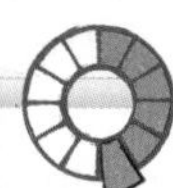

Give your drawing a clear title saying what the specimen is, and always give the magnification, e.g. ×100. (See page 3 to help you calculate the magnification.)

Now try this

The photo shows some cells in a blood smear seen under a light microscope at ×1000.
Draw and label one example of each cell in the smear. **(3 marks)**

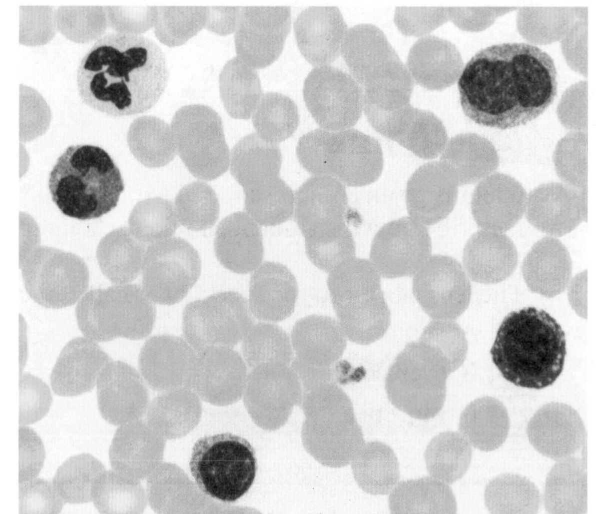

Enzymes

Enzymes are biological **catalysts** that control reactions in the body. Each enzyme is **specific** (only works with one substrate) to its substrate and the **activity** of enzymes is affected by temperature, substrate concentration and pH.

Effect of temperature and substrate concentration

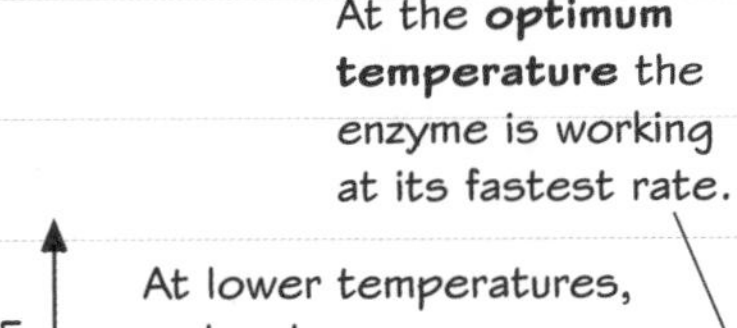

At the **optimum temperature** the enzyme is working at its fastest rate.
Higher temperatures cause the active site to change shape, so it can't hold the substrate as tightly and the reaction goes more slowly.
At lower temperatures, molecules move more slowly. So substrate molecules take longer to fit into and react in the active site.
At very high temperatures the active site breaks up and the enzyme is **denatured**.
Rate of reaction
10 20 30 40 50 60
Temperature (°C)

Adding more substrate at this point has little effect because the active site of every enzyme molecule is busy.
At this point not every active site of each enzyme molecule is busy, so adding more substrate increases the rate of reaction.
Rate of reaction
Substrate concentration

Worked example

The diagram shows an enzyme-controlled reaction.

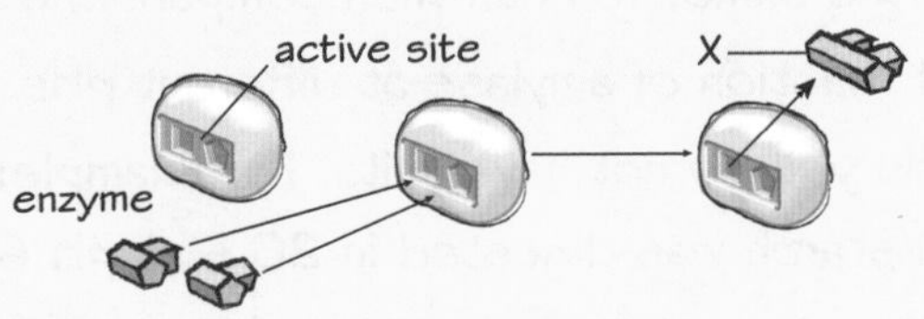

active site
X
enzyme
two different substrate molecules

(a) State the name of the part labelled X. **(1 mark)**

product molecule

(b) Explain the role of the active site in an enzyme-controlled reaction. **(4 marks)**

The shape of the active site matches the shape of the substrate molecules and holds them close together so bonds can form between them to make the product. The product molecule doesn't fit the active site well so it is released from the enzyme.

The **substrate** fits like a 'key' into the **active site** (the 'lock'). Enzymes are specific because only a substrate with the right shape can fit the active site.

Worked example

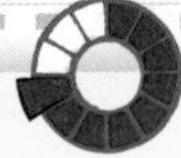

Draw a graph of rate of reaction against pH for an enzyme with an optimum pH of 6. Label your graph to explain what you have drawn. **(2 marks)**

Changing the pH can change the shape of the enzyme's active site, and so change its ability to bond with the substrate.

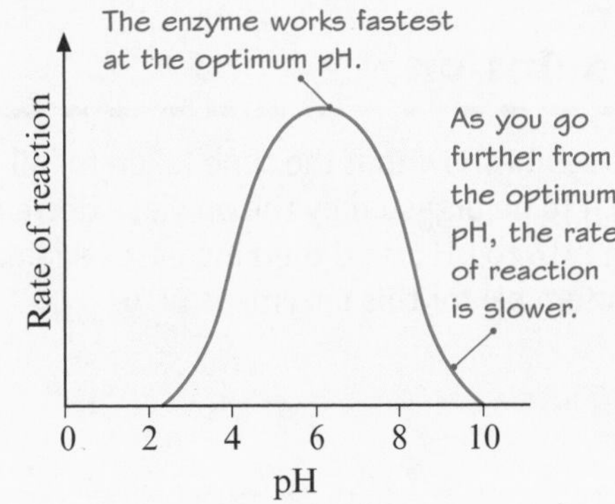

The enzyme works fastest at the optimum pH.
As you go further from the optimum pH, the rate of reaction is slower.
Rate of reaction
0 2 4 6 8 10
pH

Now try this

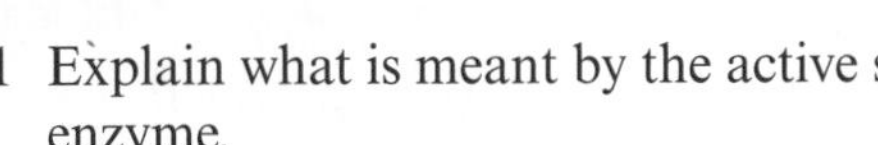

1 Explain what is meant by the active site of an enzyme. **(2 marks)**

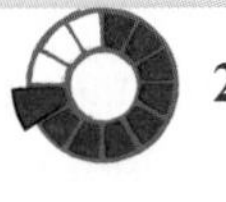

2 Enzymes in the human liver have an optimum temperature of about 37 °C. Explain why our body temperature is controlled to stay at about 37 °C. **(2 marks)**

pH and enzyme activity

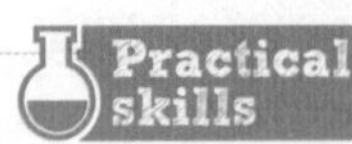

You can **investigate the effect of pH on the rate on enzyme activity** by measuring the rate of an enzyme-controlled reaction at one pH, and comparing it with the rate at other pH values. You can revise enzymes on page 7.

Core practical

Aim

To investigate the effect of pH on amylase activity.

Methods

- Add amylase to buffered starch solution in a test tube.
- Place the tube in a water bath for a constant temperature.
- Take samples of the mixture at regular intervals (e.g. every 10 s) and mix them with a fresh drop of iodine solution on a dimple tile.
- Repeat the test until the iodine solution stops changing colour when the starch/amylase mixture is added. Record the time taken for this to happen.
- Repeat the procedure at different pH values.

> Starch is broken down by amylase to sugars.

> Buffering the solution makes sure the pH doesn't change during the experiment.

> When controlling the temperature, bear in mind the effect of temperature on enzyme action. Keeping the solution at the optimum temperature for the enzyme is best.

> Iodine solution is usually yellow/orange. In the presence of starch, it turns blue/black.

Results

Record the values for each pH in a table. Then, you can draw a graph like the one given below.

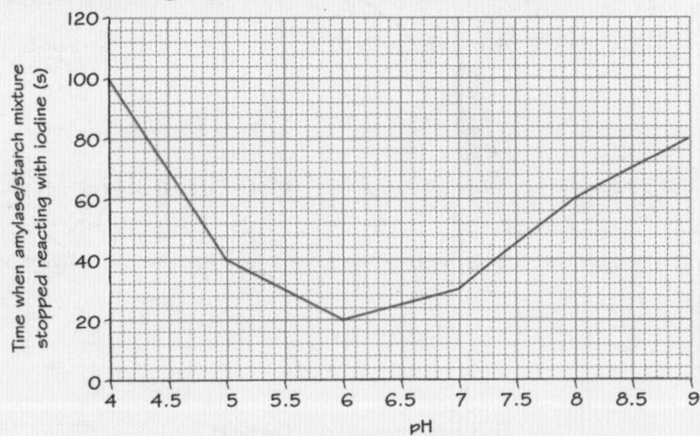

Conclusion

The results show that the time taken for all the starch to be digested by the amylase decreases from pH 4 to pH 6, and then increases again. The optimum pH for this enzyme is pH 6.

Maths skills: Reaction rate

You can calculate the relative rate of reaction for a particular pH, as $\frac{1}{\text{time}}$ because the mass of starch used at each pH is the same. You can then compare the rates of reaction of amylase at different pHs. For this you do not have units. For example: all starch was digested in 20 s at pH 6. The rate of reaction at pH 6 is $\frac{1}{20} = 0.05$.

> However, this is not a true rate. For a true rate of reaction you would need to have the mass of starch digested by the enzyme divided by the time taken. The units for this would be g/s. See page 73 for more about rates.

Improvements

This method can be improved by:

- using more accurate measuring apparatus
- taking the mean of several repeats at each pH to help reduce the effect of random variation
- taking measurements over a narrower range of pH.

Now try this

1 (a) Calculate the relative rate of reaction of amylase at pH 9 in the core practical. **(1 mark)**
(b) Explain why the graph shows that the optimum pH for this enzyme was pH 6. **(2 marks)**

2 A student repeated the experiment using solutions of pH 5.2, 5.6, 6.0, 6.4 and 6.8. Explain why the results of this experiment could produce a better answer for the optimum pH of the enzyme. **(2 marks)**

The importance of enzymes

Enzymes are biological **catalysts** that control reactions in the body. They catalyse reactions that **synthesise** large molecules from smaller ones and **break down** large molecules into smaller ones.

Enzymes as catalysts

Enzymes **speed up** the rate of a chemical reaction but are not used up in the reaction. This means they can be used over and over again.

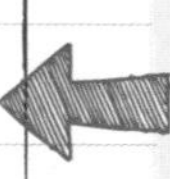

Make sure you remember at least some examples of enzymes and the reactions they catalyse.

Digestion and synthesis

Some enzymes **digest** large molecules into smaller molecules. This happens in the gut where large food molecules are broken down so that they can be absorbed into the blood.

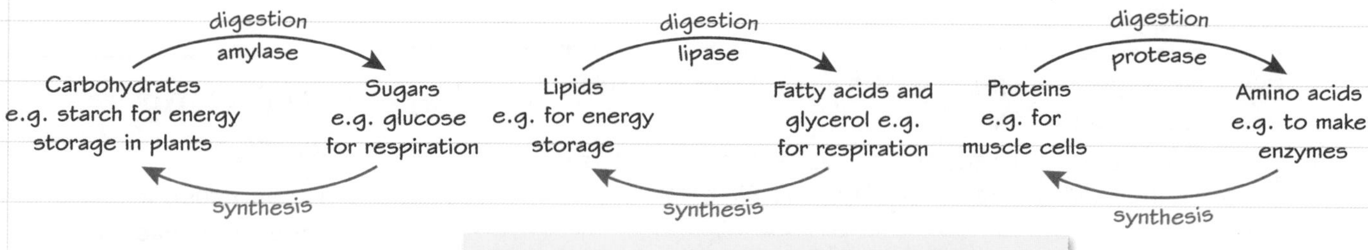

Some enzymes **synthesise** larger molecules from smaller molecules. This is important inside cells for supporting life processes and growth.

Worked example

Complete the table. **(3 marks)**

Large molecule	Smaller molecules it is broken down into
carbohydrates	sugars
proteins	amino acids
lipids	fatty acids and glycerol

Remember you need to mention **both** fatty acids **and** glycerol to get the mark.

Worked example

People with cystic fibrosis have thick mucus lining their gut. They have to take capsules containing enzymes before meals. Explain why. **(3 marks)**

The thick mucus prevents enzymes being secreted into the gut. If they didn't take enzyme capsules before meals, their food would not be digested into smaller, soluble molecules. As a result, they would not absorb enough nutrients.

Now try this

1 The enzyme that digests lipids will not digest proteins. Explain why. **(2 marks)**

2 Where in a cell would you expect to find enzymes that synthesise amino acids into proteins? **(1 mark)**

Think about what you know about cell structure (see page 1 for the generalised structures of plant and animal cells).

Using reagents in food tests

Practical skills You can use chemical reagents to **identify starch, reducing sugars, proteins and fats in food**. Each food substance has its own tests.

Core practical

Aim

To investigate the use of chemical reagents to identify substances in food.

Apparatus

- test tubes
- water bath
- iodine solution
- Benedict's solution
- 0.1 mol dm^{-3} potassium hydroxide solution
- 0.01 mol dm^{-3} copper sulfate solution
- ethanol
- water
- food

Safety note:
- Handle iodine solution carefully as it can stain skin and clothing.
- Wear suitable eye protection for all these tests.
- Work safely with hot water, to avoid scalding. Use a heat-resistant glove or tongs to handle hot equipment.

Method

To test for starch: Place a few drops of iodine solution on solid food, or mix with a solution of the food.

To test for reducing sugars: Add an equal volume of Benedict's solution to a food solution and mix. Heat the mixture in a 95 °C water bath for a few minutes.

To test for proteins (biuret test): Add an equal volume of 0.1 mol dm^{-3} potassium hydroxide solution to the food solution and mix. Add a few drops of 0.01 mol dm^{-3} copper sulfate solution and mix.

To test for fats: Add an equal volume of ethanol to the food solution, and shake thoroughly. Add water to the mixture.

Reducing sugars

These cause a reduction reaction with the reagent. They include sugars such as glucose and fructose, but not sucrose (table sugar).

Results

Test reagent	Tests for ...	Colour of reagent/ negative result	Colour if food present
iodine solution	starch	yellow/orange	blue/black
Benedict's solution	reducing sugar	blue	green→orange→red (depending on how much sugar present)
biuret test	protein	pale blue	pale purple
ethanol	fat	clear	cloudy

Now try this

The table shows the results of food tests carried out on a food sample. Identify the substances in the food. **(4 marks)**

Test reagent	Result
iodine solution	yellow/orange
Benedict's solution	green
biuret test	pale blue
ethanol	clear

Using calorimetry

You can find the **energy** in a sample of food using calorimetry.

1. The temperature of the water at the start is measured.
2. The mass of the food sample is measured.
3. The food is set alight (e.g. in a Bunsen flame), then placed immediately under the tube.
4. The temperature of the water at the end is measured, and the change in temperature is calculated.

The calorimeter contains a measured volume of water.

When all the food is burned, the increase in temperature is related to the energy released from the food.

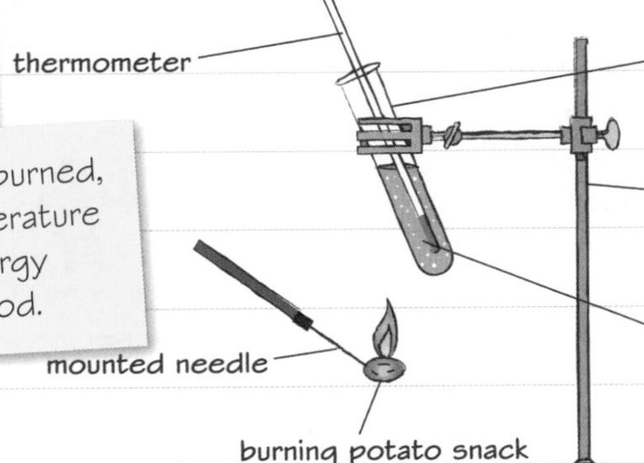

- The energy released from the food by burning is transferred to the water.
- As the water gains energy, its temperature increases.

Worked example

A student used calorimetry to measure the energy in a potato snack, using the apparatus shown above. The test tube contained 10 cm^3 water. Give **two** reasons why this may not be an accurate measurement. **(2 marks)**

Taking too long to move the burning food to under the tube, or holding the food at different distances from the tube. This would affect how much energy is transferred to the surrounding air and not the tube.

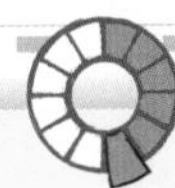

You could give other reasons, such as not measuring the mass of food/initial temperature/volume of water accurately, or the food not burning completely. You may be able to think of others.

Maths skills: Calculating the energy in food

A student burned 2g of a cereal bar underneath a test tube containing 20 cm^3 water. The water temperature was 16°C at the start. After the cereal bar had burned completely, the temperature of the water had increased to 34°C. It takes 4.2 J of energy to raise the temperature of 1 cm^3 of water by 1 °C. To calculate the energy content of the whole 125 g cereal bar you need to do the following calculation: 20 cm^3 of water was heated by 18°C.

This uses 20 × 18 × 4.2J of energy = 1512J = 1.512kJ

Therefore 1 g of cereal bar contains 1.512/2 = 0.756kJ

The whole bar weighs 125g therefore the whole bar contains 125 × 0.756 = 94.5kJ

Now try this

(a) 200 g of potato crisps were burned in a bomb calorimeter. This raised the temperature of 500 cm^3 water by 2 °C. It takes 4.2 J of energy to raise the temperature of 1 cm^3 water by 1 °C. Find the energy in 100 g crisps. Show your working. **(2 marks)**

(b) Calculate the energy in 1 g of crisps. **(1 mark)**

Getting in and out of cells

Dissolved substances (**solutes**) move into and out of cells by **diffusion** and **active transport**. Water moves into and out of cells by **osmosis**.

Diffusion

high concentration of dissolved molecules (concentrated solution)

partially permeable membrane

More molecules move from the high concentration to the lower concentration than vice versa, so the net movement is **down** the concentration gradient.

low concentration of dissolved molecules (dilute solution)

Diffusion is important in the body, for example, to move oxygen into cells and to remove carbon dioxide.

Active transport

partially permeable membrane

Active transport needs energy from respiration.

low concentration of dissolved molecules (dilute solution)

high concentration of dissolved molecules (concentrated solution)

There is net movement against the concentration gradient.

Active transport makes it possible for cells to absorb ions from very dilute solutions, e.g. root cells absorb minerals from soil water, and small intestine cells absorb glucose from digested food in the gut into the body.

Worked example

The diagram shows the results of an experiment. At the start, the level of solution inside the tube and the level of water in the beaker were the same. Name the process that caused the change and explain what happened. **(3 marks)**

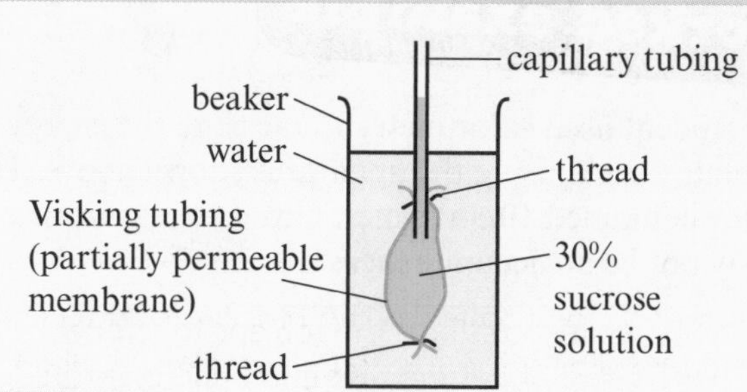

The process is called osmosis. To start with there were more water molecules in the water than in the same volume of sucrose solution, so more water molecules crossed the membrane into the tubing than going the other way. So the level of solution in the capillary rose.

Osmosis is the name given to a special case of diffusion. Osmosis is the net movement of water molecules across a partially permeable membrane.

Now try this

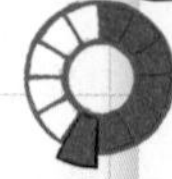

1 Define osmosis. **(2 marks)**

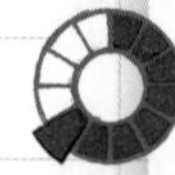

2 (a) Give one similarity between diffusion and osmosis. **(1 mark)**
(b) Give one difference between diffusion and active transport. **(1 mark)**

3 A plant root is treated with a poison that prevents respiration. Explain whether the root cells will still be able to absorb water and mineral ions from a dilute solution. **(4 marks)**

Remember that respiration provides the energy for active transport but there are other ways that substances can enter cells which do not require energy from respiration.

Osmosis in potatoes

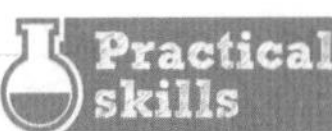

You can investigate **osmosis** by calculating the change in mass of pieces of potato that have been placed in solutions of different solute concentration.

Core practical

Aim

To investigate osmosis using potatoes.

Apparatus

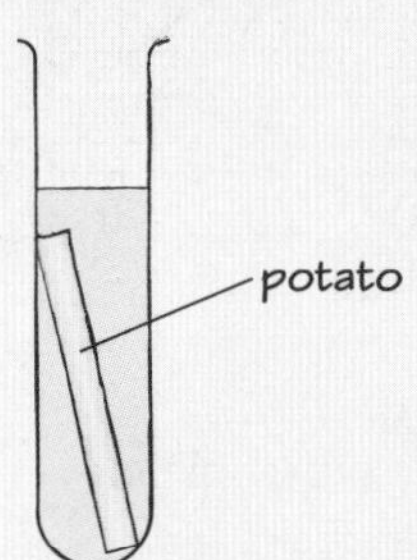

- pieces of potato about 3 × 1 × 1 cm
- boiling tubes
- accurate balance
- paper towels
- forceps
- solutions of different solute concentration (0, 0.2, 0.4, 0.6, 0.8, 1.0 mol dm^{-3})
- marker pen

Method

1 Mark the value of one solute concentration on one tube and repeat using a different tube for each concentration. Fill each tube two-thirds full of the appropriate solution.

2 Blot a piece of potato dry on a paper towel, then measure and record its mass. Use the forceps to place it into one of the tubes, and record the tube. Repeat for all tubes.

3 After 20 minutes, use the forceps to remove each piece of potato, blot it dry and measure its mass again. Record all final masses.

Results

The percentage change in mass of each potato slice is calculated and recorded, indicating whether mass was gained or lost.

Conclusion

The results show that when the solution concentration is very dilute, water enters the potato cells. This is due to osmosis because the solute concentration of the potato cells is greater than the surrounding solution. As the solute concentration of the solution increases above that inside the potato cells, osmosis causes water to be lost from the potato.

Worked example

The initial mass of a potato slice was 13.54 g. After soaking in a solution the final mass was 14.66 g. Calculate the percentage change in mass. **(4 marks)**

% change in mass =

$$\frac{\text{final mass} - \text{initial mass}}{\text{initial mass}} \times 100\% =$$

$$\frac{14.66 - 13.54}{13.54} \times 100 = 8.27\% \text{ gained}$$

(or +8.27%)

The change in mass may be very small. You should measure to 2 d.p.

The solute in the solutions must be something that is too large to diffuse across the cell membrane. Sucrose is often used.

Blotting removes surface water, and can help to increase the accuracy and repeatability of measurements.

Repeating the test at each solute concentration, and calculating the mean of the results, can help to reduce the effect of random variation.

Now try this

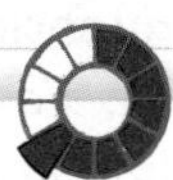

The table shows the results of an osmosis experiment using potato pieces.

(a) Calculate the percentage change in mass of potato at each concentration. **(2 marks)**

(b) Use your answers to draw a conclusion about the solute concentration of the potato cells. Explain your conclusion. **(2 marks)**

Solution concentration (mol dm^{-3})	Initial mass (g)	Final mass (g)
0	16.52	20.15
0.2	15.90	16.70
0.4	17.06	15.69
0.6	16.88	14.36
0.8	16.23	12.32

Extended response – Key concepts

There will be one or more 6 mark questions on your exam paper. For these questions, you will need to think scientifically, and structure your answer logically showing how the points you make are related to each other. For the questions on this page, you can revise the topics on **enzyme activity** on pages 7 to 9.

Worked example

The graph shows the results of an experiment into the effect of temperature on the activity of the enzyme amylase on starch. The enzyme had been isolated from a bacterium. Explain the results shown in the graph. **(6 marks)**

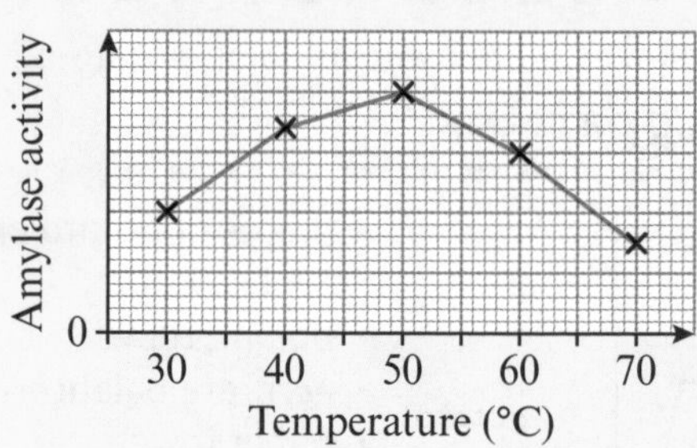

The graph shows that activity of the bacterial amylase increased from 30 °C up to a maximum at 50 °C, and then decreased as the temperature increased further to 70 °C. The maximum activity is at the optimum temperature, which is about 50 °C for this enzyme.

Before you explain the results, describe what the graph shows. Use values on the graph to add details to your answer. Remember to include important science words that are relevant in your answer.

Enzyme activity increases with increasing temperature up to the optimum because particles move faster. Starch molecules fit into the active site of enzyme molecules more quickly and are broken down more quickly, releasing the active site for another starch molecule.

Enzyme activity should be linked to how the active site of the enzyme and the substrate interact.

Beyond the optimum temperature, the shape of the active site starts to change, making it more difficult for the substrate to fit into it. So activity slows down. The active site shape changes more as temperature increases further, until the enzyme becomes denatured and stops being able to catalyse the reaction.

Make sure you explain each part of the graph clearly, linking your knowledge and understanding to give a good explanation of what is happening.

Command word: Explain

An **explain** question requires a reason for what is happening. Use a word such as 'because' to clearly link a description with its reason.

Now try this

The graph on the right shows the effect of starch concentration on the activity of a bacterial amylase. Explain the results shown in the graph. **(6 marks)**

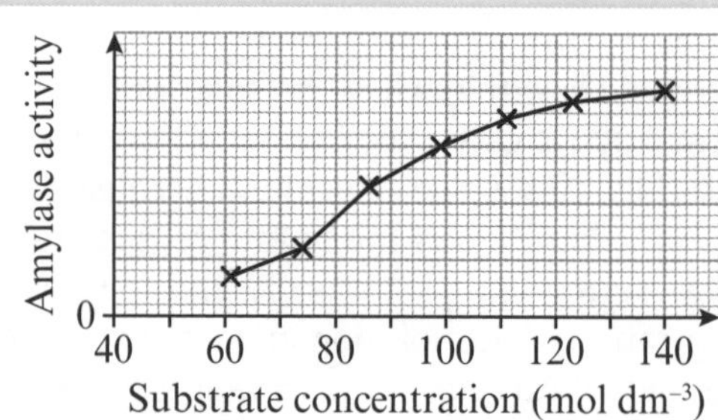

Mitosis

There are two types of cell division, **mitosis** and meiosis. Mitosis is covered here; meiosis is covered on page 27.

Mitosis is a type of **cell division** that takes place in several stages. There are two types of **cell division**. **Mitosis** is the cell division that happens in body cells. A **body cell** is any cell except those that produce **gametes** (sex cells).

The cell that is dividing is called the **parent cell** and the two new cells that are formed are called **daughter cells.** The daughter cells are identical to the parent cell, so if the parent cell is diploid then the daughter cells will be diploid too. You should be clear about the differences between meiosis and mitosis.

Three things to remember

- Mi-to-sis makes two cells
- MiTosis makes genetically idenTical cells
- Diploid means Double (two sets of) chromosomes

Stages of mitosis

Each chromosome consists of two chromatids.

The chromatids separate and one chromatid from each pair is pulled to each pole of the cell. The chromatids can now be called chromosomes.

The cell splits into two. This is called **cytokinesis**

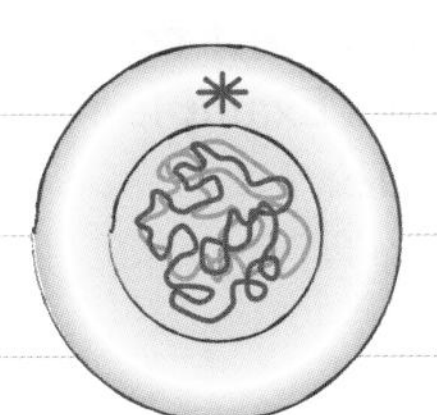
Interphase

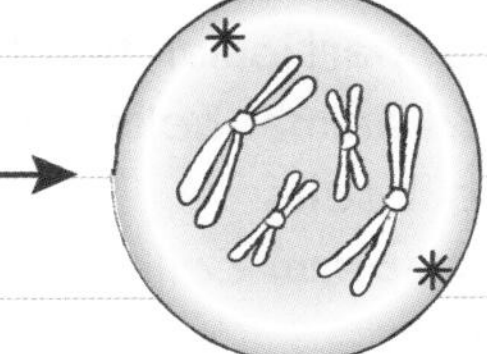
Prophase

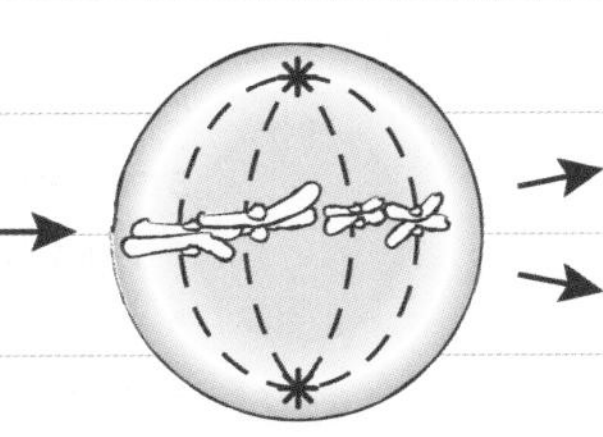
Metaphase

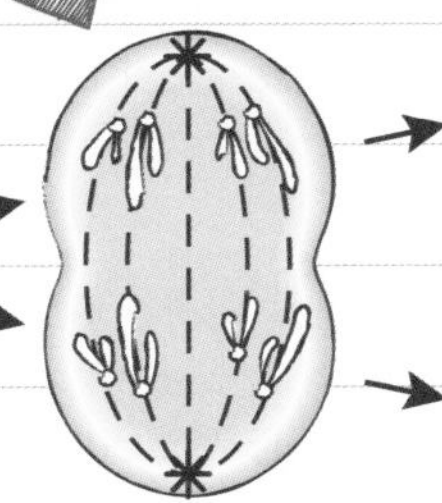
Anaphase

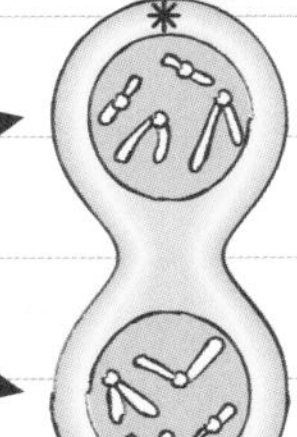
Telophase

At the end of interphase, chromosomes start to become visible. The DNA has already been copied.

The nuclear membrane breaks down. Chromosomes line up along the middle of the cell.

Spindle fibres disappear and a new nuclear membrane forms round each group of chromosomes.

Remember the stages of mitosis using the mnemonic IPMAT:
Interphase
Prophase
Metaphase
Anaphase
Telophase

Worked example

(a) Body cells have two sets of chromosomes. Explain how this happens. **(2 marks)**

One set of chromosomes comes from the mother and one set comes from the father.

(b) Explain how the daughter cells are genetically identical. **(2 marks)**

Each chromosome is copied; one copy of each chromosome goes into each daughter cell.

Interphase

A cell is in interphase most of the time.

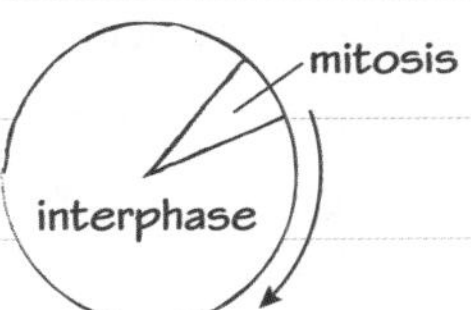

Now try this

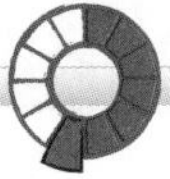

A cell divides by mitosis. Describe the daughter cells. **(2 marks)**

Cell growth and differentiation

Mitosis is used for growth, repair and asexual reproduction. After growth, cells can then **differentiate** into specialised cells. Growth and differentiation happen in different ways in plants and animals.

When does mitosis happen?

Normally cells only divide by mitosis when new diploid cells are needed for:

- growth
- repair (replacement of damaged cells)
- asexual reproduction.

Uncontrolled cell division

Cancer cells are abnormal cells that divide uncontrollably by mitosis to form a **tumour**.

Cells usually stop dividing when growth has finished, except when repair is needed. Sometimes the controls that tell cells when to stop dividing go wrong which leads to cancer.

Worked example

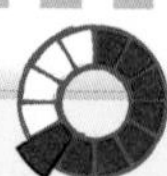

Aphids are insects that are pests of crop plants. In the summer they reproduce rapidly by asexual reproduction. Will the offspring of a single aphid be varied? Explain your answer. **(3 marks)**

The offspring will be produced by mitosis, so they will all be genetically identical to the parent aphid. They will all be diploid like the parent aphid.

Mitosis is used for asexual reproduction. This also occurs in plants, for example, when plants reproduce using bulbs or runners.

Growth in animals

In **animals**, a fertilised egg, or zygote, divides by mitosis to produce genetically identical daughter cells. These cells grow and divide by mitosis, and eventually **differentiate** into different types of cells to make up a whole organism. Differentiation creates **specialised cells** adapted to carry out a particular function. Examples of specialised animal cells include:

- red blood cells
- egg and sperm cells
- nerve cells
- bone cells
- smooth muscle cells.

Growth in plants

Plant cells divide by mitosis, just behind the tips of shoots and roots. After this the cells grow by enlarging. Young cells have small vacuoles which take in water by osmosis and enlarge, causing the cells to **elongate**. These cells can differentiate into specialised cell types. Most plant cells can **continue** to grow and differentiate throughout life.

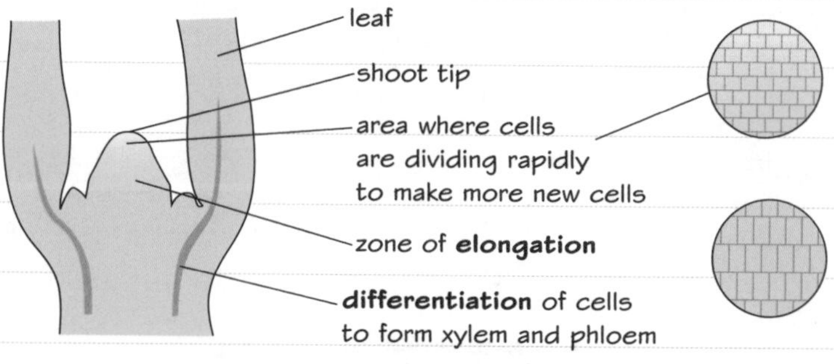

Examples of specialised plant cells include:

- xylem
- phloem
- mesophyll cells
- root hair cells
- stoma cells.

Now try this

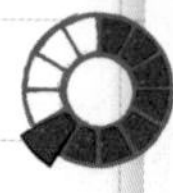

1 One drug that is used to treat cancer stops spindle formation in mitosis. Suggest how this drug helps to prevent the growth of a cancer. **(2 marks)**

2 State what is meant by a specialised cell. **(1 mark)**

3 Explain why cell differentiation is important. **(2 marks)**

Growth and percentile charts

When organisms **grow** they get bigger. Growth can be measured in different ways.

Estimating growth

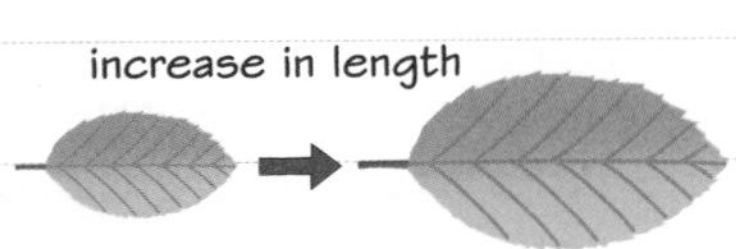

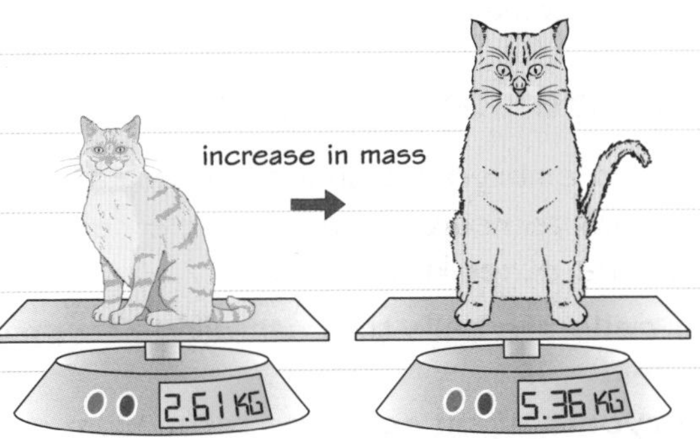

Growth is a **permanent** increase in size. For example, a balloon that is blown up a little more has not 'grown' in size.

Percentile charts

Percentile charts can help to show if a child is growing faster or slower than is normal for their age.

Babies with a mass above the 95th line or below the 5th line may not be growing properly.

A baby whose mass decreases by two or more percentile categories over their first year may not be growing normally.

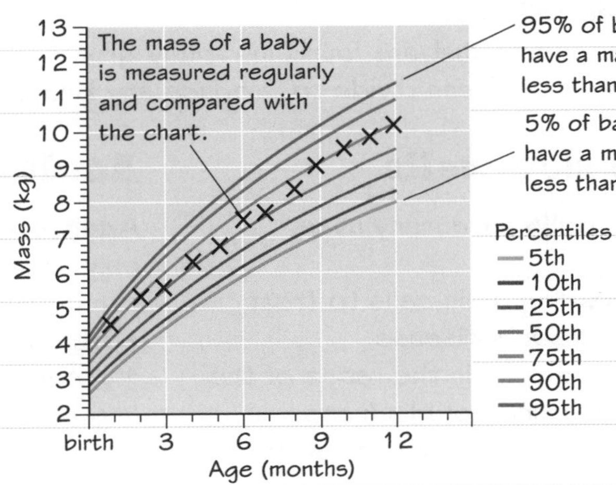

This chart is for baby girls. The chart for baby boys is similar, but they grow at a slightly different rate to girls.

Worked example

Look at the percentile chart. The crosses mark the mass of a baby girl measured each month.

(a) State the percentile that she belonged to in her first month. **(1 mark)**

75th percentile

(b) Do you think there was concern about this baby's mass increase in her first year? Explain your answer. **(2 marks)**

No, because her mass varied only between the 75th and 50th percentiles, and this amount of variation is normal.

Worked example

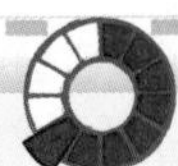

The government has produced percentile charts for BMI in children. A child is said to have a clinically healthy weight if their BMI is between the second and ninety-first percentile. A parent has been told that her child is on the 70th percentile for BMI. Explain to her what this means. **(2 marks)**

This means the child has a higher BMI than 70% of children and a lower BMI than 30% of children. Because this falls between the 2nd and 91st percentile, the child has a clinically healthy weight.

Now try this

1 Describe one way in which you could measure the growth of a plant. **(2 marks)**

2 Describe what a percentile chart is used for. **(2 marks)**

3 Explain why an increase in the size of a balloon is not an example of growth but an increase in the size of a child is. **(2 marks)**

Stem cells

Stem cells have different functions in plants and animals. In humans, they have many potential uses in medicine.

What are stem cells?

Cells in an embryo are unspecialised. They divide to produce all the **specialised cells** in the body, such as neurones and muscle cells. Once the cells have differentiated they cannot divide to produce other kinds of cell.

Stem cells are cells that can divide to produce many types of cell. There are three kinds of stem cell:

- **Embryonic stem cells** are taken from embryos at a very early stage of division (e.g. 8 cells).
- **Adult stem cells** are found in differentiated tissue, such as bone or skin – they divide to replace damaged cells.
- Plants have **meristems** that are found in rapidly growing parts of the plant, e.g. tips of roots and shoots. These cells can divide to produce any kind of plant cell.

Embryonic stem cells

Embryonic stem cells have many uses, including:

- replacing or repairing brain cells to treat people with Parkinson's disease
- replacing damaged cells in the retina of the eye to treat some kinds of blindness
- growing new tissues in the lab to use for transplants or drug testing.

Adult stem cells

Adult stem cells (from bone marrow) can only form a limited number of cell types. They can be used for:

- treatment of leukaemia
- potentially growing new tissues that are genetically matched to the patient.

Using stem cells

embryonic stem cells

✓ easy to extract from embryo

✓ produce any type of cell

✗ embryo destroyed when cells removed – some people think embryos have a right to life

all stem cells

✓ replace faulty cell with healthy cell, so person is well again

! stem cells may not stop dividing, and so cause cancer

adult stem cells

✓ no embryo destroyed so not an ethical issue

✓ if taken from the person to be treated, will not cause rejection by the body

✗ produce only a few types of cell

✓ – Advantage ✗ – Disadvantage ! – Risk

Now try this

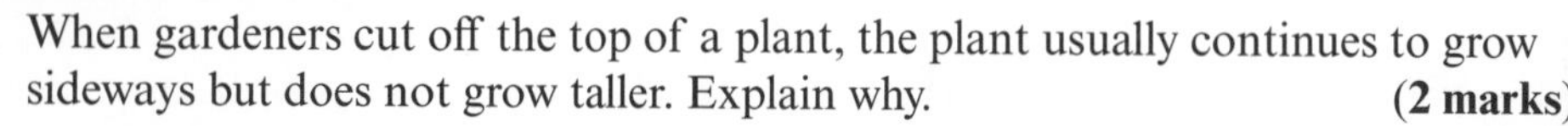

1 When gardeners cut off the top of a plant, the plant usually continues to grow sideways but does not grow taller. Explain why. **(2 marks)**

2 Explain two disadvantages of research into embryonic stem cells. **(2 marks)**

3 (a) State why embryonic stem cells could be more useful than adult stem cells to replace faulty cells. **(1 mark)**

(b) Describe one practical advantage of using adult stem cells from the patient instead of embryonic stem cells to replace faulty cells. **(2 marks)**

If an exam question asks for **two** advantages or disadvantages, make sure you give two **different** examples.

The brain and spinal cord

The brain and the spinal cord make up the **central nervous system.**

Parts of the brain

The cerebral hemispheres control **voluntary movement**, **interpret** sensory information and are responsible for **learning** and **memory**.

The medulla oblongata regulates the **heart beat** and **breathing**.

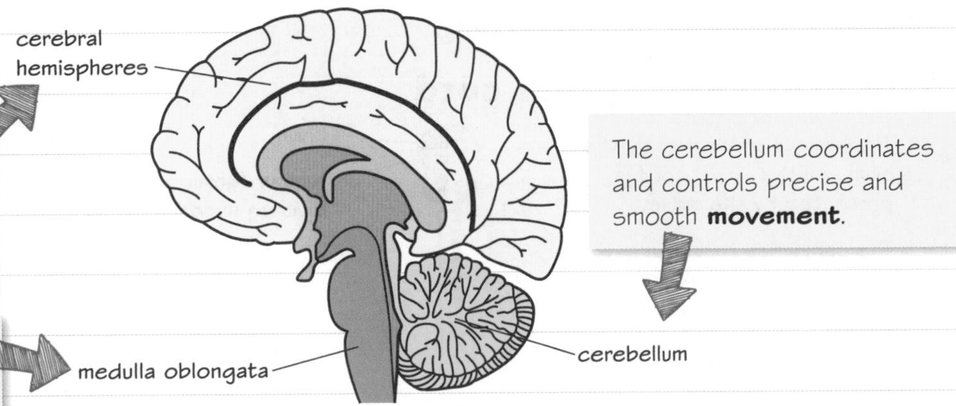

The cerebellum coordinates and controls precise and smooth **movement**.

CT (computerised tomography) scans

- The patient is given a **radioactive** tracer which allows different parts of the brain to show up.
- A CT scan is carried out, taking many different **X-rays** of the skull and brain from different angles.
- A computer puts all these images together to give a **three-dimensional** image.

PET (positron emission tomography) scans

- The patient is given a small amount of a **radioactive** form of glucose.
- This travels to parts of the body where respiration is occurring rapidly.
- This shows up changes in parts of the body such as the brain that might indicate damage or disease.
- The scanner detects the radioactivity and builds up images showing where the radioactive tracer is most concentrated.

Worked example

A person who has broken their spinal cord is paralysed from the point of the damage downwards. This means they cannot feel anything from the lower part of their body or move it. Explain why. **(2 marks)**

Nerve impulses to and from the lower part of the body pass through the spinal cord. If these nerves are damaged there is no way that impulses can be sent between the brain and the lower part of the body.

To answer this question fully, you will need to describe both the **role** of the spinal cord and the **effect** of damage to it.

Worked example

A patient has to lie very still while a CT or PET scan is taking place. Explain why. **(2 marks)**

Lots of different images are taken to build up into a 3D image. If the person moves, the different images won't fit together properly.

Now try this

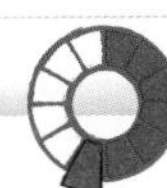

Complete the table to show the part of the brain responsible for each activity. **(2 marks)**

Part of brain	Activity
	increasing heart rate during exercise
	reading a book
	balancing on a skate board
	recognising a person from a photograph

Treating damage and disease in the nervous system

It is difficult to **treat** damage and disease in the brain and other parts of the nervous system because they are so well protected.

The brain and spinal cord

The brain is protected by the skull and the spinal cord is protected by the spine.

The capillaries that supply the brain are not as leaky as normal capillaries. This is called the 'blood-brain barrier'. This makes it difficult to get medicines into the brain.

Neurones are specialised cells and so cannot divide to replace damaged cells.

brain

tumour (group of cells dividing uncontrollably)

The brain and spinal cord are protected by bone, making it very hard to access them for surgery. (Surgery is when diseased tissue is removed during an operation.)

spinal cord

When doctors treat brain tumours with radiotherapy or surgery, this can not only remove the tumour but also cause **damage** to healthy nervous tissue.

Watch out! Don't confuse the **spine**, which is the bony structure in your back, with the **spinal cord**, which is made of nerves. The spinal cord lies inside the spine for protection.

Worked example

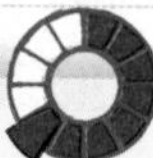

If a person has been in a road accident and damage to their vertebral column is suspected, paramedics will not move them until they have been strapped to a spinal board. This causes minimum movement of the vertebrae while the patient is moved. Explain what might happen if a spinal board was not used. **(3 marks)**

If the bones move, this could break the spinal cord. This would stop nerve impulses passing to the parts of the body below the break. The patient would be unable to control or move parts of the body below the break, causing paralysis.

You need to state that the spinal cord could be broken, and what effect this would have both on a small scale (the nerve impulses cannot pass) and on the patient (paralysis).

Now try this

Explain two reasons why it is difficult to treat a brain tumour. **(4 marks)**

This is an **explain** question so it's not enough to just give two reasons, you need to explain why this makes it difficult. So, for example, as well as stating that the brain is protected by bone, you need to say why this makes it difficult to treat.

Neurones

Stimuli are detected by sensory **receptors** that send impulses along sensory **neurones** to the central nervous system. Neurones are specialised cells that carry nervous impulses.

Types of neurones

There are three main types of neurones. **Sensory neurones** carry impulses to the central nervous system. **Motor neurones** carry impulses from the central nervous system to effector organs. **Relay neurones** are found only in the central nervous system.

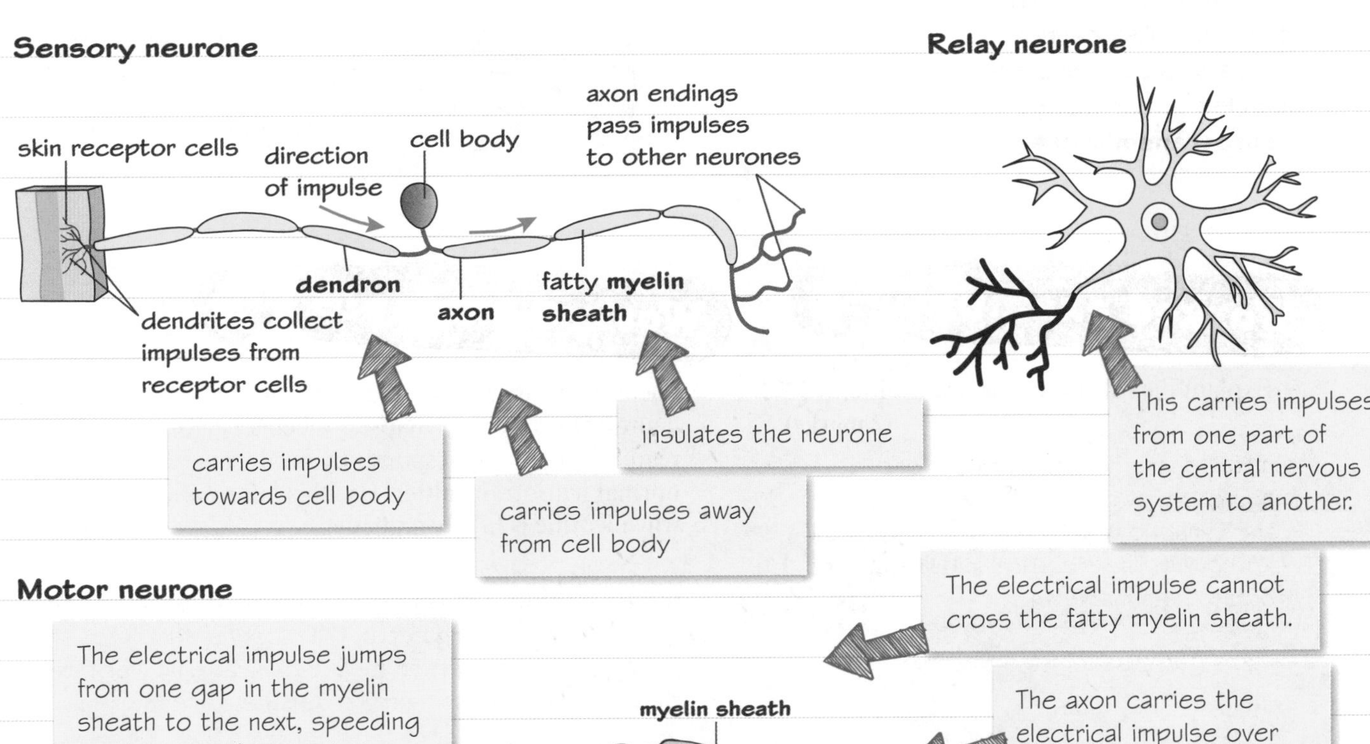

Motor neurone

The electrical impulse jumps from one gap in the myelin sheath to the next, speeding up the rate of transmission.

The electrical impulse cannot cross the fatty myelin sheath.

The axon carries the electrical impulse over long distances through the body.

The nerve ending transmits the impulse to an effector, such as a muscle or gland.

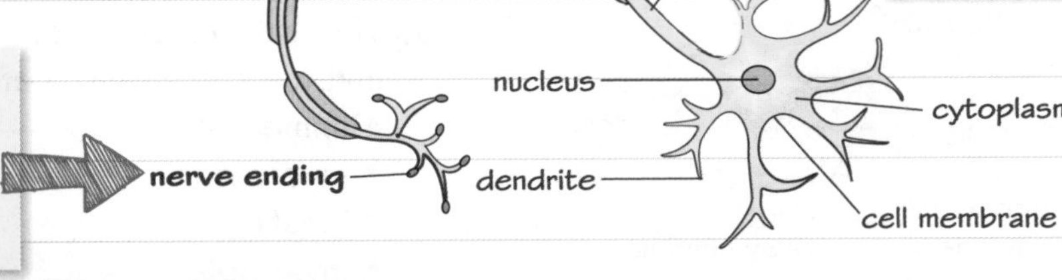

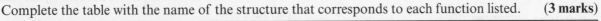

Worked example

Complete the table with the name of the structure that corresponds to each function listed. **(3 marks)**

Structure	Function
axon	carries impulses away from the cell body
dendron	receiving impulses from other neurones
myelin sheath	a fatty layer that provides electrical insulation around the neurone

Now try this

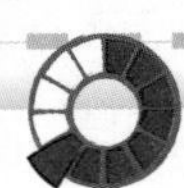

1 Compare the roles of sensory, motor and relay neurones in the nervous system. **(3 marks)**
2 Explain how the structure of a sensory neurone is related to its function. **(2 marks)**

Responding to stimuli

Sensory neurones **carry impulses** from receptors to the central nervous system.

Synapses

The point where two neurones meet is called a **synapse**. There is a small gap between the neurones. The electrical nerve impulse cannot cross this gap, and the impulse is carried by **neurotransmitters**.

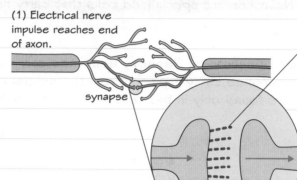

(1) Electrical nerve impulse reaches end of axon.

synapse

(2) Electrical impulse causes chemical neurotransmitter to be released from vesicles in the neurone into gap between neurones.

(3) Neurotransmitter diffuses across the gap and fits into receptors, causing a new electrical impulse in next neurone.

Worked example

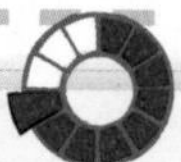

Explain the role of a neurotransmitter. **(2 marks)**

It is a chemical released from one neurone that carries the impulse across the synaptic gap to the next neurone. Without it, the electrical impulse cannot cross the synaptic gap.

Worked example

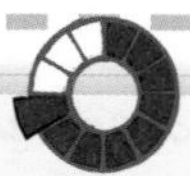

Nicotine in cigarettes is the same shape as a common neurotransmitter in synapses. When a person smokes regularly, the body responds by producing less of the normal neurotransmitter. Use this information to explain why nicotine is highly addictive. **(3 marks)**

When the synapse produces less neurotransmitter, the body does not function as well as usual. When the person smokes a cigarette, the nicotine stimulates the synapse and the person feels better again. Over time, they need to smoke more to get the same feeling.

The reflex arc

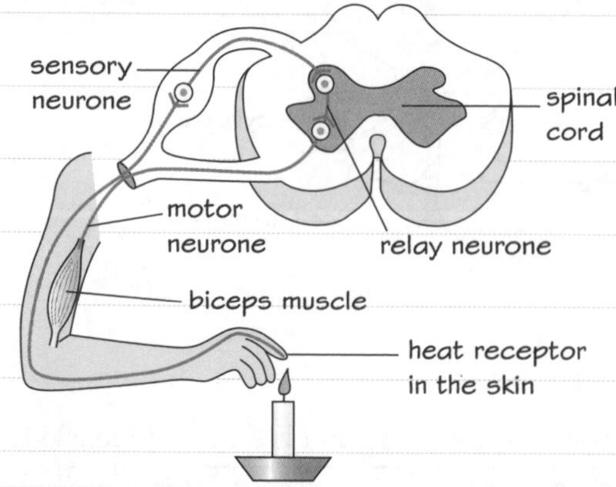

Reflex arcs involve only three neurones, and impulses pass to and from the spinal cord. This provides a fast response that does not involve the brain. Reflex arcs are:

- immediate
- involuntary
- innate
- invariable.

These reflexes help protect us from immediate harm, such as the eye blink reflex which protects the eye if something comes close to it.

If the impulses had to go to the brain to be processed, there would be many more synapses, so the response would take longer.

Now try this

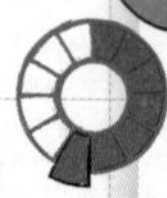

1 Sketch a flow chart to show the neurones in a reflex arc, from the receptor to the effector. **(4 marks)**

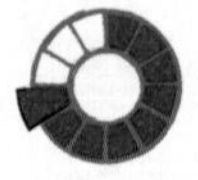

2 Synapses make sure that nervous impulses can pass in one direction only. Explain how. **(2 marks)**

The eye

The eye is a **sensory receptor** that detects light and sends electrical impulses along sensory neurones to the brain.

Parts of the eye

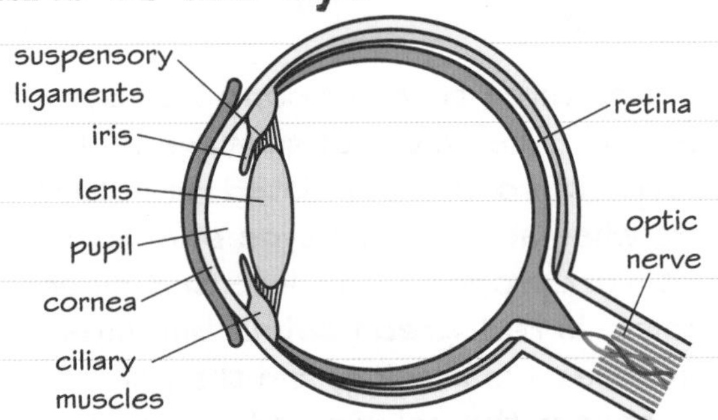

Light enters the eye through a hole called the pupil. The **cornea** and the **lens** focus the light to form a sharp image on the **retina**. The retina contains special receptor cells called rods and cones that detect the light and form an image. The nerves in the retina convert the image into electrical signals that are sent to the brain along the optic nerve.

Focusing the image

The eye lens changes shape to produce a sharp image on the retina.

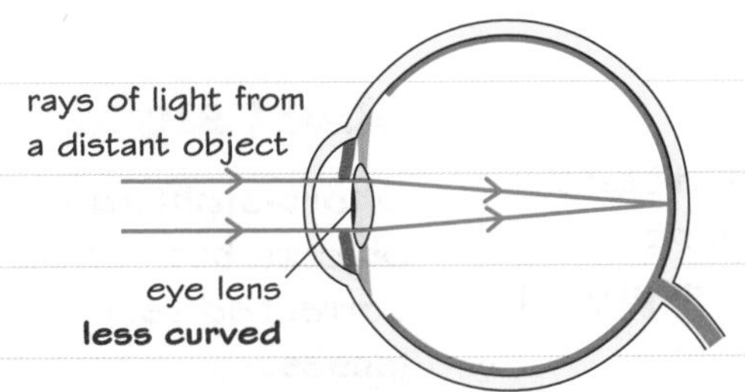

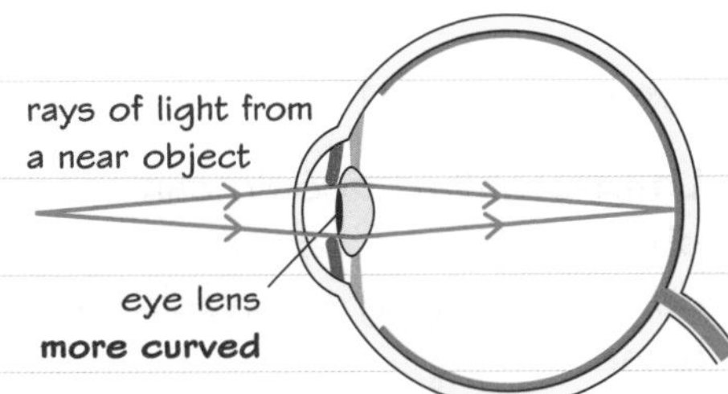

Object	Ciliary muscles	Suspensory ligaments	Shape of lens
near	contracted	slack	fat and rounded
far	relaxed	tight	thin and flattened

Worked example

Explain the role of the two different kinds of receptor cells in the retina. **(2 marks)**

Cone cells are sensitive to bright light and respond to different colours. Rod cells are sensitive at low light intensity and respond only to how dark or light something is.

You are asked for the two different kinds of cells so name both, then give the role for each.

The iris

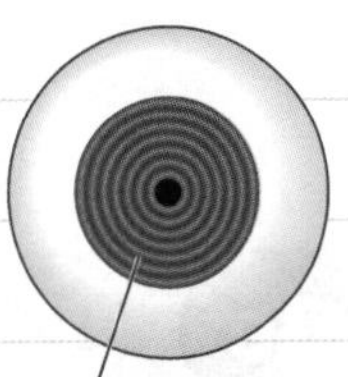

In bright light the circular muscles in the iris contract to make the pupil smaller.

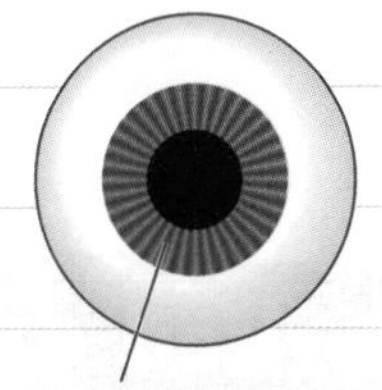

In dim light the radial muscles contract to make the pupil larger.

The **iris** is a ring of muscle that controls the size of the pupil. It does this to protect the rods and cones in bright light and to let more light in when light is dim.

Now try this

1 (a) Which part of the eye is a hole that allows light to enter the eye?

☐ **A** iris ☐ **B** pupil
☐ **C** cornea ☐ **D** retina **(1 mark)**

(b) Which is the coloured part around the hole (a)?

☐ **A** iris ☐ **B** pupil
☐ **C** rods ☐ **D** retina **(1 mark)**

2 Explain why it is difficult to detect the colour of cars driving along a road at night. **(2 marks)**

3 Describe the function of the cornea and lens. **(2 marks)**

Eye problems

Problems with the eye include **colour blindness**, **long-** or **short-sightedness**, or **cataracts**. Some of these can be corrected with lenses.

Cataracts

Cataracts occur when the lens becomes cloudy, so light cannot pass through it properly. The person receives a blurred image on the retina. Cataracts can be treated by replacing the cloudy lens with a clear **artificial lens**.

Colour blindness

A normal retina contains three types of **cone** that detect red, green and blue light. The colour of an image is detected by how much each type of cone is stimulated. In **colour blindness**, it occurs when at least one type of cone is missing or does not work properly. This inherited disorder occurs mostly in males. In **red–green colour blindness**, either red or green cones are missing, and the person cannot distinguish between the colours red and green.

Long sight

Long-sighted people can focus on distant objects but not near ones. This can be corrected using spectacles with **converging** lenses.

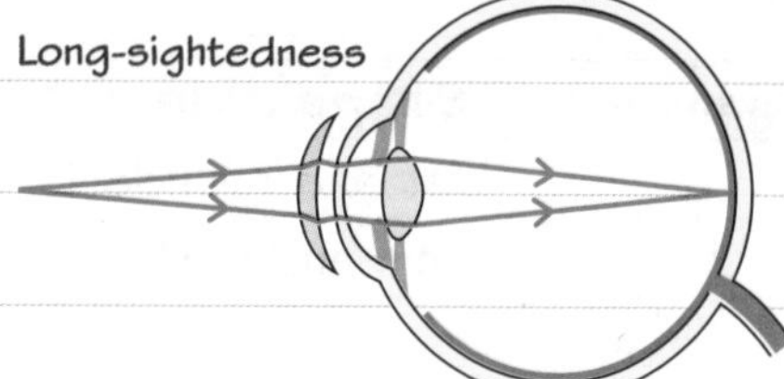

A **converging** lens brings the rays together so light is focused on the retina.

Short sight

Short-sighted people can focus on close objects but not distant ones. This can be corrected using spectacles with **diverging** lenses.

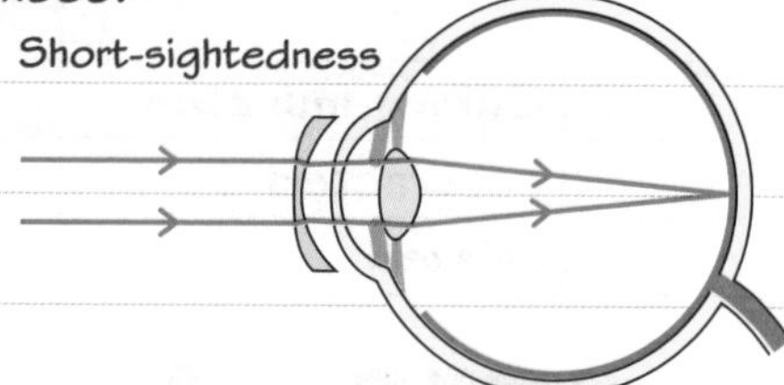

A **diverging** lens makes the rays come together further away, so light is focused on the retina.

Long and short sight can also be corrected with laser surgery and with contact lenses that work with the eye's own lens to adjust the path of the light through the eye.

Worked example

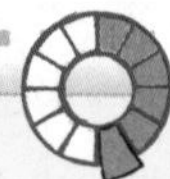

What are the causes and symptoms of
(a) short sight **(2 marks)**
(b) long sight? **(2 marks)**

(a) A short-sighted person may have eyeballs that are too long, or eye lenses that are too powerful even when the muscles are relaxed. A person with short sight can focus on close objects but not distant ones.

(b) A long-sighted person may have eyeballs that are too short, or eye lenses that are not powerful enough. This often happens as we get older and the lens does not bend enough. A person with long sight can focus on distant objects but not close ones.

Now try this

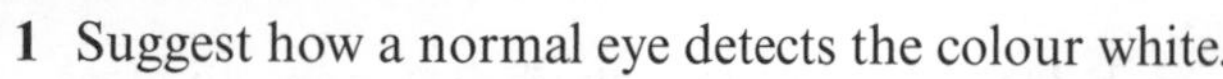

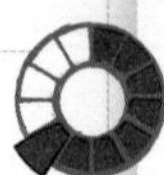

1 Suggest how a normal eye detects the colour white. **(1 mark)**

2 Suggest how the eye can detect the colour yellow. **(2 marks)**

3 The lens in the eye gets stiffer as people get older. Use this information to explain why people are more likely to need spectacles as they get older. **(2 marks)**

Extended response – Cells and control

There will be one or more 6 mark questions on your exam paper. For these questions, you will need to think scientifically, and structure your answer logically showing how the points you make are related to each other. You can revise the topic for this question, which is about **stem cells** in medicine, on page 18.

Worked example

Parkinson's disease causes some cells of the nervous system to die and stop releasing neurotransmitter. At the moment, patients with the disease are treated with a drug. This slows the disease, but this cannot stop it. Scientists are investigating whether skin cells, turned into stem cells, could be used to treat the disease.

Discuss whether this stem cell treatment could replace drug treatment for Parkinson's disease.

(6 marks)

Stem cells are unspecialised cells that can divide to produce many kinds of specialised cell. This means they could be used to produce new nerve cells to replace those that have died in a person with Parkinson's disease. So, stem cell treatment may be able to cure the disease, while the drug treatment only slows down how quickly the disease develops.

Turning skin cells into stem cells is useful because skin cells are easy to get at. If the skin cells are taken from the person with the disease then, when the stem cells from those skin cells are put back into the body, the person's immune system will recognise the stem cells made from those skin cells as belonging to their body and will not attack them. This should increase the chances of successful treatment.

Using stem cells to treat Parkinson's disease is still being tested. The treatment might not work if the stem cells do not behave properly in the body. They may make the wrong kind of specialised cell, or they may develop into cancer.

Planning an answer

Try planning out your answer before you start writing, e.g. note down a different idea for each paragraph. This can help order the answer, and make sure you do not miss anything important.

A good start is to explain any key words in the question. In this case, explaining what stem cells do will prepare for why this treatment could be better than using drugs.

Command word: Discuss

The answer to a **discuss** question should include all aspects of the issue in the question. You are not expected to draw a conclusion from the discussion.

If stem cell treatment is to replace drug treatment, there must be evidence that it is better. Look for places in your answer where you can compare the two treatments.

When discussing all aspects of using stem cells, remember to include their risks as well as their benefits.

Now try this

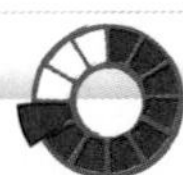

Heart disease can involve heart muscle cells, epithelial (surface) cells and other blood vessel cells. Embryonic stem cells have been shown to replace several types of damaged heart cell in mice with heart disease. Discuss the potential benefits and problems involved with developing this treatment for use in humans with heart damage.

(6 marks)

Asexual and sexual reproduction

Reproduction is the production of new individuals. There are two forms of reproduction. Each has advantages and disadvantages.

Sexual reproduction

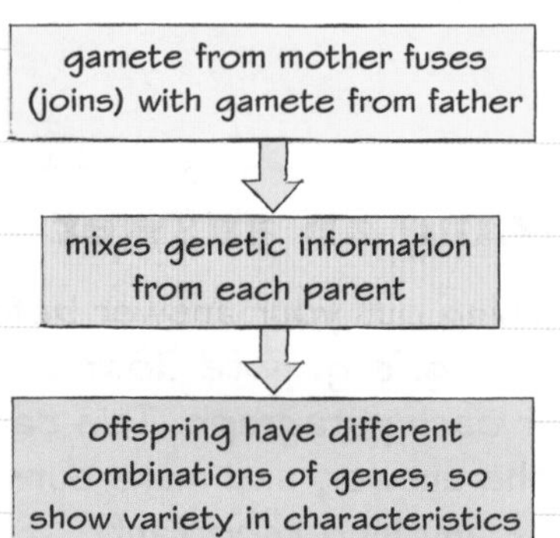

gamete from mother fuses (joins) with gamete from father
mixes genetic information from each parent
offspring have different combinations of genes, so show variety in characteristics

Advantages

- Offspring are genetically different to parents and each other, so there is **variation**. This means that if the environment changes, then some individuals may survive.

Disadvantages

- The organism has to **find** a mate to reproduce, which takes time and energy.

2 Asexual reproduction

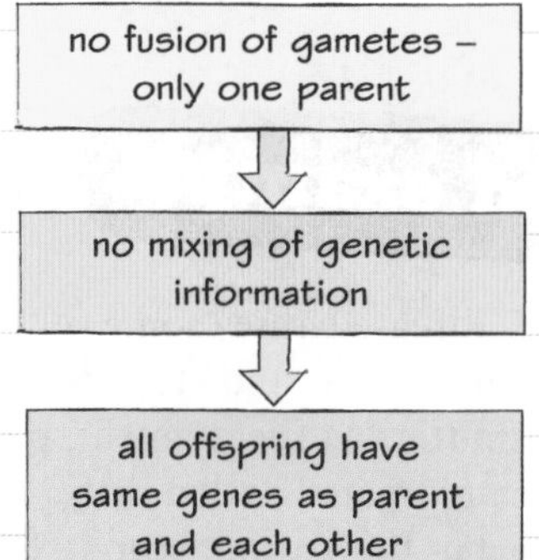

Advantages

- Only one parent – no need to find a mate and reproductive cycle is **faster**.
- Offspring are **genetically identical** to each other and to the parent. This is an advantage in organisms that are very well adapted to an unchanging environment. If the parent is well adapted to the environment, then offspring will be too.

Disadvantages

- All offspring are genetically identical, so there is **no variation** in the population and if the environment changes then all may die.

Worked example

It isn't enough to say mitosis – you need to say that this gives genetically identical cells

1 Describe how asexual reproduction produces genetically identical offspring. **(1 mark)**

This involves mitosis, which produces genetically identical cells.

2 Aphids are insects that are pests of crop plants. They reproduce asexually in the summer but by sexual reproduction in the autumn. Explain the advantage to aphids of having both sexual and asexual reproduction. **(2 marks)**

Asexual reproduction in the summer means they produce lots of offspring very quickly while there is plenty of food available. In the autumn, they reproduce sexually so that the offspring show variation. This means that at least some of the offspring are likely to survive if the environment is harsh.

Now try this

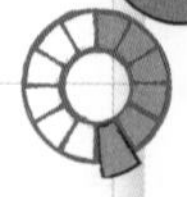

1 Which of these is a disadvantage of sexual reproduction?

☐ **A** Only one parent
☐ **B** Organism needs to find a mate
☐ **C** Offspring genetically identical
☐ **D** Offspring show variation **(1 mark)**

2 Explain one advantage of sexual reproduction. **(2 marks)**

Explain means 'give a reason'. Use 'because' in your answer.

Meiosis

Meiosis is a type of cell division that produces four **daughter cells**, each with half the number of chromosomes. Meiosis only happens in gamete-producing cells, producing genetically different **haploid** gametes. The other type of cell division, mitosis, is covered on page 15.

Stages of meiosis

The parent cell is a diploid cell. So it has two sets of chromosomes.

The parent cell divides in two and then in two again. Four daughter cells are produced.

one set of chromosomes

the other set of chromosomes

pair of chromosomes

Before the parent cell divides, each chromosome is copied.

Each daughter cell gets a copy of one chromosome from each pair.

Each daughter cell has only one set of chromosomes. So these are **haploid** cells. The daughter cells are not all identical – meiosis results in variation.

Remember: haploid cells, produced by meiosis (me-1-osis), have 1 set of chromosomes.

The cells produced by division are always called 'daughter cells', even if they will eventually turn into sperm cells.

Worked example

Compare mitosis and meiosis. (4 marks)

Meiosis produces four daughter cells, but mitosis only produces two.

Meiosis produces genetically different daughter cells, but in mitosis the daughter cells are identical to each other and to the parent cell.

Meiosis produces haploid cells, but mitosis produces diploid cells.

Mitosis occurs in body cells, but meiosis occurs only in germ cells.

Be careful to spell mitosis and meiosis correctly. If you write something like 'meitosis' or 'miosis' it won't be clear which kind of cell division you are referring to.

Now try this

1 Describe the outcome of meiosis of a diploid parent cell. **(3 marks)**

2 Explain the importance of meiosis occurring before fertilisation. **(3 marks)**

You need to say enough for 3 marks here. It may help to think about what would happen if gametes were produced by mitosis and not meiosis.

3 Distinguish between the terms 'haploid' and 'diploid'. **(2 marks)**

4 The cells produced by meiosis are

☐ **A** diploid
☐ **B** genetically different
☐ **C** embryos
☐ **D** identical **(1 mark)**

DNA

DNA is the **genetic material** found in the chromosomes in the nuclei of cells.

DNA in the cell

The nucleus contains chromosomes.

Most cells have a nucleus.

cell

chromosome

A chromosome consists of a string of genes.

A **gene** is a short piece of **DNA** that codes for a specific **protein**. You have genes for hair structure, eye colour, enzymes and every other protein in your body.

DNA

Each gene is a length of DNA. DNA is a long, coiled molecule formed from two strands. The strands are twisted in a **double helix**.

The two strands of the double helix are joined by pairs of **bases**. There are four different bases in DNA:
A = adenine T = thymine
C = cytosine G = guanine

Bases form **complementary pairs**:
A always pairs with T
C always pairs with G.

Remember: straight A with straight T; curly C with curly G.

G C
A T
C G
A T
T A

Weak hydrogen bonds between the base pairs hold the DNA strands together.

The **genome** is the base sequence of all the DNA in an organism.

DNA structure

DNA is a **polymer** made of many **monomers**, called **nucleotides**, joined together.

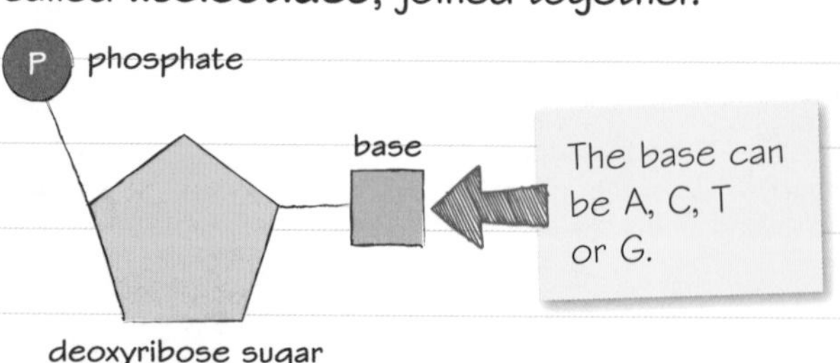

The base can be A, C, T or G.

Practical skills: DNA from fruit

DNA can be extracted from fruit by:

1. grinding the fruit with sand, using a pestle and mortar, to separate the cells
2. adding a detergent to break open the membranes
3. adding ice-cold alcohol so that the DNA precipitates out.

Now try this

You do not need to know the names of the bases. You just need to know their letters are A, C, T and G.

1 Write a sentence to define each of these words:
(a) gene (b) base. **(2 marks)**

2 The sequence of bases on one strand of DNA is CGAT. Write down the sequence of bases on the complementary strand, and explain how you worked out your answer. **(2 marks)**

3 Describe the structure of DNA. **(4 marks)**

This question has 4 marks, so the answer needs 4 different ideas.

Protein synthesis

Protein synthesis consists of two separate stages: transcription and translation. **Transcription** takes place in the nucleus. The strand of **messenger RNA (mRNA)** that is formed then moves out of the nucleus into the cytoplasm. **Translation** takes place in the cytoplasm when the mRNA strand attaches to a **ribosome**.

Transcription

1 A section of DNA is unwound and the two strands separate

2 The enzyme RNA polymerase binds to non-coding DNA in front of the gene

3 Free complementary bases pair with the open bases on one DNA strand. The free nucleotides are joined together by the enzyme RNA polymerase to make a strand of complementary mRNA.

direction of RNA polymerase

free bases

The base pairs that produce the strand of mRNA are the same as in DNA, except that T in DNA is replaced by U in RNA. So A and U pair, and G and C pair.

Translation

A polypeptide is one piece of a protein.

1 The mRNA attaches to a ribosome. Ribosome moves along the mRNA in this direction reading one **triplet of bases (codon)** at a time.

2 tRNA molecules bring amino acids to the ribosome. The amino acid attached to each tRNA molecule depends on the order of bases in the tRNA.

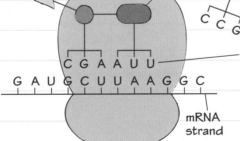

3 Complementary bases of tRNA pair with the bases on the mRNA strand.

4 Amino acids that are close together are joined to make an amino acid chain (a **polypeptide**).

5 tRNA free to collect another amino acid

6 Every protein is formed from a specific number of amino acids in a particular order. The order of the bases in the DNA defines the order in which the amino acids are joined together. So one section of DNA codes for one particular protein.

The proteins then fold to produce specifically shaped proteins such as enzymes.

amino acids

C C G

C U A

C G A A U U

G A U G C U U A A G G C

mRNA strand

To **transcribe** means to copy – the base order in DNA is copied to make the base order in mRNA. To **translate** is like changing to another language – translating from bases to amino acids.

Now try this

1 Name the two stages in protein synthesis. **(2 marks)**

2 Describe the role of the following in protein synthesis:
(a) mRNA (b) tRNA. **(2 marks)**

3 Explain the link between the order of the bases on the DNA and the order of the amino acids in a polypeptide. **(3 marks)**

Gregor Mendel

Gregor Mendel was an Austrian monk who studied genetics. He was the first person to discover the basics of **inheritance**.

Mendel's experiment

Mendel cross-bred peas to determine which traits were **dominant** and which traits were **recessive**.

So although the trait for tall peas was dominant, the first generation of offspring still retained some information about the trait for dwarf peas. Mendel had discovered **genes**.

pure-bred peas
Mendel created **pure-bred** peas to use in his experiments. These would always produce identical offspring when bred with a pea of the same type.

1st generation
He crossed pure-bred **dwarf peas** with pure-bred **tall peas** and discovered that all the offspring were tall. The trait for tall peas was **dominant** and the trait for dwarf peas was **recessive**.

2nd generation
Mendel then removed the pure-bred peas and cross-bred the offspring with themselves. In the **second generation** about **one quarter** of the offspring were dwarf peas.

Mendel's work is important because he set up his experiments scientifically.

He used peas because his earlier work showed a repeatable pattern of results.

He developed pure-breeding lines of peas to use in his experiments.

These produced offspring that were all identical to the parent for that particular trait. This meant he could repeat the experiments and know that he would get similar results each time.

He pollinated each plant by hand, so he knew which plants had been crossed.

He repeated his experiments many times, and kept detailed notes of his results.

Worked example

(a) Mendel crossed a pure-breeding tall pea with a pure-breeding dwarf pea. He obtained 128 offspring and they were all tall. Explain why Mendel had to prepare pure-breeding tall and dwarf plants before he started his experiment. **(3 marks)**

This was so that he knew the tall plants were all genetically the same and that the dwarf plants were also genetically the same. It meant he could repeat his results.

(b) He bred the offspring together and got 3980 tall and 1302 dwarf plants. Explain what Mendel could conclude from these results. **(3 marks)**

There was a factor for tallness that was dominant over the factor for dwarfness, because although there were no dwarf plants after the first cross, some dwarf plants appeared in the second generation.

You need to state a conclusion and give a reason why the results support this conclusion.

Before Mendel

At the time Mendel was working, nobody knew about DNA, genes or chromosomes. Many people thought that offspring resulted from a 'blending' of the parents' characteristics.

Another idea, common at the time, was that sperm cells carried a miniature but perfectly formed offspring, and the female's egg provided an 'essence' that allowed the offspring to grow.

Now try this

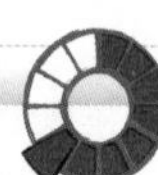

1 Explain why it was difficult for Mendel to understand inheritance before the mechanism was discovered. **(1 mark)**

2 Explain why Mendel carried out each of his crosses many times. **(1 mark)**

Genetic terms

You need to be able to explain all of the **genetic terms** in bold on this page.

Inside a cell

When **gametes** fuse at fertilisation, they form a diploid **zygote**. Each zygote inherits different alleles (genetic variants) of their genes from their parents. This produces variation in inherited characteristics between different individuals.

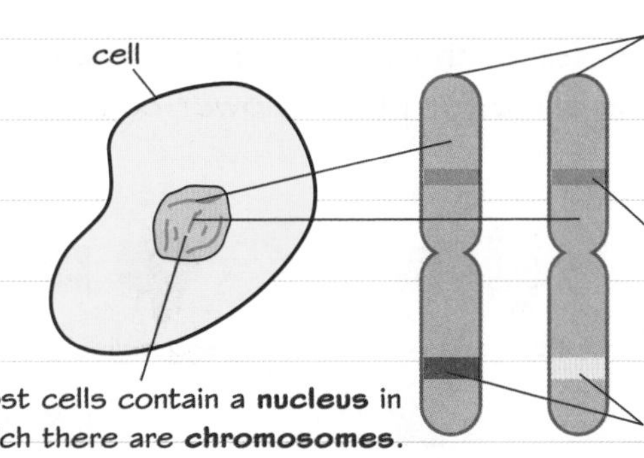
cell
Most cells contain a **nucleus** in which there are **chromosomes**.
There are two copies of each **chromosome** in body cells – each copy has the same genes in the same order along its length (except chromosomes that determine sex).
A **gene** is a short piece of DNA at a particular point on a chromosome – a gene codes for a characteristic, e.g. eye colour.
A gene may come in different forms, called **alleles**, that produce different variations of the characteristic, e.g. different eye colours.

Alleles

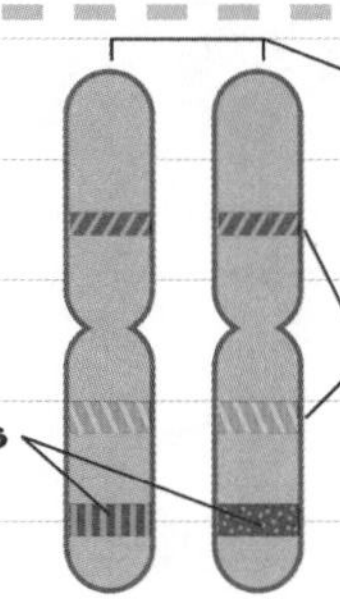
Chromosomes of the same pair have the same genes in the same order.
different alleles of the same gene – the person is **heterozygous** for this gene
these genes have the same allele on both chromosomes – the person is **homozygous** for these genes

Genetic definitions

The gene for coat colour in rabbits has different alleles. The allele for brown colour (B) is dominant over the allele for black colour (b). The table shows all the possible genotypes and phenotypes for these alleles.

Genotype shows the alleles (forms of the genes) in the individual. Remember that each body cell has two genes for each characteristic – either two alleles that are the same or two that are different.

Genotype	Phenotype
BB	brown coat
Bb	brown coat
bb	black coat

Phenotype means the characteristics that are produced, including what the individual looks like.

The effect of the **dominant** allele will show when at least one copy is present in the genotype.

The effect of the **recessive** allele will only show when two copies are present in the genotype.

Now try this

Make sure you know the difference between a gene and an allele. This is a common mistake that students make.

1 Define the terms *chromosome*, *gene* and *allele*. **(3 marks)**

2 A pea plant has a recessive allele for white flower colour and a dominant allele for purple flower colour.
(a) Identify if the plant is homozygous or heterozygous for flower colour, and explain your answer. **(2 marks)**
(b) State the phenotype of the plant for flower colour. Explain your answer. **(2 marks)**

Monohybrid inheritance

Monohybrid inheritance can be explained using **genetic diagrams** and **Punnett squares**.

Genetic diagrams

Body cells contain two alleles for each gene. In this example, both parent plants are heterozygous – they have one allele for purple flower colour and one allele for white flower colour.

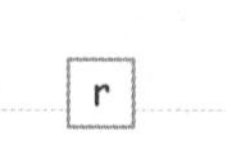

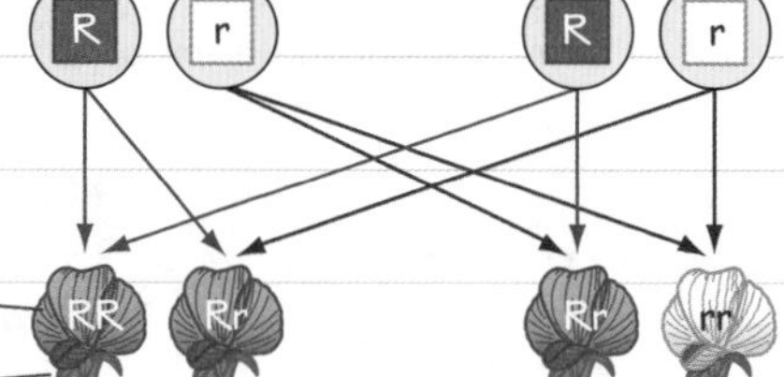

Worked example

Green seed pod (G) is dominant to yellow seed pod (g). Complete the Punnett square to show the possible offspring for plants heterozygous for seed pod colour, and calculate the (a) ratio, (b) probability and (c) percentage of possible offspring genotypes and phenotypes. **(4 marks)**

		parent genotype Gg	
	parent gametes	G	g
parent genotype Gg	G	GG green	Gg green
	g	Gg green	gg yellow

(a) Genotype 1 GG : 2 Gg : 1 gg
Phenotype 3 green : 1 yellow

(b) Genotype 1/4 (1 out of 4) GG, 2/4 (1/2) Gg, and 1/4 gg
Phenotype 3/4 green and 1/4 yellow

(c) Genotype 25% GG, 50% Gg, 25% gg
Phenotype 75% green and 25% yellow

A **Punnett square** is a different way of showing the same information about how genotype is inherited and what effect this has on the phenotype.

Genetic diagrams and Punnett squares only show **possible** offspring, not the **actual** offspring from these parents.

Now try this

Remember to use a Punnett square when answering this question.

A heterozygous rabbit with a brown coat was bred with a rabbit with a black coat (homozygous recessive). The four baby rabbits were all black.

(a) Use a diagram to calculate the predicted outcome of this cross. **(3 marks)**

(b) Comment on the difference between this and the actual outcome. **(2 marks)**

Family pedigrees

Cystic fibrosis (CF) is a genetic condition caused by a recessive allele. **Pedigree analysis** can be used to study the inheritance of dominant and recessive alleles.

Family pedigree showing inheritance of cystic fibrosis

You can use a **family pedigree** to show the inheritance of a genetic condition within a family, and to **predict** the chance that someone will inherit the faulty allele.

In the family pedigree below, both Ethan and Mia have CF. Ethan inherited his alleles from Arun and Beth. But they don't have the disease, so they must both be **carriers** (have one copy of the faulty allele).

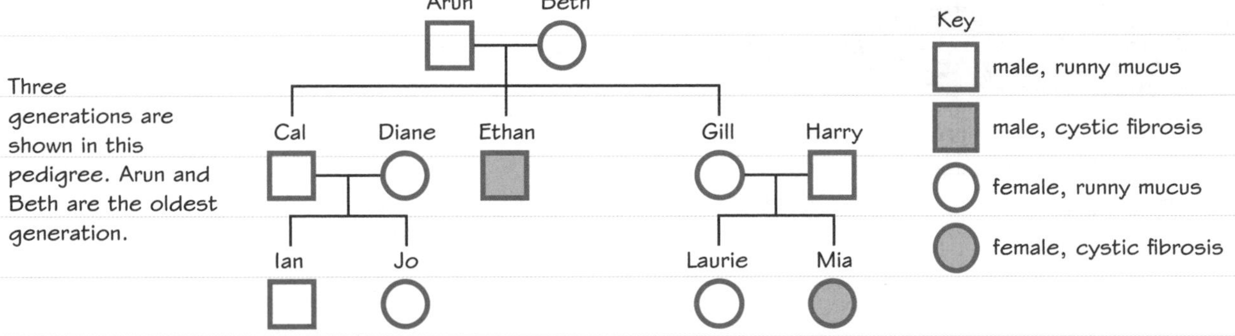

Ethan and Mia must have two copies of the recessive allele, as they have the disease.

Worked example

The ability to taste phenylthiocarbamide (PTC) is a dominant condition. The diagram shows the inheritance of PTC tasting in one family. Describe the evidence that PTC tasting is controlled by a dominant allele. **(2 marks)**

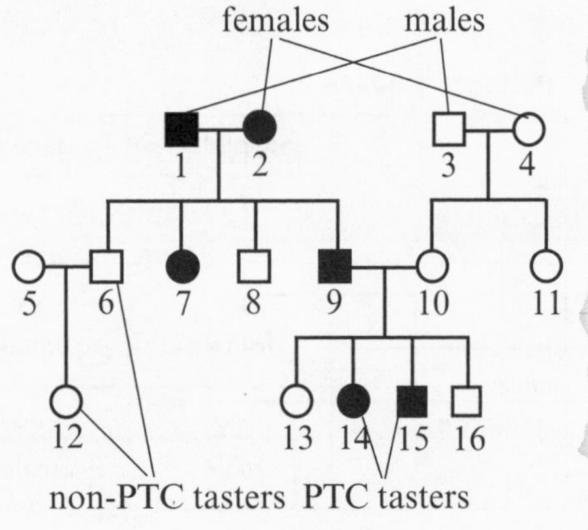

1 and 2 are both PTC tasters but they have two children who are non-tasters. Therefore PTC tasting must be dominant and non-tasting is recessive.

You are asked for **evidence** so make sure you refer to **specific individuals** in the pedigree.

Maths skills: Pedigree analysis

Look at the family pedigree above. You can calculate the **probability** of Gill and Harry having a third child with cystic fibrosis using a Punnett square.

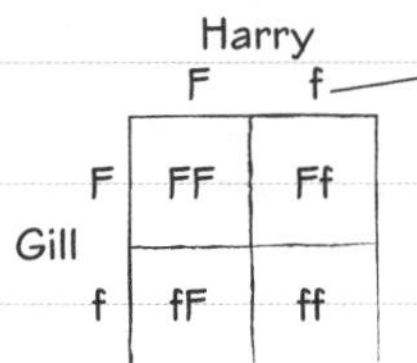

Mia has the disease, so Harry and Gill must both have one copy of the faulty allele.

There is one outcome (ff) that would lead to a child having CF, and three that would not:

P(third child has CF) = $\frac{1}{4}$ or 25%

There is more about Punnett squares on page 34.

Now try this

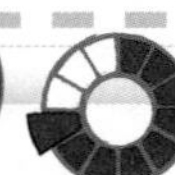

Look at the family pedigree in the worked example above.

(a) Give the genotype of individual 2. **(1 mark)**

(b) Individuals 9 and 10 have a fifth child. Calculate the probability that the child will be a PTC taster. **(2 marks)**

Remember that the trait is **dominant** so each person only needs **one copy** of the allele in order to be a PTC taster.

Sex determination

The sex of humans is determined at fertilisation and can be expressed using **genetic diagrams** and **Punnett squares**.

Sex chromosomes

The sex of humans is controlled by one pair of **sex chromosomes**. The genotype **XX** produces the **female** phenotype. The genotype **XY** produces the **male** phenotype.

Genotype and phenotype

The genotype is all the genes of the individual. The phenotype is what the individual looks like.

Worked example

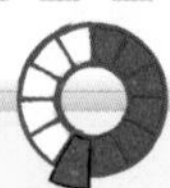

Explain the proportions of the different sex chromosomes in the gametes of men and women. **(3 marks)**

Gametes are haploid because they are produced by meiosis. As the sex chromosomes in a woman's diploid body cell are both X, all the eggs she produces will contain one X chromosome. The sex chromosomes in a man's diploid body cells are XY, so 50% of his sperm will contain one X chromosome and the other 50% will contain one Y chromosome.

Genetic diagrams and Punnett squares

We can use a **genetic diagram** or **Punnett square** to show that the sex of an individual is determined at fertilisation.

Genetic diagram

parent's phenotype	male		female	
parent's genotype	XY		XX	
gametes	X	Y	X	X
possible offspring	XX	XY	XX	XY

Punnett square

		possible female gametes	
		X	X
possible male gametes	X	XX female	XX female
	Y	XY male	XY male

You can usually use either a Punnett square or a genetic diagram to answer a question about inheritance. Use the one that works best for you.

Both diagrams show that, at fertilisation, there is an equal chance of producing a male or a female:

- 50% male XY: 50% female XX
- ratio of 1 : 1 male : female
- 1 out of 2 chance of either male or female.

Use a Punnett square like this.

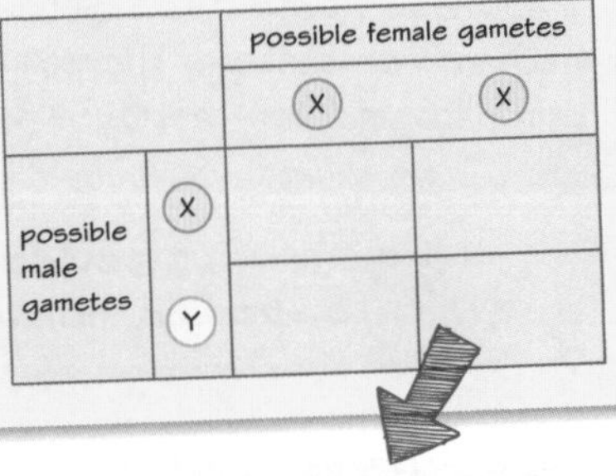

Now try this

1 At which of the following stages is the sex of a baby determined?

☐ **A** When the egg is fertilised
☐ **B** As the foetus develops in the womb
☐ **C** When the baby is born **(1 mark)**

2 A couple have two sons. The woman is pregnant with another child. Draw a genetic diagram to show the % chance of this child being a girl. **(4 marks)**

3 Explain why human eggs all contain one X chromosome. **(2 marks)**

Inherited characteristics

The human ABO blood group is an example of an inherited characteristic controlled by a single gene that has **multiple alleles**. Sex-linked genetic disorders are **inherited**.

Blood groups

There are four ABO blood groups controlled by three different alleles:

Phenotype (blood group)	Genotype
A	I^AI^A or I^AI^O
B	I^BI^B or I^BI^O
AB	I^AI^B
O	I^OI^O

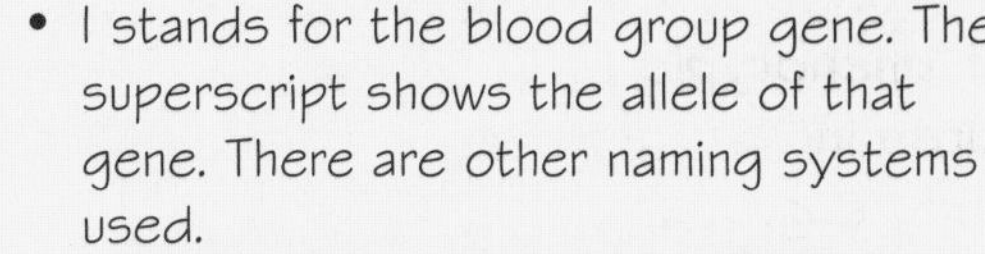

- I stands for the blood group gene. The superscript shows the allele of that gene. There are other naming systems used.
- I^O is recessive to I^A and I^B because it is not expressed in the heterozygote.
- I^A and I^B are **codominant**. This occurs when the heterozygous individual shows the effect of both alleles that they carry for the gene.

Worked example

A woman of blood group O has a baby with blood group B. Her partner has blood group AB.
Use a Punnett square to explain how a baby can have a different blood group to both parents. **(3 marks)**

The woman must have the genotype I^OI^O and her partner must have the genotype I^AI^B.

The woman's gametes are all I^O but the man has two types of gamete: I^A and I^B.

	I^A	I^B
I^O	I^AI^O	I^BI^O
I^O	I^AI^O	I^BI^O

Sex-linked inheritance

The sex chromosomes, X and Y, are not a matching pair. Males only have one X chromosome. A recessive allele on this chromosome will affect the phenotype as it is not matched by a dominant allele on the Y chromosome. This produces a different pattern of inheritance in men and women, and is said to be **sex-linked**.

Haemophilia

Haemophilia is a sex-linked genetic disorder.

The alleles for the gene are:
- X^H – allele on the X chromosome that produces normal blood clotting
- X^h – the **recessive** haemophilia allele that causes poor blood clotting.

There is no gene for haemophilia on the Y chromosome. Boys can only inherit haemophilia if their mother is a haemophiliac or a **carrier** for the disease.

For sex-linked inheritance, you must show the X chromosome as well as the allele.

		mother: genotype X^HX^h	
	gametes	X^H	X^h
father: genotype X^HY	X^H	X^HX^H female, normal clotting	X^HX^h female, normal clotting (carrier)
	Y	X^HY male, normal clotting	X^hY male haemophilia

genotypes and phenotypes of possible offspring

Chance of inheriting haemophilia from a father with normal blood clotting and a carrier mother:
- probability: daughter 0/2, son 1/2
- ratio: daughter 0, son 1 : 2
- percentage: daughter 0%, son 50%.

Now try this

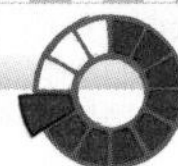

Explain the role of co-dominant alleles in human ABO blood groups. **(3 marks)**

Variation and mutation

Causes of **variation** that influence phenotype include genetic variation and environmental variation. Genetic variation happens through **mutation**.

Causes of variation

Most phenotypic features in humans, e.g. hair colour, are caused by many genes. Each of these genes may have several alleles, so the phenotype is the result of the **combination** of different alleles for different genes. This combination of alleles that an organism inherits is the result of sexual reproduction.

differences between individuals of the same kind

caused by differences in alleles they have inherited, e.g. eye colour (**genetic variation**)

combination of both causes, e.g. weight, skin colour

caused by differences in conditions in which they developed, e.g. riding a bike, scars (**environmental variation**)

Most variations are caused by a combination of genes and environment.

Mutation

A **mutation** or **genetic variant** is created if the sequence of bases in a gene is changed. A mutation in the gene's coding DNA can affect the phenotype of an organism. If the amino acid sequence is altered, the activity of the protein produced may also be altered. However:

- most genetic mutations have no effect on the phenotype
- some mutations have a small effect on the phenotype
- a single mutation can, rarely, significantly affect the phenotype.

A mutation may cause:

- a large change in the protein produced
- a small change in the protein
- no change at all in the protein produced.

The bigger the change to the protein, the larger the effect on how the body works.

Non-coding DNA

A mutation in the non-coding DNA can also affect the phenotype. This may increase or decrease the ability of RNA polymerase to bind to DNA. A change like this can increase or decrease the amount of protein produced.

Worked example

Enzymes have a very specific shape that allows them to work effectively. Explain why a gene mutation can change the activity of an enzyme. Refer to the active site in your answer. **(3 marks)**

A gene mutation can change the base sequence in DNA. If this change produces a different amino acid sequence, this may change the shape of the active site. The shape of the active site controls how well an enzyme works. If the shape of the active site matches the shape of the substrate better, then the enzyme will work better. But if the shape of the active site is not as good a match, then the enzyme will not work so well.

Now try this

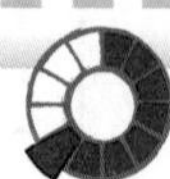

1 Identical twins are produced when a fertilised egg cell divides in two on its first division. Use this information to explain why identical twins share many, but not all, of their characteristics. **(2 marks)**

2 Explain why a mutation in a body cell will not affect a person's phenotype. **(2 marks)**

Most mutations occur when DNA replicates before cell division. Most of them cause no change in the phenotype.

The Human Genome Project

The **Human Genome Project** is a collaboration between scientists to decode the **human genome** (the order of bases on all human chromosomes). The project was completed quickly because so many scientists worked on it at the same time. The work was published in 2003 and made freely available to scientists all over the world. The results are being used to develop new medicines and treatments for diseases.

Advantages and disadvantages of the Human Genome Project

Advantages

- Alerting people that they are at particular **risk** of certain diseases, e.g. types of cancer or heart disease. The person may be able to make lifestyle changes to reduce the chances of the disease developing.
- Distinguishing between different forms of diseases such as leukaemia or Alzheimer's disease, as some drugs are beneficial in some forms of these diseases but not in others.
- Allowing doctors to **tailor treatments** for some diseases to the individual, where specific alleles affect how a person will respond to treatment.

Disadvantages

- People who are at risk of certain diseases, e.g. cancer, may have to pay more to obtain life insurance.
- It may not be helpful to tell someone they are at risk of a condition for which there is currently no cure.

Worked example

Describe two possible developments as a result of decoding the human genome, and discuss the implications of these developments. **(4 marks)**

One development is the identification of genes that can cause disease. Knowing if you have a faulty gene could help a person and their family prepare for its effects, but some people would prefer not to know if they have a faulty gene because then they would worry about it.

Another development is gene therapy. This involves replacing faulty alleles in body cells with healthy ones. This would allow the affected person to live a normal life. However, people will have to decide whether the faulty alleles are replaced in gametes, so that the healthy alleles could be passed on to children.

There are many possible answers for this question, because there are many new developments. Other possibilities include: creating personalised medicines, and identifying evolutionary relationships between humans and other organisms. As well as learning about new developments you need to be able to say what the implications are.

Now try this

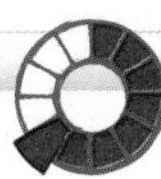

Humans all share the same genes, but think carefully about alleles and base sequences.

1 The Human Genome Project means that soon we might be able to tell a child that they are at increased risk of developing high blood pressure in early middle age.
Give one advantage and one disadvantage of this. **(2 marks)**

2 The genome of two different humans is not exactly the same. Explain why. **(2 marks)**

Extended response – Genetics

There will be one or more 6 mark questions on your exam paper. For these questions, you will need to think scientifically, and structure your answer logically showing how the points you make are related to each other. You can revise the topics for this question, which is about **monohybrid inheritance** and **blood group inheritance**, on pages 32 and 35.

Worked example

A woman is blood group A (I^AI^O) and her husband is blood group B (I^BI^O). With reference to this information, explain how inheritance of ABO blood group is different from examples of monohybrid inheritance where the gene has two alleles. **(6 marks)**

This Punnett square shows the possible offspring from these parents.

		father's gametes	
		I^B	I^O
mother's gametes	I^A	I^AI^B blood group AB	I^AI^O blood group A
	I^O	I^BI^O blood group B	I^OI^O blood group O

This shows that each child of these parents has an equal probability of any of the four possible blood groups.

Monohybrid inheritance usually shows the inheritance of a single gene that has two possible alleles, and one allele is dominant to the other (recessive) allele.

Blood group inheritance is different to normal monohybrid inheritance because the gene for ABO blood group has three alleles, I^A, I^B and I^O. This makes it an example of a gene with multiple alleles. It is also different to normal monohybrid inheritance because the I^A and I^B alleles are codominant. This means that they both have an effect on the phenotype when they are present together in the genotype.

When a question tells you to use information, make sure you include it in your answer.

Even in long-answer questions, a good way to display genetic information clearly is in a Punnett square or genetic diagram.

When you use a Punnett square or genetic diagram, remember to explain the possible outcomes in terms of probability, ratio or percentage.

Use the correct science words where appropriate, such as multiple allele, codominant, phenotype and genotype.

Now try this

Duchenne muscular dystrophy is an inherited disorder that causes increasing muscle weakness.
About 1 in 3500 men develop the disorder, but it is almost never seen in women.
Explain how this disorder is inherited. **(6 marks)**

Evolution

Alfred Russel **Wallace** and Charles **Darwin** separately developed theories of evolution by means of natural selection, based on their own work and that of previous scientists. They presented their theory jointly in 1858, and it is still important in modern biology.

Natural selection

Individuals of a species show variation. This can mean that some individuals will be better able to survive in their environment and produce more healthy offspring than others. This is **natural selection**, where the environment (including climate and other organisms) selects which individuals pass on their **alleles** to the next generation.

Theory of evolution in modern biology

The theory of evolution is very important in modern biology:

- ✓ It helps us understand the relationships between different species of organisms.
- ✓ It explains how new species evolve.
- ✓ It explains how different species adapt to changes in their environment.

Darwin's theory

Adults usually produce more young than the environment can support when they are adults (**overproduction**). This produces a **'struggle for existence'** by the young.

→ Some individuals have inherited **advantageous variations** in characteristics that are better adapted to the environment. These individuals will have a better chance of **survival** to adulthood.

→ Individuals with advantageous variations will pass their genes on to their young. The young may inherit the advantageous variations.

→ More individuals will have these advantageous variations in the next generation.

→ Individuals with variations that are not as well adapted to the environment will be less likely to survive.

→ These individuals will not produce young.

One example of Darwin's theory is the development of antibiotic resistance in bacteria.

Doctors tell you to complete the full course of antibiotics, even if you feel better before the course is finished. If you do not finish taking a complete course of antibiotics, the bacteria resistant to the antibiotic can reproduce. This can result in an infection of antibiotic-resistant bacteria that is much harder to treat.

Worked example

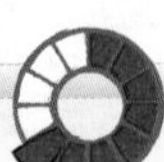

African Elephants are hunted illegally by poachers for their tusks. Elephants may be born tuskless due to a mutation. In 1930 in Uganda, only 1% of elephants were born without tusks. In 2010, 15% of females and 9% of male elephants were born without tusks. Explain this change using the theory of evolution. **(3 marks)**

Elephants with tusks are more likely to be poached and killed, so do not survive to pass on their alleles. Tuskless elephants are more likely to survive to pass on the allele for no tusks, so the allele for no tusks increases in frequency in the population.

This is an example of where you may be asked to apply your understanding to a specific example that you may not be familiar with.

Now try this

Remember to use scientific terms like mutation and alleles, as well as explaining the effects on survival and passing on alleles.

In a recent study, scientists tested 321 samples of head lice and found that 82% of the lice were resistant to chemicals used to treat head lice infestations. Use your knowledge of natural selection to explain how this has happened. **(4 marks)**

Human evolution

Some of the evidence we have for evolution leading to modern humans (*Homo sapiens*) comes from **fossils**. These include fossils of bones and teeth.

Species	**Ardi** (*Ardipithecus ramidus*)	**Lucy** (*Australopithecus afarensis*)	*Homo habilis* ('handy man')	*Homo erectus* ('upright man')	*Homo sapiens* ('wise'/modern man)
height	120 cm	107 cm	< 130 cm	179 cm	wide variety but generally taller than other species
when existed	4.4 million years ago	3.2 million years ago	2.4–1.4 million years ago	1.8–0.5 million years	since c. 200 000 years ago
brain size	350 cm^3	400 cm^3	500–600 cm^3	850–1100 cm^3	approx. 1200 cm^3
other details	tree climber, also walked upright	walked upright, face ape-like	flat face like modern humans, used simple stone tools	long-distance walker, strongly built	user of complex tools

You do not need to remember details such as brain sizes but you do need to remember the names and the general trends.

Homo habilis and *Homo erectus* fossils were found by the archaeologists **Leakey** and his family. They wrote the first description of these early humans.

Stone tools

Stone tools also give us evidence of human evolution. The earliest stone tools are around 2.4 million years old. Over time more complex tools were made, and a greater range of tool types.

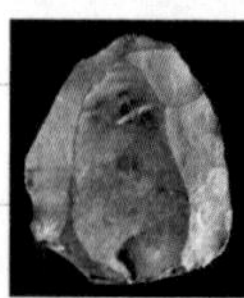

c. 2 million years old. A large stone that has had some chips flaked off it, e.g. simple hand axes

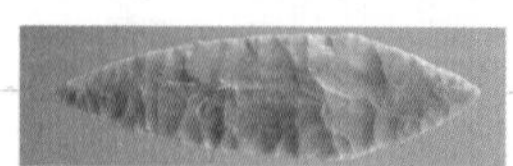

c. 40 000 years old. Made from fine flakes split from larger stones; many types of tool made this way, e.g. arrow head, spear head, scraper, knife

Worked example

Explain how stone tools can be dated from their environment. **(3 marks)**

The amount of radiation in samples of sediment just above and below the layer in which the tools are found can be used to date the sediment and so give a range of dates when the tools were left there.

The stone used to make the tools is much older than the tools, so cannot be used to date when the tool was made.

Now try this

1 Describe two ways that human-like species have evolved over the past 4.4 million years which can be seen from fossils. **(2 marks)**

2 Suggest what the development of stone tools implies about human evolution over the last 2.5 million years. **(2 marks)**

Classification

Scientists used to classify living organisms into the following five big groups, called **kingdoms**. The kingdoms were Plants, Animals, Fungi, Protists and Prokaryotes. Scientists have now classified organisms into three **domains**.

Five-kingdom system

Carl Linnaeus originally proposed the classification of organisms into just two kingdoms, but this was later developed into five kingdoms. These are:

1 Plants
2 Animals
3 Fungi
4 Protists
5 Prokaryotes.

Three-domain system

Research on genes shows that the organisms which were grouped as prokaryotes in the kingdom system should be separated into two groups, which have been named **Eubacteria** and **Archaea.** This is because the genes of organisms in Archaea work more like those in the eukaryotes, while the genes of organisms in Eubacteria work a little differently.

Eubacteria

Eukaryota includes **Plants**, **Animals**, **Fungi**, **Protoctista**

prokaryotes

Archaea mainly bacteria that live in very warm or salty conditions

This grouping forms the **three-domain** system of classification.

Worked example

The diagram shows the bones of the forelimbs of two living vertebrates. Explain how these pentadactyl limbs are evidence for evolution. **(4 marks)**

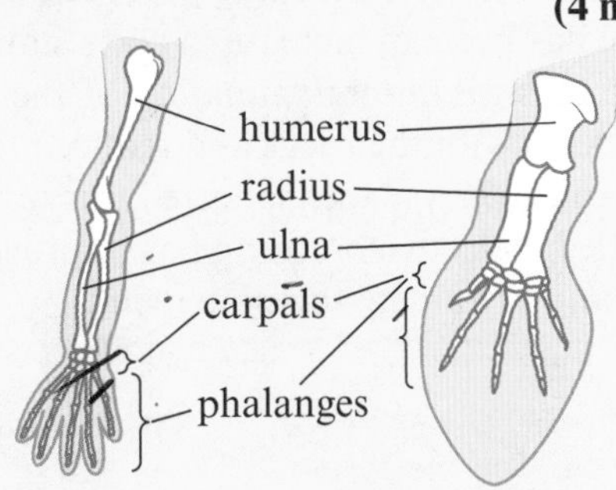

human arm – for holding and working with objects

whale flipper – for swimming underwater

The limbs show the same basic pentadactyl structure. They have long bones supporting carpal bones and phalanges. This suggests that the human and the whale evolved from a shared ancestor. The differences between the limbs can be explained by evolution. The limbs have developed in different ways because they have adapted to different uses.

Many living vertebrates have the same **pentadactyl** (five-fingered) limb structure.

Notice that this answer explains ways in which DNA differs between different groups of organisms, and points out that closely-related organisms have more similarities in their DNA.

Worked example

Suggest how studying DNA can help scientists to work out the evolutionary relationships between different groups of organisms. **(3 marks)**

Scientists can examine the structure of the DNA in the cells, e.g. whether it is formed into linear chromosomes or is circular. They can also find out how much non-coding DNA it contains. Then they can find the base sequence in the DNA of different organisms. The more closely related the organisms are, the more similarities there will be in their DNA base sequences.

Now try this

1 Describe the three-domain system of classification. **(3 marks)**

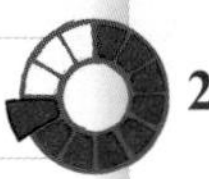

2 Explain why the five-kingdom system of classification has been replaced by the three-domain system. **(2 marks)**

Selective breeding

Selective breeding is when plants or animals with certain desirable characteristics are chosen to breed together, so that offspring will be produced that **inherit** these characteristics. This produces **new breeds** of animals and **new varieties** of plants. Selective breeding has taken place over thousands of years, but more recently **genetic engineering** has been developed as a way of manipulating genetics. You can learn about this on page 43.

Selective breeding in plants

Plants with good features are crossed, e.g. plants that have good yield, are drought tolerant, or need less fertiliser. → Plants grown from seeds of these crosses are selected for their good features and crossed with each other. → Selection and crossing is repeated many times until a high-yielding variety is produced.

Reasons for selective breeding

Plants and animals are selectively bred for:

- disease resistance
- increased yield
- better ability to cope with difficult conditions
- faster growth
- better flavour.

Worked example

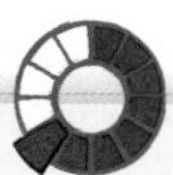

Describe how a farmer would breed cattle that have a large milk yield. **(4 marks)**

The farmer would choose a cow that produced lots of milk and cross her with a bull whose mother produced a lot of milk. The farmer would then choose the female offspring who produce lots of milk and cross them with a male whose mother had a high milk yield. The farmer would do this for many generations.

Worked example

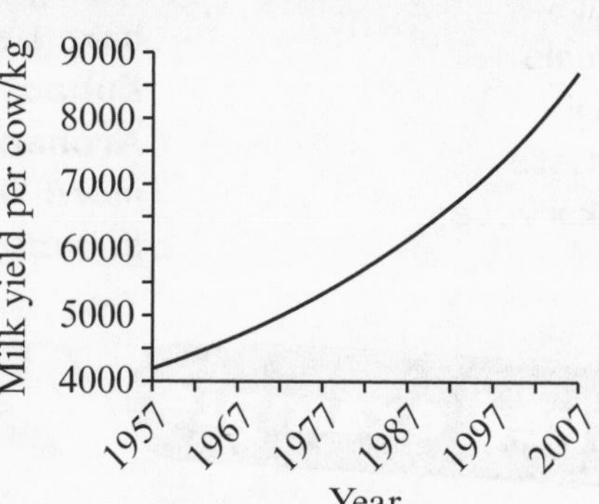

The graph shows the average milk yield per cow from 1957 to 2007. The increase is mainly the result of selective breeding. Over the same period there has been an increase in cows suffering from mastitis (an inflammation of the udders), problems with their legs and reduced fertility. A farming newspaper reported this in an article entitled 'Selective breeding has improved dairy farming'. Evaluate this statement. **(4 marks)**

The graph shows that the milk yield per cow has more than doubled over these 50 years so this is useful for the farmer. *(Advantage)*

However, the cows are having more problems with their legs and udders which may be because they are producing so much milk, so this is an animal welfare issue. *(Ethical issue)*

It also costs the farmer more in veterinary bills. *(Practical issue)*

I think that selective breeding to produce a high-yielding breed of cows is a good thing, but this should not be done at the expense of animal welfare.

You can draw your own conclusion as long as it clearly relates to the information given and the benefits and risks identified.

Now try this

1 Give one advantage and one disadvantage of selective breeding. **(2 marks)**

2 Explain the differences between natural selection and selective breeding. **(2 marks)**

3 Describe one problem of selective breeding in crop plants. **(2 marks)**

Genetic engineering

Genetic engineering is changing the **genome** (the DNA) of an organism, often by introducing genes from another to create **genetically modified organisms** (GMOs). See page 45 for more details of the processes involved in genetic engineering.

How genetic engineering works

Genes can be transferred from any kind of organism to any other kind of organism, e.g. bacteria, humans, other animals, plants.

The gene for a characteristic is 'cut out' of a chromosome using enzymes. → The gene is inserted into a chromosome inside the nucleus of a cell in a different organism. → The cell of this organism now produces the characteristic from the gene.

Worked example

Human insulin is a hormone used by many patients with diabetes. Bacteria have been genetically modified to carry the human insulin gene. The bacteria are then grown in large quantities to produce the human insulin. Explain why bacteria had to be modified to make human insulin and describe how the GM bacteria were produced. **(3 marks)**

Bacteria don't normally produce human insulin, so they had to be modified to make it. The gene for making insulin was cut out of a human chromosome. The gene was then inserted into the bacterial chromosome, so that the bacterium made the insulin.

GM crops

GM crop plants have been genetically modified to give them new characteristics, such as:

- resistance to attack by insects
- resistance to **herbicides**, so that fields can be sprayed to kill weeds, but not the crop.

These characteristics can help the crop grow better and produce more food (an increased **yield**).

Evaluating something means identifying advantages and disadvantages, then comparing them to draw a conclusion about whether the example is worth doing. You need to consider issues such as:

- How effective is it and is it worth the effort?
- Is it right/wrong/fair to do this?

Worked example

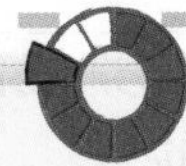

A sheep has been genetically modified to produce a protein in its milk that can be used to treat serious lung diseases in humans. Evaluate the advantages and disadvantages of this. **(4 marks)**

The protein is secreted in milk so the sheep is not harmed to produce the protein, although some people think it is unethical to use animals for the benefit of humans. The protein treats serious lung disease so is very beneficial to human health. However, in developing the genetically modified sheep a lot of embryos would have been made that did not successfully express the gene, so a lot of embryos are wasted to produce a GM sheep. However, I think this is worth doing as it treats serious disease in humans and the sheep is not harmed because the protein is produced in its milk.

Now try this

1 Define **genetic engineering**. **(2 marks)**

2 Describe how a GM crop with herbicide resistance could be developed. **(2 marks)**

3 Some mice have had a gene inserted that gives them a human disease. At the same time, the scientists inserted a gene for a fluorescent protein, so modified mouse cells glow when exposed to ultraviolet light. These mice are then used for testing new treatments for the disease.

(a) Suggest **one** advantage of using a glow gene joined to the disease gene. **(1 mark)**

(b) Describe how lots of mice with the human disease gene could be produced. **(2 marks)**

Tissue culture

Plant and animal tissue can be used to produce **cell cultures.** This means you can make many identical copies of a special organism, for example, one that has been genetically modified. It also means that drugs can be tested on cell cultures instead of animals.

Plant tissue culture

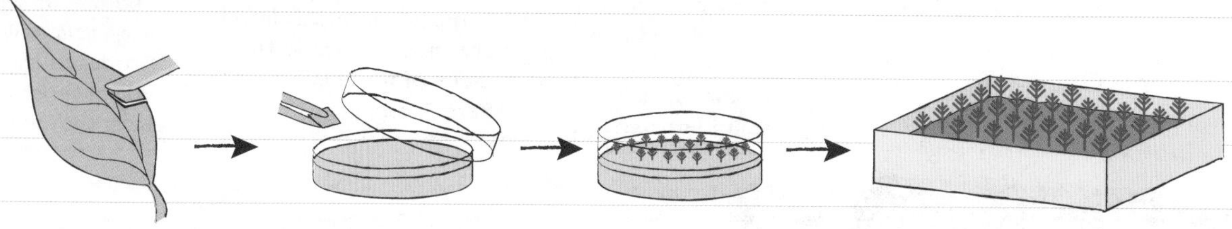

This process is similar for other kinds of cells.

Advantages of using cell cultures

Uses of animal cell cultures	Uses of plant cell cultures
test the effect of drugs and other chemicals on cells	produce hundreds or thousands of identical plants (clones) from just one parent plant, e.g. genetically modified plants
check for cancer cells in a sample from a patient	cells can be grown in culture to make plant products, e.g. paclitaxel used to treat cancer
produce important proteins, e.g. antibodies	produce disease-free plants

Worked example

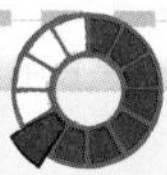

Suggest an advantage of testing drugs on animal cell cultures rather than on animals. **(2 marks)**

Testing drugs on animals means using a lot of animals and it may cause them harm. It also takes up a lot of space to test drugs on animals and cell cultures use very little space. You can test drugs on large numbers of cells in cell cultures and there are no ethical issues if the drug damages the cells.

There are several advantages but you can get full marks for just one advantage as long as you explain why it is an advantage.

Worked example

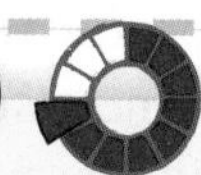

Scientists have made a genetically modified cotton plant which contains a protein that kills insect pests. The scientists want to make many copies of this plant so they can test the plant grows well. Explain the advantage of tissue culture in this process. **(3 marks)**

Thousands of identical plants can be made from just one parent plant. They can be grown quickly in a small space. As they are genetically identical to the parent plant they are very useful for testing.

Remember you need to make 3 points to gain 3 marks.

Now try this

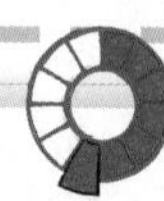

1 Explain why the plantlets produced by plant tissue culture are genetically identical. **(2 marks)**

2 Describe how tissue culture can be used to make many identical cauliflower plants. **(2 marks)**

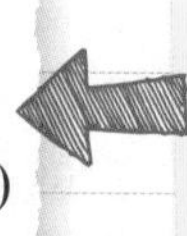

This question checks that you really understand what is going on in plant tissue culture.

Stages in genetic engineering

You need to know the processes involved in **genetic** engineering used to make **genetically modified organisms.**

Making human insulin

Human insulin can be made in large quantities from bacteria that have been genetically modified to contain the gene for human insulin.

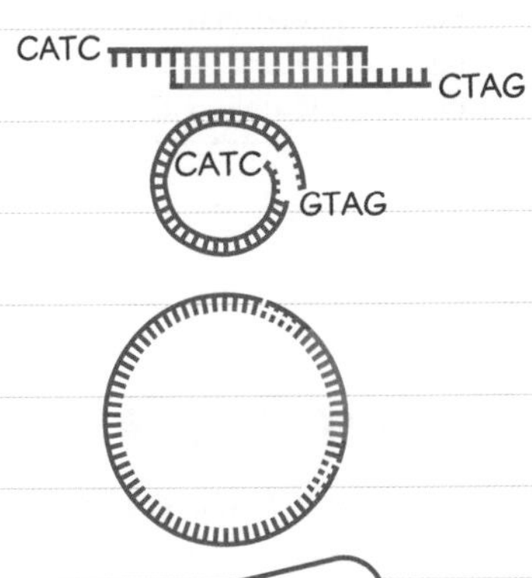

1. DNA from a human cell is cut into pieces using enzymes called **restriction enzymes**. These make staggered cuts across the double-stranded DNA, leaving a few unpaired bases at each end, called **sticky ends**.
2. Bacteria cells contain small circles of DNA called plasmids. The same restriction enzymes are used to cut plasmids open, leaving sticky ends with matching sets of unpaired bases.
3. The pieces of DNA containing the insulin gene are mixed with the plasmids. The bases in the sticky ends pair up. An enzyme called DNA **ligase** is added, linking the DNAback into a continuous circle.
4. The plasmids are inserted into bacteria. The bacteria can now be grown in huge fermenters, where they make human insulin.

Worked example

Describe the role of enzymes in the formation of genetically modified bacteria. **(3 marks)**

Restriction enzymes cut the required gene out of the human DNA. They leave 'sticky ends' on the gene. The same restriction enzymes cut open the plasmid, creating matching sticky ends. The DNA ligase enzyme joins the matching sticky ends of the human gene and the plasmid, to make one complete modified plasmid.

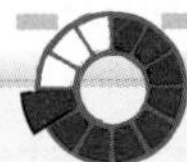

The plasmid must be removed from a bacterium before the gene is inserted. The plasmid is then inserted into another bacterium. The sticky ends allow the insulin gene and the plasmid to join together properly.

Vectors

A **vector** is the name for anything that carries the new gene into a cell. In the case of insulin above, the vector is a **plasmid**. Other kinds of vectors may be used, such as viruses.

Now try this

There are four stages you should include.

1. Describe all the stages in producing genetically modified bacteria that make insulin. Use a bullet point list or flow chart in your answer. **(4 marks)**
2. Explain why it is useful to make human insulin using genetically modified bacteria. **(2 marks)**
3. 'Glow mice' have been produced by transferring a gene that produces a chemical which glows in blue light into a mouse. The glow gene is joined to a gene that causes a human genetic disease. These mice are then used for testing new treatments for the disease.
   (a) Suggest one advantage of using a glow gene joined to the disease gene. **(1 mark)**
   (b) Describe how lots of mice with the human gene could be produced. **(2 marks)**

Insect-resistant plants

An example of genetic engineering in crop plants is the introduction of genes that give **insect resistance**.

Creating Bt plants

The bacterium ***Bacillus thuringiensis*** naturally produces a chemical that is poisonous to insect pests such as caterpillars. This chemical is called **Bt toxin**.

→ The gene for Bt toxin can be cut out of the bacterial DNA and inserted into the DNA of a plant cell using *Agrobacterium tumefaciens*.

→ Plants grown from these cells produce the Bt toxin. When an insect tries to eat them, the poison kills the insect pest.

Agrobacterium tumefaciens naturally infects plant cells, and so is a useful vector for making transgenic plants.

Using Bt plants

There are advantages and disadvantages of introducing genes for insect resistance into crop plants.

Advantages	Disadvantages
crop damage is reduced so crop yield should increase less chemical insecticide is needed so other harmless and useful insects are less likely to be harmed (better for biodiversity)	seed from transgenic plants is more expensive than seed from non-transgenic varieties insect pests may become resistant to Bt toxin Bt gene may transfer to closely related wild plants by pollination, which would make those plants resistant to pests too

Worked example

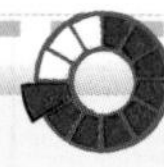

Explain how genetic modification with the Bt toxin gene could increase food production. **(2 marks)**

Damage to a plant's leaves by an insect pest will reduce the amount of food that a plant makes by photosynthesis. This will reduce the rate of plant growth, including growth of the parts of the plant that we eat. Bt toxin kills insect pests that eat the leaves, so crop yield should increase.

You need to explain how insects reduce crop yields as well as understanding that the Bt toxin gene kills insects.

Now try this

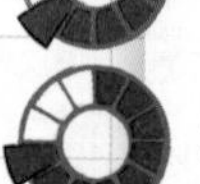

1 State why insect-resistant crop plants are less likely to be grown in poorer countries. **(1 mark)**

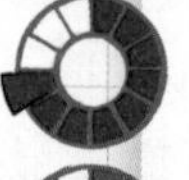

2 Describe how a wheat plant could be genetically modified to produce Bt toxin. **(5 marks)**

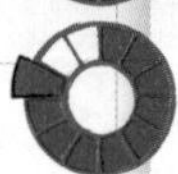

3 Explain how insect-resistant plants could be beneficial to the numbers of animals in a food web. **(3 marks)**

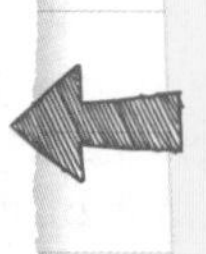

Remember to include key terms like restriction enzyme, sticky ends, ligase, and plasmid.

Meeting population needs

A growing human **population** needs more food. Agricultural solutions to this include using **fertilisers** and **biological control**.

Advantages and disadvantages of fertilisers

- 👍 fertilisers contain nutrients, including nitrogen, phosphorus and potassium, that help crops to grow well
- 👍 they increase crop yields providing more food for people
- 👍 it is a good way to use animal waste (manure) from farms
- 👎 excess fertiliser can pollute waterways, causing **eutrophication**
- 👎 artificial fertilisers are expensive to make
- 👎 artificial fertilisers can reduce soil biodiversity

See page 110 for more information on eutrophication.

Advantages and disadvantages of biological control

Biological control uses a natural predator, parasite or disease of the pest to keep the pest population low.

- 👍 the pest cannot become resistant
- 👍 if well chosen, the control agent is **specific** to the pest
- 👍 avoids using chemical pesticides which can leave harmful residues and kill useful organisms
- 👎 biological control does not get rid of the pest completely
- 👎 the control agent may become a pest itself

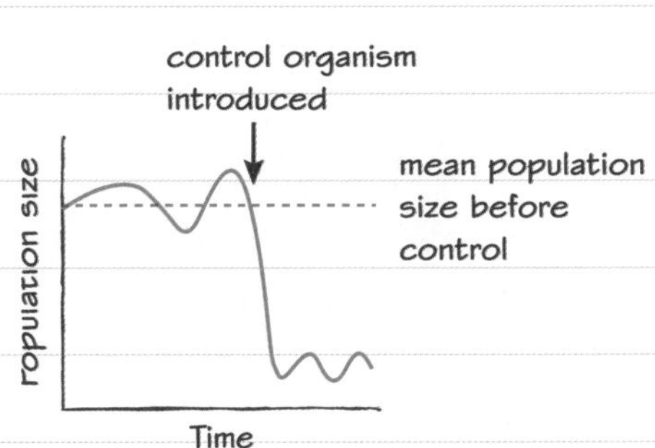

Worked example

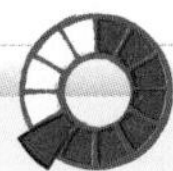

Red spider mite is a pest of greenhouse crops. A predatory mite that feeds on the pest can be used as a biological control. Explain the advantages and disadvantages of this. **(3 marks)**

The predatory mite feeds on the red spider mite so it gets rid of the pest but not other useful insects. The red spider mite cannot develop resistance to it, and the predatory mite only needs to be introduced once because it reproduces in the greenhouse. A disadvantage is that it does not get rid of the red spider mite completely. When the red spider mite population falls, the predatory mite runs out of food so its population falls as well.

You need to apply your understanding of biological control to specific examples like this.

Now try this

1 Give **one** advantage and **one** disadvantage of using artificial fertilisers. **(2 marks)**

2 Explain how the use of biological control could help to provide more food for a growing human population. **(3 marks)**

Had a look ☐ Nearly there ☐ Nailed it! ☐

Extended response – Genetic modification

There will be one or more 6 mark questions on your exam paper. For these questions, you will need to think scientifically, and structure your answer logically showing how the points you make are related to each other. You can revise the topics for this question, which is about the **advantages and disadvantages of genetic modification of crops**, on pages 43 to 46.

Worked example

Some crop plants have been genetically modified to produce Bt toxin when their cells are damaged. This toxin kills caterpillars when they eat it. Explain how using crops that have been genetically modified in this way could affect farmers and the environment.

(6 marks)

Caterpillars are pests because they eat the crop plants. This reduces how well the crops grow, which reduces how much the farmer earns from selling the crop. Killing the caterpillars by growing GM crops should increase crop yield.

A good start to this answer is to identify the problem with caterpillars for crops, as it explains why farmers want to get rid of them.

Seeds of GM crop plants are more expensive than for normal crops, so they will cost the farmer more.

To answer this question fully, you need to **evaluate** the benefits and problems to farmers and to the environment of using these GM crops.

Using crops that make insecticide inside them means the farmer will not need to spray the crop with insecticide as much. This will reduce time and some costs for the farmer. It should also be good for the environment because insecticide spray can kill other insects, which can harm the food web in the area, such as by reducing food for animals that eat them.

Consider what the alternative to using the GM crop would be, and what difference that would make to farmers and the environment. This will make it easier to identify benefits and problems.

There is a risk, though, that the gene for Bt toxin might get into wild plants by fertilisation. This could harm the environment by killing caterpillars on other plants and reducing the food for animals that usually eat them.

Other answers

The answer to this question could have covered other issues, such as how the development of resistance to Bt toxin by insects will affect the benefits of using GM crops. It could also have covered the problem that many people will not buy food from GM crops as they do not trust that it is safe. What matters in this answer is that it covers all that the question asks, and is presented in a clear and logical order.

Now try this

The gene for Bt toxin was found in the bacterium *Bacillus thuringiensis.* Describe how wheat plants could be modified so that they produce the toxin. **(6 marks)**

Health and disease

The World Health Organization defines **health** as 'a state of complete physical, mental and social well-being'. There are many different **diseases** with different causes.

What is health?

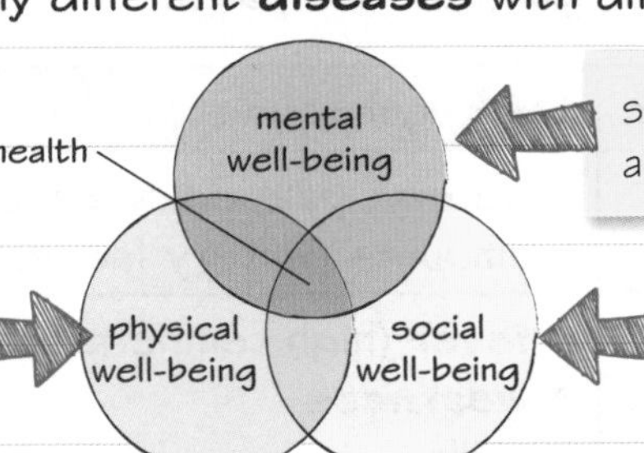

such as how you feel about yourself

such as eating and sleeping well, and being free from disease

such as how well you get on with other people

Types of disease

Diseases may be **communicable** (they can be passed from one person to another) or **non-communicable** (not passed between people). A **pathogen** is an organism that causes an infectious disease.

Communicable	Non-communicable
rapid variation in number of cases over time	number of cases changes only gradually
cases are often localised	cases may be more widely spread
e.g. malaria, typhoid, cholera	e.g. cancer, diabetes, heart disease

Worked example

Chalara fungus sometimes kills ash trees directly, but sometimes it makes the tree more likely to be infected by other pathogens which kill the tree. Suggest how this happens. **(2 marks)**

The fungus damages the bark and the cells of the ash tree, making it easier for other pathogens to infect the tree.

HIV is a pathogen that makes it easier for other pathogens to infect a person. In the case of HIV, this happens because of damage to the immune system.

Pathogens

Pathogens include bacteria and viruses, fungi and protists. When a few pathogens **infect** you (get inside your body) they can reproduce very rapidly. Large numbers of pathogens make you ill.

Bacteria are much smaller than human cells.

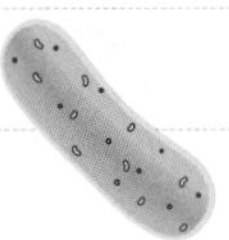

bacterium

Bacteria may release **toxins** (poisons) that make us feel ill. Some types of bacteria invade and destroy body cells.

Viruses are much smaller than bacteria.

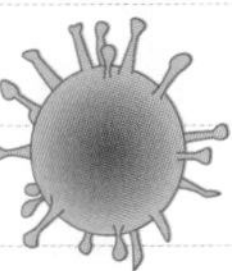

virus

Viruses take over a body cell's DNA, causing the cell to make **toxins** or causing damage when new viruses are released from cells.

fungi

Fungi are eukaryotic organisms.

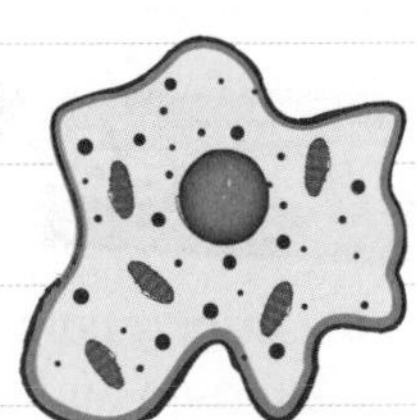

protist

Protists are eukaryotic organisms. Many are free-living but some are pathogens.

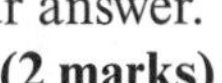

Pathogens make you feel ill when they damage cells or change how they work.

Now try this

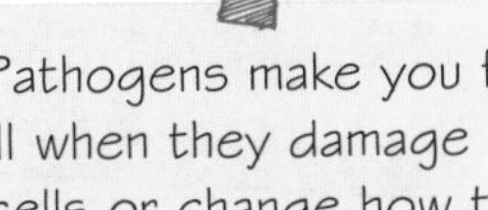

1 A stroke is caused when a blood clot blocks an artery in the brain. This stops oxygen reaching part of the brain and nerve cells die. State whether a stroke is a communicable or non-communicable disease. Give a reason for your answer. **(2 marks)**

2 Explain why an infectious disease may affect a lot of people in a community, and then fall to a very low level again. **(2 marks)**

Common infections

Different kinds of pathogens can cause different diseases with different symptoms. You need to be able to describe the **infections** given on this page.

Infection	Type of pathogen	Main symptoms
cholera	bacterium	• watery, pale-coloured **diarrhoea**, often in large amounts (watery faeces)
malaria	protist	• **fever** (high temperature) • **weakness** • chills • sweating
HIV/AIDS	virus	• mild flu-like symptoms may occur when first infected • often, no symptoms for a long time • eventually, **repeated infections** (e.g. TB) that would not be a problem if their immune system was working properly
tuberculosis (TB)	bacterium	• lung damage seen in **blood speckled mucus** • **weight loss** • **fever** and chills • night sweats
Ebola	virus	• internal bleeding and fever (**haemorrhagic fever**) • severe headache • muscle pain • vomiting • diarrhoea (frequent watery faeces)
stomach ulcers	bacterium	• **inflammation** in stomach causing pain • bleeding in stomach
ash die-back *Chalara*	fungus	• leaf loss • bark **lesions** (damage) • **dieback** of top of tree (crown)

Worked example

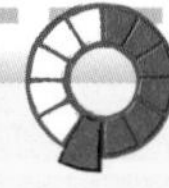

Describe a communicable disease caused by a bacterium and the symptoms of the disease. **(3 marks)**

TB is a communicable disease. Two of its symptoms are blood speckled mucus and weight loss.

You could choose any of the other communicable diseases in the table. One mark is for naming the disease, then two marks for two symptoms.

Now try this

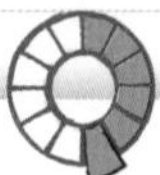

Give one example of a pathogen from each of the following groups, describing two signs of the infection it causes:

(a) virus **(2 marks)**
(b) protist **(2 marks)**
(c) fungus **(2 marks)**

Make sure you know which group each pathogen belongs to.

How pathogens spread

Understanding how pathogens are spread can help us to find ways of **reducing** or **preventing** their spread.

Malaria

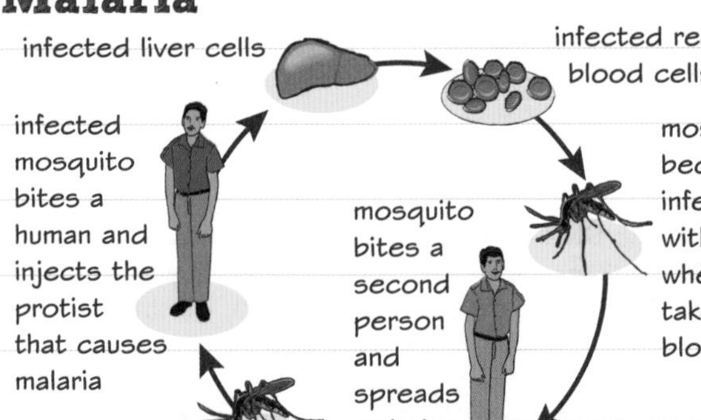
infected liver cells
infected red blood cells
infected mosquito bites a human and injects the protist that causes malaria
mosquito becomes infected with parasite when it takes a blood meal
mosquito bites a second person and spreads malaria

The protist that causes malaria is spread by a **vector**, the mosquito.

Watch out! Vectors are not pathogens. Vectors carry pathogens from one person to another. Vectors are one way infectious diseases are spread.

HIV

The human immunodeficiency virus, **HIV**, enters the blood and reproduces inside white blood cells, causing white blood cell destruction.

Eventually so many white blood cells are destroyed that the immune system cannot work properly. This stage is called **AIDS**. The person becomes ill with a disease, such as tuberculosis, that would not be a problem if their immune system was working properly.

Ebola virus

The **Ebola virus** causes **haemorrhagic fever**. The virus infects humans from other infected people, infected animals or objects that have been in contact with the virus. The virus infects:

- liver cells
- cells from the lining of the blood vessels
- white blood cells.

It multiplies inside these cells and destroys them. This causes fever, severe headache, muscle pain, extreme weakness, vomiting, diarrhoea, and internal and external bleeding.

Reducing the spread of pathogens

Disease (cause)	Ways to reduce or prevent its spread
cholera (bacteria)	• boil water to kill bacteria before drinking • wash hands thoroughly after using toilet to prevent spread by touch
tuberculosis (bacteria)	• ventilate buildings adequately to reduce chance of breathing in bacteria in droplets of mucus coughed out by an infected person • diagnose infected people promptly and give antibiotics to kill tuberculosis bacteria • isolate infected people so they cannot pass the infection to others
malaria (protists)	• prevent mosquito vectors biting people, by killing mosquitoes or keeping them off skin (e.g. by using a sleeping net)
stomach ulcers (bacteria)	• cook food thoroughly to kill bacteria • wash hands thoroughly before preparing food to avoid transfer
Ebola haemorrhagic fever (virus)	• keep infected people isolated because the virus is easily spread • wear fully protective clothing while working with infected people or dead bodies

Now try this

Using malaria as an example, explain the difference between a pathogen and a vector. **(2 marks)**

STIs

Chlamydia and HIV are sexually transmitted infections (**STIs**) spread by sexual activity. *Chlamydia* is a bacterium, and HIV is a virus.

Virus lifecycle

Viruses infect host cells. They multiply by the **lytic** cycle or the **lysogenic** cycle.

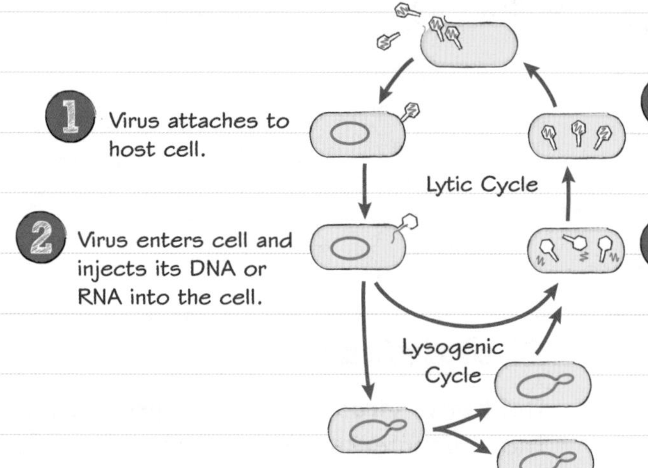

1 Virus attaches to host cell.
2 Virus enters cell and injects its DNA or RNA into the cell.
Lytic Cycle
Lysogenic Cycle
3 Virus RNA or DNA copies itself and causes new virus proteins to be made, using the organelles in the host cell.
4 The DNA or RNA and virus proteins are packaged together to make new viruses. These are released from the cell, which usually destroys the host cell.

The virus is actually much smaller than this compared to the host cell.

In the lysogenic cycle, the virus inserts its DNA into the chromosomes of the host cell. It is called a **provirus**. The provirus replicates with the rest of the host DNA every time the host cell divides. The provirus can stay dormant for a long time like this. At some stage, the provirus can become active and make new viruses in the lytic cycle.

Spread of STIs

Chlamydia bacteria can be spread by contact with sexual fluid from an infected partner. An infected mother can pass *Chlamydia* to her baby during birth.

Common methods of **HIV transmission** are:
- unprotected sex with an infected partner
- sharing needles with an infected person
- transmission from infected mother to foetus
- infection from blood products.

Reducing or preventing STIs

The spread of many STIs can be reduced or prevented by:
- using **condoms** during sexual intercourse
- **screening people**, including pregnant women
- **screening blood** transfusions
- supplying intravenous drug abusers with **sterile needles** (HIV)
- treating infected people using **antibiotics** (for *Chlamydia* and other bacterial infections).

Worked example

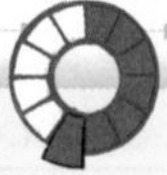

A newborn baby's eyes are infected with *Chlamydia*. Explain how this could happen. **(1 mark)**

During birth, the baby's eyes and lungs may become contaminated with vaginal fluid containing the bacteria.

Pathogens enter the body through natural openings, so the baby's eyes, nose and mouth are places where pathogens can enter the body easily.

Now try this

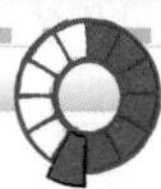

1 State what STIs are and how they are spread. **(2 marks)**

2 During sexual intercourse a man places a condom over his penis. Explain how this reduces his risk of being infected with an STI. **(1 mark)**

Human defences

The human body has both physical barriers and chemical defences to give protection against pathogens. **Physical barriers** make it hard for pathogens to enter the body. **Chemical defences** are chemicals that are produced to kill or make pathogens inactive.

Chemical and physical defences

Chemical defences

Lysozyme enzyme in tears kills bacteria by digesting their cell walls.

Lysozyme enzyme is also present in saliva and mucus.

Hydrochloric acid in stomach kills pathogens in food and drink.

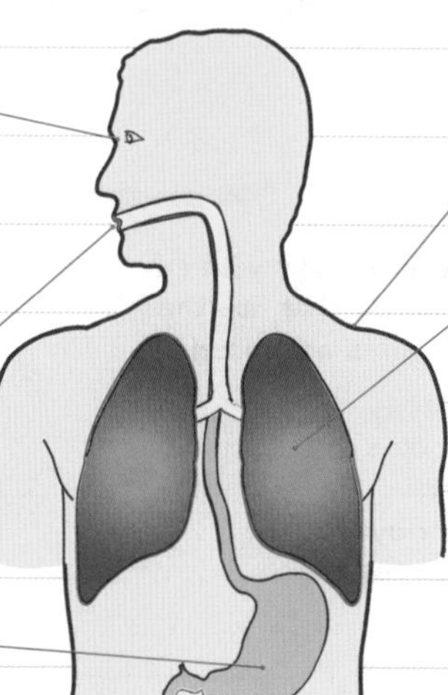

Physical barriers

Unbroken **skin** forms a protective barrier because it is too thick for most pathogens to get through.

Sticky **mucus** in the breathing passages and lungs traps pathogens. **Cilia** on the cells lining the lungs move in a wave-like motion, moving mucus and trapped pathogens out of lungs towards the back of the throat where it is swallowed.

Remember that epithelial cells line the surface of tubes.

Worked example

Cilia move mucus away from the lungs. Describe how this protects the body from pathogens. **(3 marks)**

It stops pathogens entering the lungs where they can cause disease. When the mucus gets to the throat it is swallowed and the pathogens are destroyed by the acid in the stomach.

Cilia are tiny hairs on the surfaces of cells that move together in a rhythm to move substances along, such as mucus. Their movement is a bit like a crowd of people doing a Mexican wave.

Worked example

Chemicals in cigarette smoke paralyse the cilia in the epithelium of the airways. Smokers are more likely than non-smokers to suffer from lung infections. Explain why. **(2 marks)**

When the cilia are paralysed, they cannot move the mucus containing pathogens back up to the throat. The mucus travels down into the lungs, carrying pathogens with them.

Now try this

1 Give one example of a physical barrier and one example of a chemical defence that prevents pathogens entering the body. **(2 marks)**

2 A burn damages the skin, and a bad burn can completely break through the skin. First aid advice for a person who has suffered a burn includes covering the burn with clean cling film or a plastic bag. Explain why. **(2 marks)**

The immune system

The **immune system** helps to protect the body by attacking pathogens if they manage to enter the body. **Lymphocytes** are part of this immune system.

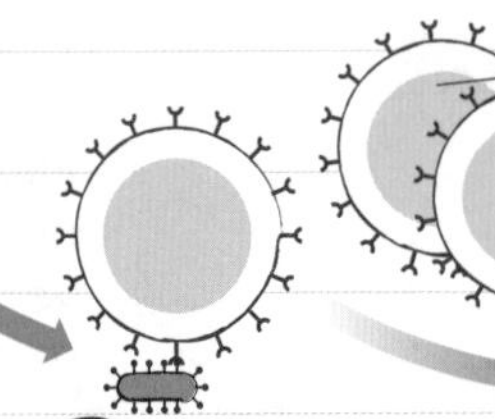

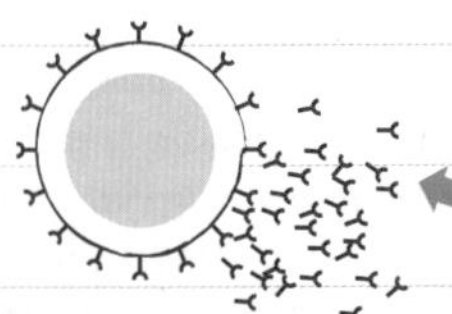

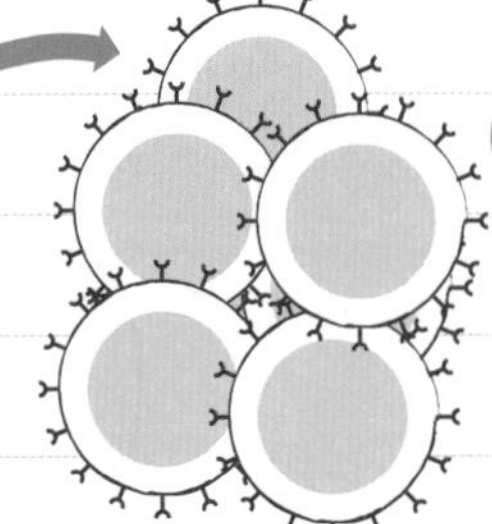

1 Each pathogen has unique **antigens** on its surface.

2 A **lymphocyte** with an **antibody** that fits the antigen is activated.

3 The lymphocyte **divides** many times to produce clones of identical lymphocytes.

4 Some of the lymphocytes produce lots of antibodies which stick to the pathogen and destroy it. Other lymphocytes stay in the blood as **memory lymphocytes**, ready to respond immediately if the same antigen returns.

Antibodies

The antibodies produced by a white blood cell are **specific** for one particular kind of pathogen. This means they can only destroy that kind of pathogen. They cannot destroy another kind of bacterium or virus.

Immunity

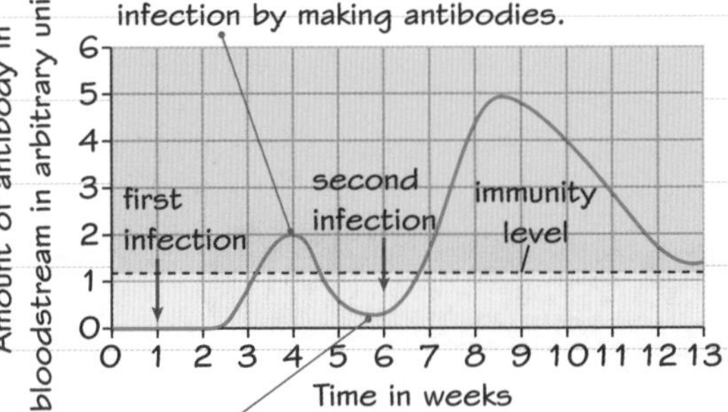

This is called the **secondary response**.

Worked example

Explain why there is a delay of a few days between a person becoming infected by a pathogen for the first time and antibodies being made. **(2 marks)**

It takes time for lymphocytes to identify the antigens on the pathogen, and to secrete specific antibodies.

The secondary response is much faster because memory cells are already present, and can secrete specific antibodies immediately.

Worked example

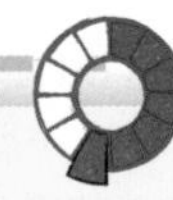

Pathogens have antigens that are foreign to the body. When a pathogen enters the body, the body is exposed to these antigens. Describe two responses triggered by the antigens. **(2 marks)**

The antigens trigger an immune response which causes the production of antibodies.
They also trigger the production of memory lymphocytes.

Now try this

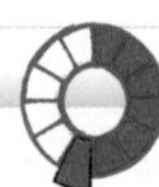

Describe how the immune system helps to fight infection. **(3 marks)**

Immunisation

Immunisation is when you give a person a vaccine to prevent them becoming ill from a disease.

How vaccines work

A **vaccine** contains antigens from the pathogen, often in the form of dead or weakened pathogens. → The person's lymphocytes produce antibodies against the pathogen and also memory lymphocytes. → If the person becomes infected with the real pathogen, the memory lymphocytes will give a very rapid secondary response to the pathogen. This means the person is very unlikely to become ill.

This form of the pathogen is **inactive** and cannot cause the disease in the person receiving the vaccine.

Advantages and disadvantages of immunisation

- Immunity is produced without being ill.
- Immunity lasts a long time, often for life.
- If most people are immune, then the few people who are unvaccinated are also less likely to catch the disease. This is called **herd immunity**.

- Some people get a mild reaction of swelling or soreness, or a mild form of the disease.
- Very rarely, a person has a major harmful reaction.

Worked example

Describe how a vaccine can protect you for life. **(2 marks)**

Once you have received the vaccine, the immune system makes antibodies but also memory lymphocytes which stay in the body for a long time. If you ever catch the disease 'for real', these memory cells divide very quickly and produce huge numbers of antibodies.

Make sure you refer to memory lymphocytes being formed as a result of vaccination.

Worked example

Explain why immunisation only protects you against one particular disease. **(2 marks)**

Each pathogen has a particular antigen. The immune system produces antibodies that are exactly the right shape to fit on to these antigens. Other pathogens have antigens of a different shape, so one kind of antibody cannot bind to a different kind of antigen.

You sometimes hear people say that a vaccine is a 'small dose of the disease'. This is wrong. The vaccine contains antigens from the pathogen and is not necessarily a small amount. However it is in a safe form, e.g. the pathogen is dead or weakened. And you are not given the disease, just antigens from the pathogen that causes the disease.

Now try this

1 Describe the difference between a vaccine and immunisation. **(2 marks)**

Immunisation and vaccination mean the same thing.

2 Explain why people who have not been vaccinated against a particular disease are protected if most people are immune to that disease. **(2 marks)**

Treating infections

Antibiotics can be used to treat bacterial infections.

Antibiotics

Antibiotics are medicines that **kill bacteria** inside the body. Specific bacteria are only killed by a specific antibiotic, so the correct antibiotic must be used. Deaths from bacterial diseases have greatly decreased where antibiotics are used. **Penicillin** is an example of an antibiotic.

Some bacteria are becoming **resistant** to some antibiotics. This means that the antibiotic is no longer effective at killing or inhibiting them.

Worked example

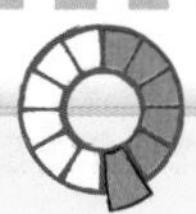

Describe how antibiotics kill bacteria. **(2 marks)**

Antibiotics inhibit cell processes in the bacterium but not the host organism. For example, some antibiotics stop bacterial cell walls forming properly. This does not harm the host animal because animal cells do not have cell walls.

Do not confuse **antibiotics** and **antibodies**. They are very different things!

Effect of antibiotics on bacteria

The effect of antiseptics, antibiotics or plant extracts on the growth of bacteria can be studied on a **bacterial culture** in a **Petri dish**.

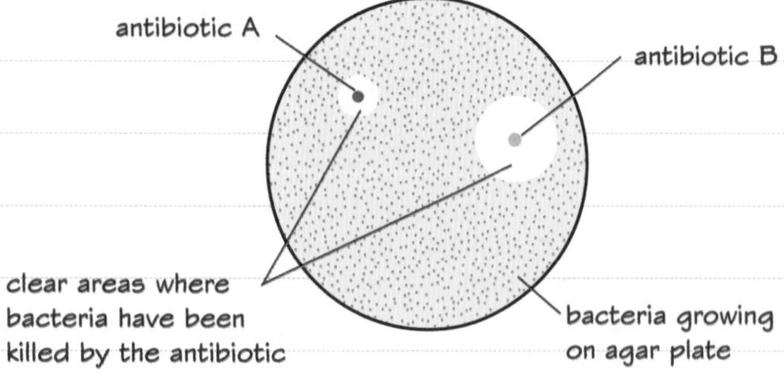

Maths skills: Comparing the effects of antibiotics

You can **calculate** the cross-sectional area of the clear zone using the formula πr^2 (where r = the radius of the circle of the clear zone). This allows you to **compare** how effective different antibiotics are. So if, in the example on the left, r = 8 mm for antibiotic A and 14 mm for antibiotic B, then

Area for antibiotic A = $\pi \times 8^2 = 201\,\text{mm}^2$

Area for antibiotic B = $\pi \times 14^2 = 615\,\text{mm}^2$

Antibiotic B is the more effective antibiotic for this bacterial culture.

Now try this

1 Explain why doctors do not prescribe antibiotics if a patient has the flu virus. **(1 mark)**

2 Some antibiotics work by binding to bacterial ribosomes so that proteins cannot be made. Bacterial ribosomes are smaller than human ribosomes and have a different structure. Explain why these antibiotics do not harm human cells. **(2 marks)**

Aseptic techniques

When working with microorganisms, you need to use **aseptic techniques**. These help to prevent other microorganisms from the air and surfaces from contaminating cultures when they are being prepared. Several techniques can help prevent this.

1 Sterilising dishes and culture media

Sterilisation kills microorganisms.

- Petri dishes can be **sterilised** by autoclaving or heating to a high temperature.
- Culture media (the substances that the microorganisms grow on, such as nutrient agar) are sterilised by heating to a high temperature.

2 Sterilising inoculating loops

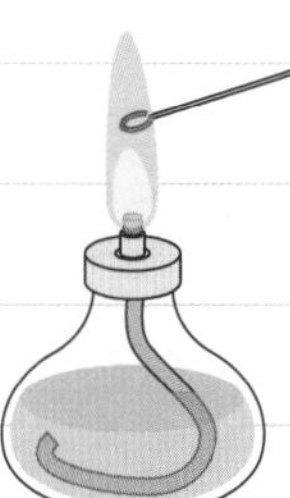

The loop is sterilised in a hot flame and then cooled, before using it to transfer microorganisms to the growth medium.

3 Sealing Petri dishes

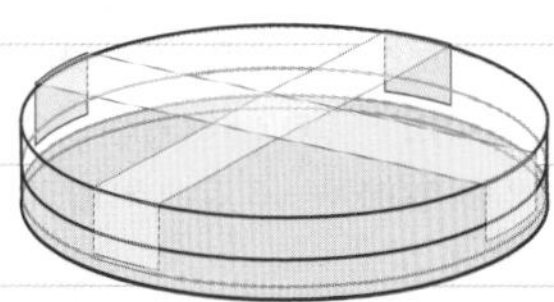

The lid is secured to the dish with adhesive tape to stop microorganisms from the air getting in. Vials containing bacteria must be kept covered for the same reason.

The Petri dish is not completely sealed as this would encourage the growth of anaerobic bacteria which are likely to be pathogens.

Worked example

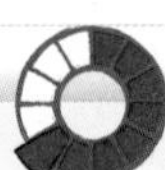

Cultures of microorganisms should be incubated at a maximum temperature of 25 °C in school and college laboratories. Explain why. **(2 marks)**

Temperatures higher than this encourage rapid growth in bacteria. This includes pathogenic bacteria that are harmful to humans.

When microorganisms are grown in industry, they are cultured at higher temperatures than 25 °C because they are not handled by people. The microorganisms grow more quickly at these higher temperatures, but there is no risk that people will get infected by the bacteria.

Now try this

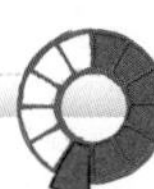

1 Give **three** ways in which cultures of microorganisms can easily be contaminated with other microorganisms during preparation. **(3 marks)**

2 Describe fully how you would prepare a culture of microorganisms so that you could investigate the action of a plant extract on the microorganisms. **(4 marks)**

Investigating microbial cultures

Practical skills You can investigate the **effect of antiseptics, antibiotics or plant extracts on the growth of bacteria** by placing paper discs of the test substances on to a bacterial lawn (a Petri dish of nutrient agar covered in a layer of bacteria) and incubating them for a few days.

Core practical

Apparatus

- bacterial lawn plate
- paper discs soaked in test substances
- sterile forceps
- sticky tape
- marker pen
- Bunsen burner + heat-resistant mat

You might investigate how effective different concentrations of the same substance are at killing bacteria. Or you might investigate different kinds of antiseptic, antibiotic or plant extract. If comparing different substances, think about how to prepare the extracts so the test is fair.

Remember: aseptic techniques are needed to help prevent contamination. You can revise these on page 57.

Method

1 Turn the bacterial plate upside down and mark the base into sections – one section for each test disc. Label each section with the substance or concentration used.

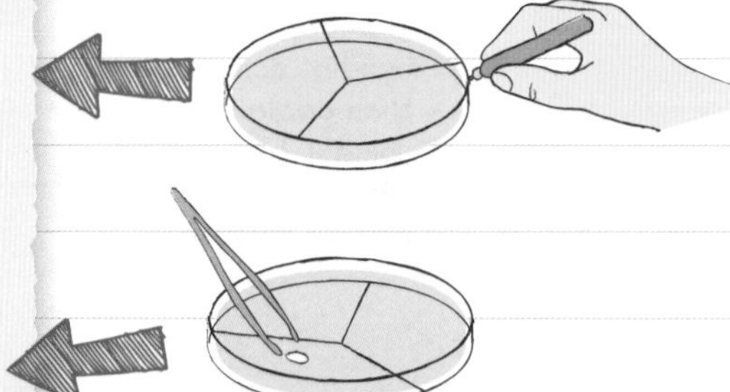

2 Turn the plate the right way up. Lift the lid of the dish just enough to be able to place a disc on the lawn.

3 Use the sterile forceps to place one paper disc on to the bacterial lawn in the correct section. Then briefly flame the forceps in a blue Bunsen flame to sterilise them again.

4 Repeat step 3 for each disc.

5 Tape the lid to the base of the dish without completely sealing it, to avoid the risk of harmful anaerobic bacteria growing.

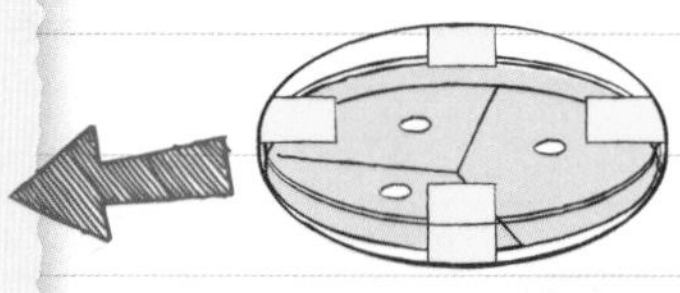

6 Incubate the plate for a few days at 25 °C.

Results

Accurately measure the diameter of any clear area in mm.

There are different ways to measure the diameters, e.g. squared paper, ruler. Choose a way that will give you the most precise values.

Conclusion

The larger the diameter of a clear area around a disc, the better the test substance was at killing bacteria.

Maths skills Calculate the cross-sectional area of each clear area using πr^2. (Remember to change the diameter to radius by dividing by 2.)

Now try this

The table shows the results of one investigation into the effect of some plant extracts on bacterial growth.

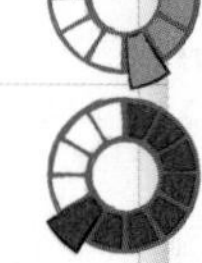

(a) Calculate the cross-sectional area for each substance. **(4 marks)**
(b) Display your calculations on a chart. **(2 marks)**
(c) Draw a conclusion from the results. **(1 mark)**

Plant extract	Diameter of clear area (mm)
neem	15
oregano	17
lemongrass	5
thyme	10

New medicines

Medicines are chemicals that are used to treat the cause or signs of an illness. Scientists are continually developing new medicines. New medicines must be extensively tested before doctors can **prescribe** them to patients. There are several steps of testing.

Development and testing

1 Discovery

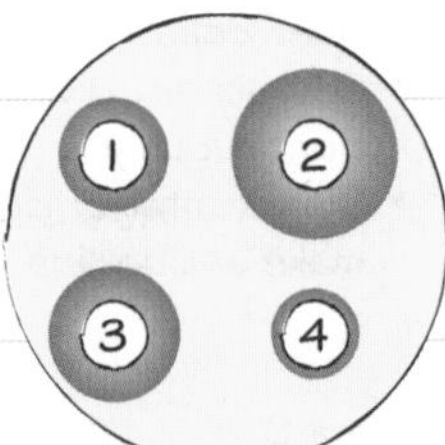

New medicines are **discovered**, e.g. by screening organisms to see if they produce antibiotics that kill bacteria. They are then **developed** through a series of stages.

2 Preclinical testing (in the lab)

cultures of cells

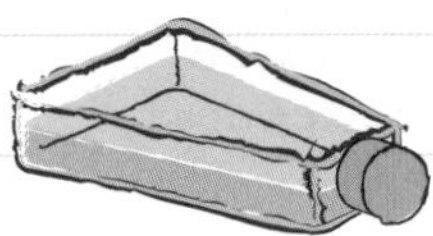

cultures of tissues

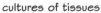

animals

Antibiotics are **tested** in the lab to make sure the medicine gets into cells without harming them, and damages pathogens inside cells.

3 Clinical trials: stage 1

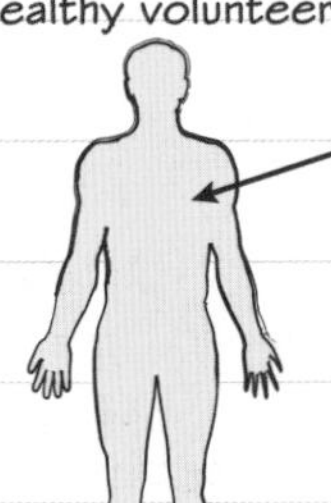

To check that the drug is not **toxic** (harmful).

Medical drugs are prescribed (given) by doctors to help patients who are ill.

4 Clinical trials: stage 2

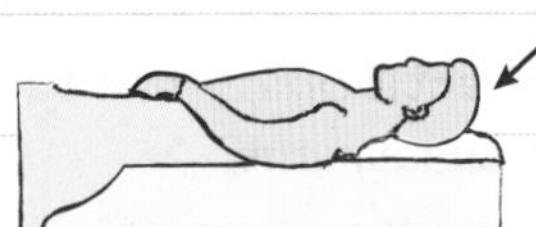

To test **efficacy** (whether it works) and to find the **optimum** dose (the dose that works best).

Worked example

Explain why a new medicine is not tested on lots of people straight away. **(3 marks)**

This is to make sure there are no harmful side effects and also to make sure it works on people. It would be unethical to give the medicine to lots of people before it was tested for safety and to see if it works on people.

Now try this

There are several different possible answers here, but you only need to think of two of them.

1 There are two antibiotics, A and B, that are effective against a particular bacterial infection. Antibiotic A produces a larger clear zone around it than antibiotic B when tested on a Petri dish of bacteria. However, the doctor chooses to prescribe antibiotic B to the patient. Give two possible reasons for this. **(2 marks)**

2 Suggest **one** advantage and **one** disadvantage of using animals as models for testing new drugs rather than direct testing on humans. **(2 marks)**

Monoclonal antibodies

Monoclonal antibodies are antibodies that carry useful chemical markers or treatments. A set of monoclonal antibodies are identical because they are produced in large quantities from the same **hybridoma cells**.

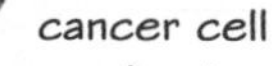

B lymphocyte from mouse
- advantage: makes particular antibodies continuously
- disadvantage: B lymphocytes don't divide

cancer cell
- advantage: divides continuously
- disadvantage: doesn't make antibodies

- hybridoma cell formed by fusing a B lymphocyte cell and a cancer cell
- the hybridoma cell divides and produces antibodies that are all the same

Uses of monoclonal antibodies

1. In **pregnancy tests** to identify if the pregnancy hormone is present in urine. The monoclonal antibody matches the hormone and causes a reaction with an indicator.
2. In **diagnosis** of diseases. Monoclonal antibodies can stick to blood clots or cancer cells so they can be detected. Blood clots need to be detected and treated to prevent blockage of arteries, especially in the heart and brain.
3. In **treatment** of diseases. As well as aiding detection, the way monoclonal antibodies can target specific cells can be used to target treatment.

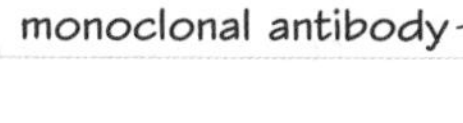

monoclonal antibody with a cancer drug can target cancer cells

Worked example

Remember that monoclonal antibodies carry drugs directly to cancer cells. Other treatments affect healthy cells not just cancer cells.

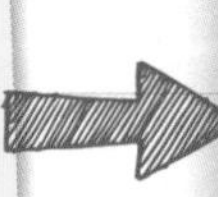

Describe the advantages of using monoclonal antibodies in cancer treatment compared to drug and radiotherapy treatments. **(3 marks)**

The cancer drug can be attached to a monoclonal antibody that only binds to cancer cells. This means the drug is 'delivered' to the cells that need to be killed, so the drug has a much reduced effect on healthy cells. This means a lower dose of the drug is needed, and therefore fewer side effects.

Now try this

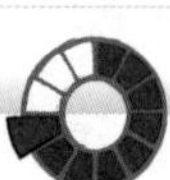

1 Explain why monoclonal antibodies can bind to cancer cells but not other body cells. **(2 marks)**

2 Explain why hybridoma cells must be created in order to produce sufficient amounts of monoclonal antibodies. **(3 marks)**

Non-communicable diseases

Many non-communicable diseases are caused by the **interaction of several factors**. Having several factors can increase the risk of developing a disease.

Factors that affect the risk of developing non-communicable diseases

Genes (inherited factors): Different alleles of a gene may be more prone to mutation (e.g. in breast cancer) or how well you absorb nutrients (e.g. in diseases related to diet). These factors may be more common in particular ethnic groups.

Age: The older the body, the more likely that cells may develop mutations which lead to cancer.

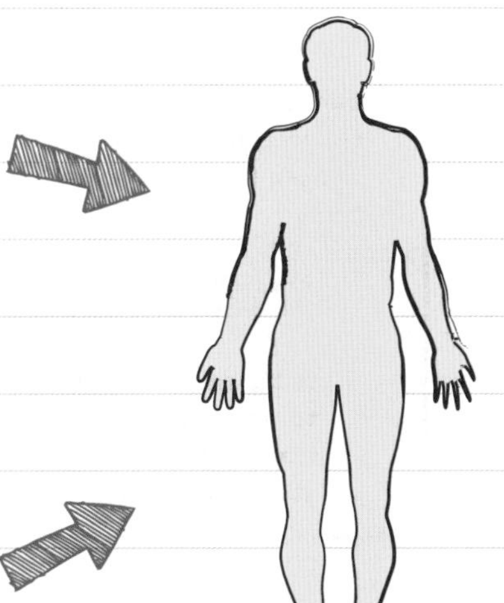

Sex: The female hormone oestrogen has protective effects that men do not get.

Environmental: Air pollution can cause lung diseases; poisons in food and drink can damage the body.

Lifestyle factors: The way we live, including diet, alcohol, smoking and exercise, can affect our risk of developing many diseases. You can find out more about lifestyle factors on pages 62 and 63.

Some non-communicable diseases caused by these factors include cancer, cardiovascular (heart) disease, lung and liver diseases, and dietary diseases. Rates of these diseases are different between different groups of people in a country, or in different countries, according to individual exposure to these risk factors.

Worked example

The graph shows the number of deaths from heart disease in the USA for one year.

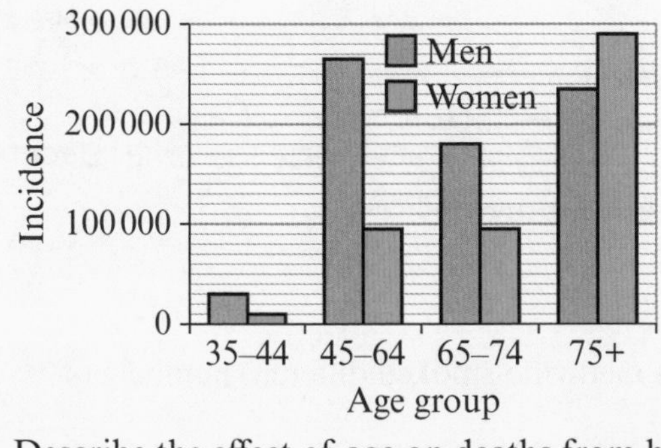

(a) Describe the effect of age on deaths from heart disease shown in the chart. **(2 marks)**

The death rate from heart disease is at least twice as high in men compared to women until the 75+ age group, when more women die from heart disease than men.

(b) Women produce the hormone oestrogen until the menopause (at about 50). Suggest whether the chart supports the idea that oestrogen can protect against heart disease. **(2 marks)**

The idea is not clearly supported, because the 65–74 category is about the same as the 40–64 group, but it does increase greatly in the 75+ group.

Now try this

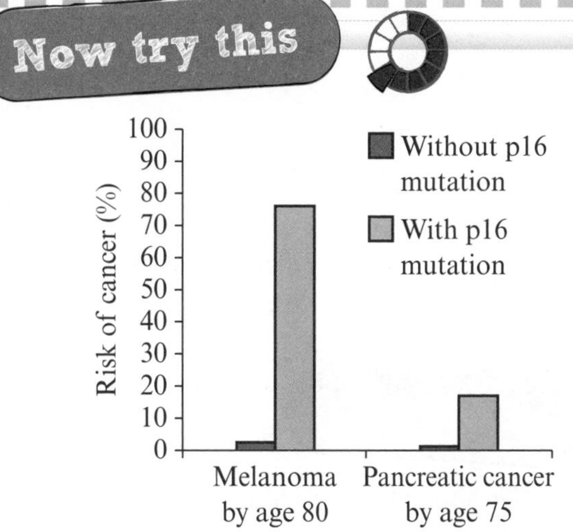

The chart shows the risk of developing some types of cancer in people with a particular mutation in the gene *p16* compared with people without this mutation.

(a) Explain why the risk of developing cancer is given as a percentage. **(2 marks)**

(b) Explain whether these data support the hypothesis that a mutation in the *p16* gene increases a person's chance of developing cancer. **(2 marks)**

Alcohol and smoking

Lifestyle factors including **drinking alcohol** and **smoking** increase the risk of non-communicable diseases by changing how the body works and increasing the levels of **toxins** (poisons) in your body.

Alcohol and disease

Ethanol (found in alcohol) is poisonous to cells. When absorbed from the gut, it passes first to the **liver** to be broken down. So liver cells are more likely than other cells to be damaged, leading to liver disease, e.g. cirrhosis.

This can lead to low birth weight in babies whose mothers smoke.

The damage caused by smoking

nicotine is addictive

carbon monoxide reduces how much oxygen the blood can carry

chemicals in **tar** are **carcinogens** that cause cancers, particularly of mouth and lungs

Substances in cigarettes can cause blood vessels to narrow, increasing blood pressure. This can lead to **cardiovascular diseases** such as heart attack or strokes.

Worked example

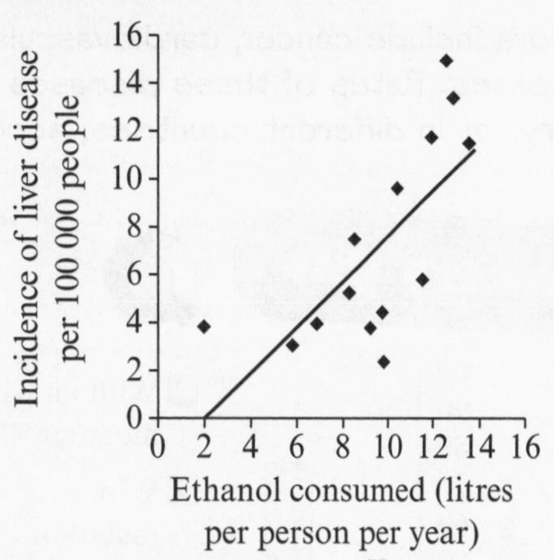

The graph shows the incidence of liver disease and the mean ethanol consumption per person per year for different countries.

Describe and explain the relationship shown in the graph. **(2 marks)**.

As the amount of alcohol consumed increases, the incidence of liver disease also increases. This is because ethanol is poisonous, particularly to liver cells.

This is a scatter diagram. It is good for showing a link (**correlation**) between two factors. This graph shows a **positive correlation**. You might also see a graph where one factor increases while the other decreases – a **negative correlation**.

Now try this

The table shows the death rate from coronary heart disease in men who smoked different numbers of cigarettes.

	Death rate			
Age group	**Non-smokers**	**Light smokers**	**Moderate smokers**	**Heavy smokers**
35–54	0.44	0.95	1.47	1.84
55–64	5.34	6.49	6.75	6.98
65–74	10.13	10.77	10.53	14.85
75 and over	15.19	20.00	22.27	24.93

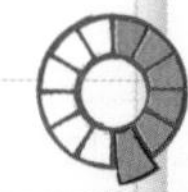

(a) Describe what these data show. **(2 marks)**

(b) Explain the relationship between smoking and deaths from coronary heart disease. **(2 marks)**

Malnutrition and obesity

Malnutrition happens when a person eats too much or too little of a nutrient. Too little of some nutrients can lead to **deficiency diseases**. If there is too much energy in the diet and not enough exercise then there will be an increase in body fat. Too much body fat leads to **obesity**.

Measuring obesity

Obesity can be measured by **BMI** or by **waist : hip** ratio.

Waist : hip ratio is calculated using this equation:

$$\text{Waist : hip ratio} = \frac{\text{waist measurement}}{\text{hip measurement}}$$

People with a high waist : hip ratio ('apples') are more at risk of some diseases than those with a lower waist : hip ratio ('pears').

Maths skills

Body mass index (BMI)

BMI is calculated using this equation:

$$\text{BMI} = \frac{\text{weight in kilograms}}{(\text{height in metres})^2}$$

Adults who have a BMI over 30 are said to be obese.

Obesity is linked with many health problems, including Type 2 diabetes.

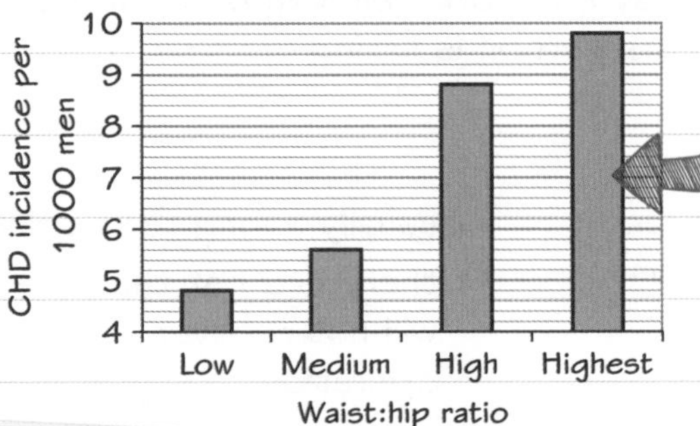

As waist : hip ratio increases, the **risk** of coronary heart disease increases.

CHD = coronary heart disease

Worked example

A scientific study showed that for a 10 g increase in wholegrain fibre that a person ate each day, there was a 10% decrease in their risk of developing bowel cancer. The scientists concluded that people should eat lots of wholegrain foods every day to help them stay healthy.

Do the results of this study support this conclusion? Give a reason for your answer. **(2 marks)**

The results do support this conclusion, because the more fibre the person eats the lower their risk of getting bowel cancer.

You will not be expected to know the effect of fibre in the diet, but you will be expected to answer questions like this about the effect of food on health from data that you are given. You will be given data to work with.

Now try this

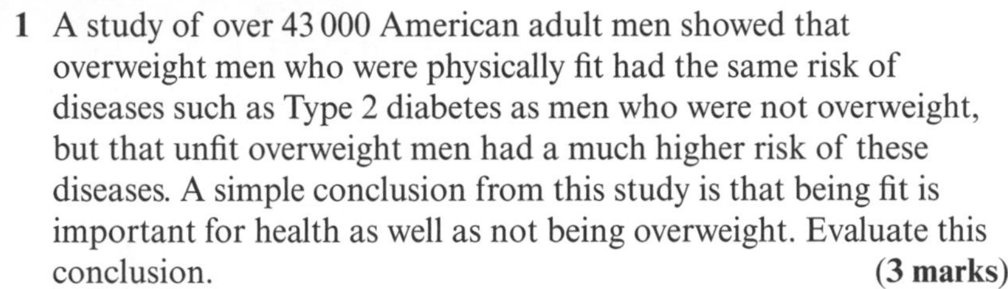

1 A study of over 43 000 American adult men showed that overweight men who were physically fit had the same risk of diseases such as Type 2 diabetes as men who were not overweight, but that unfit overweight men had a much higher risk of these diseases. A simple conclusion from this study is that being fit is important for health as well as not being overweight. Evaluate this conclusion. **(3 marks)**

For an 'evaluate' answer, use your knowledge and the information given to consider evidence for and against, and then draw a suitable conclusion from your arguments.

2 A 45-year-old woman is 160 cm high and weighs 80 kg. Calculate her BMI and state whether or not she is obese. **(1 mark)**

Cardiovascular disease

Cardiovascular disease may be **treated** using medication, surgery, or by making lifestyle changes.

Lifestyle changes

Doctors will advise the patient to:

- give up smoking
- take more exercise
- eat a healthier diet (lower fat, sugar and salt)
- lose weight.

👍 no side effects

👍 may reduce chances of getting other health conditions

👍 this is the cheapest option

👎 may take time to work or may not work effectively

Medication

If lifestyle changes do not improve the patient's health, the doctor may prescribe **medication**, such as betablockers, to reduce blood pressure.

👍 start working immediately, e.g. to lower blood pressure

👍 easy to do

👍 cheaper and less risky than surgery

👎 need to be taken long term and can have side effects

👎 may not work well with other medication the person is taking

Surgery

If an artery becomes narrowed, the drop in blood flow can cause damage to tissue beyond the blockage. A wire frame, called a **stent**, is inserted into the narrowed part of the artery.

Sometimes **heart by-pass** surgery is carried out, when a new blood vessel is inserted to by-pass blocked coronary arteries.

If the blood supply to the heart muscle is reduced or stopped, the heart muscle cells cannot get enough oxygen for respiration. This means the cells die and the person has a heart attack.

👍 usually a long term solution

👎 there is a risk the person will not recover after the operation

👎 surgery is expensive

👎 more difficult to do than giving medication

👎 there is a risk the person will develop an infection after surgery

Worked example

In a study of patients with narrowed coronary arteries, one group exercised and was given medicine, while a similar group exercised, took medicine and had a stent inserted into the narrowed artery.

In the 'without stent' group, 202 out of 1092 patients died of a heart attack within 5 years. In the 'with stent' group, 211 out of 1111 died of a heart attack within 5 years. Evaluate whether these results suggest that stent surgery is worth doing. **(3 marks)**

The percentage of deaths was 18.5% in the group without stents and 19.0% for the group with stents. This is not a big difference with such large sample sizes. This suggests that stent surgery is not worth doing if other treatments are carried out at the same time.

Maths skills You need to calculate the percentages so you can make an accurate comparison.

Now try this

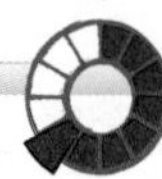

Surgery is usually only carried out if the person has serious heart disease and other treatments will not work. Explain why. **(2 marks)**

Plant defences

Plants have many adaptations to protect themselves from attack by **pests** and **pathogens**. A pest is an organism that causes damage to a crop plant, e.g. plant-eating insects.

Physical barriers

Many plants have **bark** and **thick waxy cuticles** (outer covering of a leaf) that are difficult for a pest to get through. Some have adaptations such as **spikes** and **thorns** to stop pests eating them. **Cellulose cell walls** are difficult for pathogens to break down unless they produce a suitable enzyme.

Chemical defences

Plants also protect themselves from attack by producing **chemicals**. They make:

- poisons in their cells to **deter pests** that try to eat them
- chemicals that **kill pathogens** (such as bacteria and fungi), which infect them and cause disease.

Using plant chemicals

You use some of the defence chemicals found in plants as **medicines**.

Example	Plant source	Use
quinine	cinchona tree	to treat human disease, e.g. malaria
digoxin	foxglove	to treat human disease, e.g. heart disease
aspirin	willow tree and other plants	to relieve **symptoms**, e.g. pain and fever

You only need to remember the uses, not particular examples.

A 'symptom' is what you feel when you have a disease.

Worked example

Give two ways that medicines made from plants can be used to treat people who are ill. **(2 marks)**

To treat diseases by killing pathogens in people, or to relieve symptoms such as pain or fever.

In a question like this you do not have to write full sentences. You can use bullet points if you prefer.

Now try this

1 Explain how physical barriers can protect a plant from pests and pathogens. **(2 marks)**

2 Explain the advantage to plants of producing chemicals that deter pests or kill pathogens. **(2 marks)**

3 Which of the following is NOT useful in protecting a plant against damage by pests?

☐ **A** thorns and spikes

☐ **B** thick waxy cuticle

☐ **C** sunken stomata

☐ **D** poisons in their cells **(1 mark)**

Plant diseases

Plant diseases may be caused by environmental factors, e.g. nutrient deficiency in the soil, or by pathogens such as fungi. **Detecting** and **identifying** plant diseases can be done in different ways in the lab and the field.

Visible symptoms

The first signs of plant disease are generally **visible symptoms** (changes in the plant that you can see) and will be the first step in identifying the disease.

Identify the visible symptoms:
- Change in normal appearance of plant, e.g. different colour of flowers or leaves
- Overgrowth of part of plant, e.g. swellings (gals) on roots
- Death of parts of the plant, e.g. dead leaves or roots
- Under-development of part of plant, e.g. smaller leaves than usual

Different diseases may result in the same symptoms, so other tests are needed to confirm the cause.

Distribution analysis

Looking at the way plants are **distributed** (spread) in the environment can help identify possible causes of disease. The following are some questions you can consider:

- **How many** plants are affected? All of them or only some? If they are all affected it is probably an **environmental factor**, e.g. soil pH.
- **Where** are diseased plants found? All over the area, or in one place, e.g. next to a road which might indicate pollution?
- Is just one species of plant affected or several? This might tell you whether it is a **species-specific** pathogen.
- Do the symptoms of the plant change over time? This might help you to distinguish one disease from another.

Laboratory testing

In the laboratory, scientists will use different techniques to identify a disease:

- **microscopic examination** of plant material for signs of pathogens
- **antibodies** to test for the presence of a pathogen
- **genetic testing** to identify any pathogens found
- **soil sample** testing to rule out soil factors, e.g. nutrient deficiency
- trying to **grow pathogens** on nutrient medium to produce a larger sample for identification.

Worked example

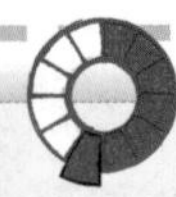

A scientist found a diseased plant. He thought the disease was caused by a fungus. Describe how he could prove this. **(4 marks)**

The scientist could place some of the diseased plant onto an agar dish to grow some of the fungus.

The scientist could then isolate some of the fungus and grow a pure culture on a new agar dish.

The scientist could infect a healthy plant with some of the fungus.

If the plant develops the same symptoms as the original diseased plant, it shows that the fungus did cause the disease symptoms in the original plant.

Now try this

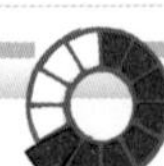

Laboratories that carry out disease identification for farmers ask for a sample of plant material and of soil in which the plant was growing. Explain why they ask for these samples. **(3 marks)**

Remember that soil can be tested to see if it is deficient in certain mineral ions, for example.

Extended response – Health and disease

There will be one or more 6 mark questions on your exam paper. For these questions, you will need to think scientifically, and structure your answer logically showing how the points you make are related to each other. You can revise the topics for this question, which is about the **advantages and disadvantages of immunisation**, on pages 54 and 55.

Worked example

The MMR vaccine protects against the diseases measles, mumps and rubella.

The graph shows the percentage of young children given the MMR vaccine in England. The World Health Organisation recommends a target percentage of 95% of children immunised. Discuss the importance of this target. **(6 marks)**

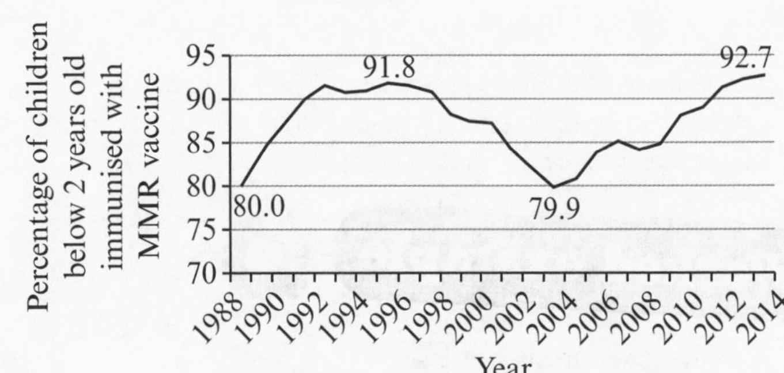

Children who are given the MMR vaccine are made immune to measles, mumps and rubella for the rest of their lives. This means they will not suffer from the diseases, and will be protected against the problems that some children develop as a result of having these diseases.

A good start is to explain why the MMR vaccine protects against infection.

A very few children are at risk of developing problems if they are given the vaccine, though these are much less than problems caused by having the disease.

Remember to cover both advantages and disadvantages in an answer to a discuss question.

The target of 95% is linked to herd immunity, which is when the chance of a non-immunised person coming into contact with someone with the disease is so low that the disease dies out in that group. This protects those children who cannot be immunised because they react badly to the vaccine.

Use scientific terminology where it is appropriate, and make sure you explain clearly what it means.

Command word: Discuss

Plan out your answer to a **discuss** question, e.g. using bullet points that cover all the issues in the question, including any benefits or risks. Arrange your bullet points into a logical order. Then use your plan to produce a well-organised answer.

Now try this

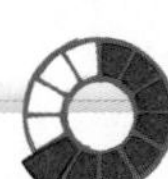

Between 1996 and 2004 the percentage of children given the MMR vaccine fell from 92% to 80%. This fall was the result of a scare that persuaded some parents that their children might be harmed by the vaccine. Discuss the effect of a fall in immunisation rate on the health of all children. **(6 marks)**

Photosynthesis

Photosynthesis is the process that plants and algae use to make their own food. Plants are called **producers** because they produce their own food. Photosynthetic organisms are the main producers of food and therefore **biomass**. Biomass is the mass of living material at a particular stage in a food chain.

Photosynthesis equation

Photosynthesis can be summarised by this equation:

carbon dioxide + water —(light energy, absorbed by **chlorophyll**)→ glucose + oxygen

- carbon dioxide: from air
- water: from soil
- glucose: a sugar
- oxygen: released to air as **by-product** (not needed)

Chlorophyll is a green substance found in the chloroplasts of some plants.

Remember that during photosynthesis there is an energy transfer from light energy to chemical energy stored in the sugars produced.

Worked example

Maths skills Light intensity is proportional to $\frac{1}{d^2}$ where d = distance between the algae and the lamp.

A student set up six bottles. Each contained the same number of gel beads containing algae, and the same volume of hydrogencarbonate indicator solution. The indicator is yellow when carbon dioxide concentration is high, orange-red when carbon dioxide concentration is the same as in normal air, and purple when carbon dioxide concentration is low. The student placed the bottles at different distances from a lamp as shown in the diagram.

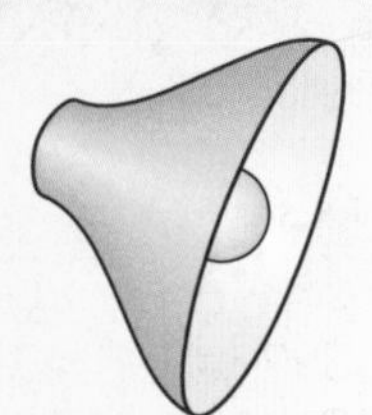

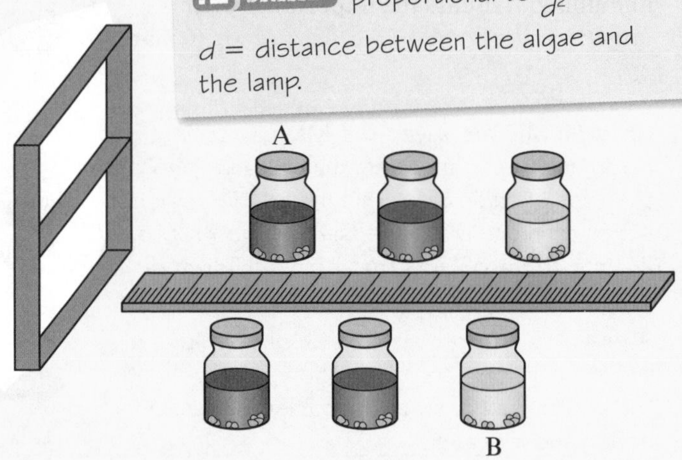

After two hours, the bottles were the colours shown in the diagram. Explain the difference in colour between bottles A and B. **(3 marks)**

Bottle A has high light intensity so photosynthesis is occurring much faster than respiration. Therefore the concentration of carbon dioxide is very low. Bottle B is too far away from the light to photosynthesise very fast, but it is respiring, so the concentration of carbon dioxide is very high.

Worked example

Explain why a leaf covered in black paper makes no food. **(2 marks)**

The black paper stops light from reaching the chlorophyll. Therefore, the leaf cannot use light energy to convert carbon dioxide and water into sugar in photosynthesis.

Plants make food in photosynthesis, but they can only do this in the light. However, plants respire all the time, whether it is dark or light.

Now try this

1 Explain why photosynthesis is an endothermic reaction. **(2 marks)**

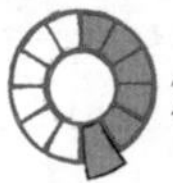

2 Explain the role of plants as producers of food. **(4 marks)**

Remember that 'endothermic' reactions take in energy from the surroundings.

Limiting factors

Low temperature, dim light and low carbon-dioxide concentration all limit the rate of photosynthesis. They are all **limiting factors** for photosynthesis

Effect of light on rate of photosynthesis

You can measure the effect of light intensity on the rate of photosynthesis by measuring the rate at which oxygen is given off by a piece of pondweed. You can use the apparatus shown to investigate the effect of light intensity using bright and dim lights.

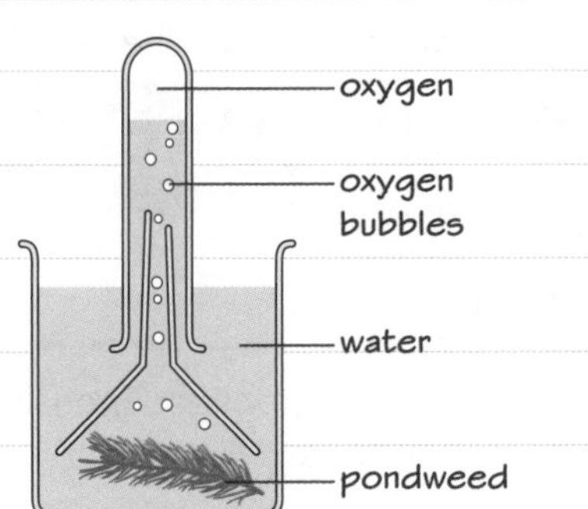

Worked example

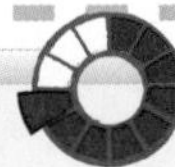

The graph shows the rate of photosynthesis of a plant at different light intensities. Explain the shape of the graph at points A and B. **(4 marks)**

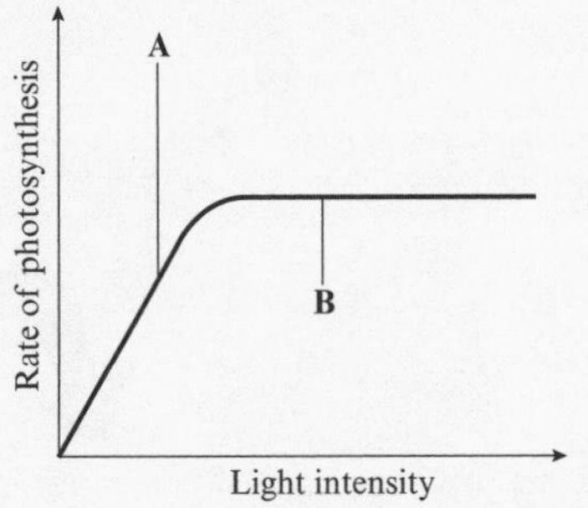

At A, light intensity is limiting photosynthesis, because increasing the light intensity increases the rate of photosynthesis. At B, light intensity is no longer the limiting factor because increasing the light intensity does not change the rate of photosynthesis. Another factor, such as carbon dioxide concentration or temperature, is limiting the rate of photosynthesis.

Increasing only carbon dioxide concentration or temperature, while keeping other factors constant, will produce a similar graph to this.

Carbon dioxide concentration

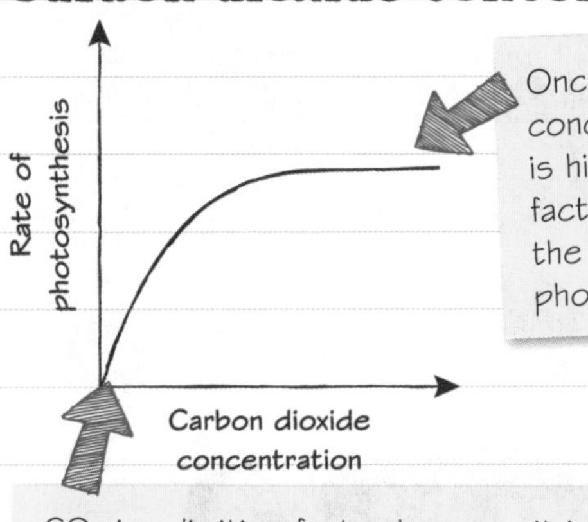

Once CO_2 concentration is high, another factor is limiting the rate of photosynthesis.

CO_2 is a limiting factor because it increases the rate of photosynthesis. There is more CO_2 to use to make sugars.

Temperature

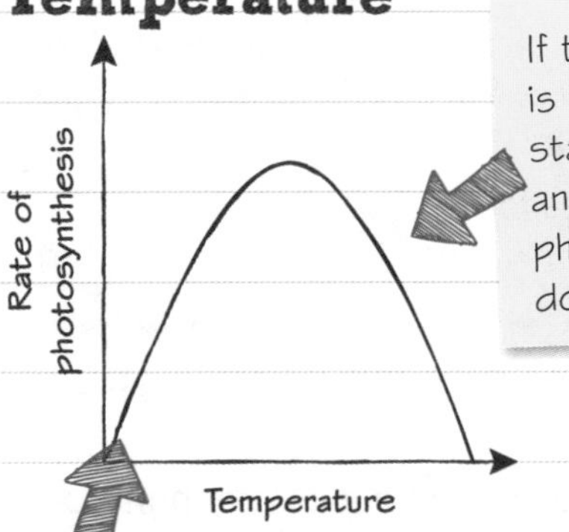

If the temperature is too high, enzymes start to denature and the rate of photosynthesis slows down.

Temperature is a limiting factor because it increases the kinetic energy of molecules and increases the rate of enzyme activity making photosynthesis faster.

Now try this

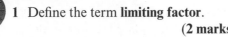

1 Define the term **limiting factor**. **(2 marks)**

2 Explain why measuring the oxygen given off by a plant is a way of measuring the rate of photosynthesis. **(2 marks)**

Light intensity

Practical skills You can investigate the **effect of light intensity on the rate of photosynthesis** by measuring the change in pH of solution around algal balls. The pH changes because carbon dioxide forms an acidic solution, and photosynthesis changes the concentration of carbon dioxide in the solution.

Core practical

Aim

To investigate how light intensity affects the rate of photosynthesis.

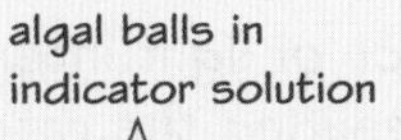

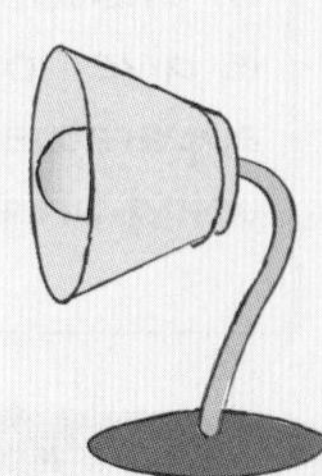

Apparatus

- screw-top bottles (one for each distance)
- algal balls (20 per bottle)
- pH indicator solution
- measuring cylinder
- foil or black paper
- bright lamp
- small tank of water (if lamp is hot)
- metre ruler
- pH colour chart for indicator

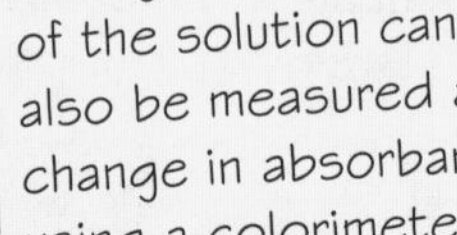

Change in the colour of the solution can also be measured as change in absorbance using a colorimeter.

Method

1 Place 20 algal balls and the same volume of indicator solution in each tube, and replace the screw tops.

2 Check the colour of the indicator against the colour chart and record the starting pH.

3 If using a hot lamp, place the water tank next to the lamp.

4 Use the metre ruler to place the uncovered tubes at specific distances from the lamp, on the opposite side of the tank.

5 Leave the tubes for 1–2 hours.

Safety: Take care if using a lamp with a hot bulb.

Using a water tank if the lamp is hot helps control for temperature, which will also vary with distance from the lamp.

Results

Record distance and pH of each tube, using the colour chart for identifying the pH.

Calculate the rate of change in pH per hour for each tube.

Draw a graph of your results to show distance against rate of change in pH.

Maths skills A graph using light intensity should show that rate of change in pH is directly proportional to light intensity.

You could also calculate the inverse square distances and draw a graph to show the relationship of that with rate of pH change. This should show that the rate of change in pH is inversely proportional to distance from the lamp.

Conclusion

As distance increases, light intensity falls and so the rate of photosynthesis decreases. This is because energy transferred by light is needed for photosynthesis to take place.

Instead of distance, light intensity could be measured directly using a light meter.

Now try this

1 Explain why rate of change in pH is a measure of the rate of photosynthesis in this experiment. **(3 marks)**

2 Explain why using a water tank is important if the lamp has a hot bulb. **(2 marks)**

3 A student covered one tube of algal balls in kitchen foil and placed it close to the tank as an addition to the method above. Explain the purpose of the tube. **(2 marks)**

Specialised plant cells

Some plant cells are **specialised** to carry out specific functions.

Phloem

Phloem contains **sieve tube elements** which have very little cytoplasm so that there is a lot of space to transport sucrose. It also contains **companion cells** which have lots of mitochondria. These supply energy from respiration for **active transport** of sucrose into and out of the sieve tubes.

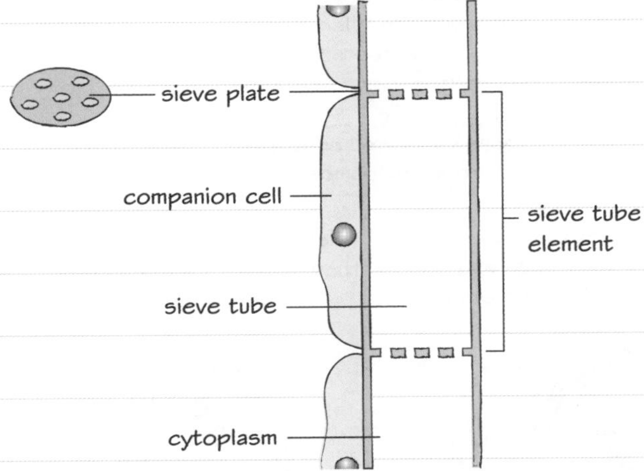

Sucrose is **translocated** around the plant in the phloem sieve tubes (see page 73 for more on translocation).

Xylem

Xylem vessels are **dead** cells which have no cytoplasm or cell contents. This means there is more space for water containing mineral ions to move through.

They have holes called **pits** in their walls to allow water and mineral ions to move out.

The walls are strengthened with **lignin** rings, which makes them very strong and prevents them from collapsing.

They have no end walls so they form a long tube that water can flow through easily.

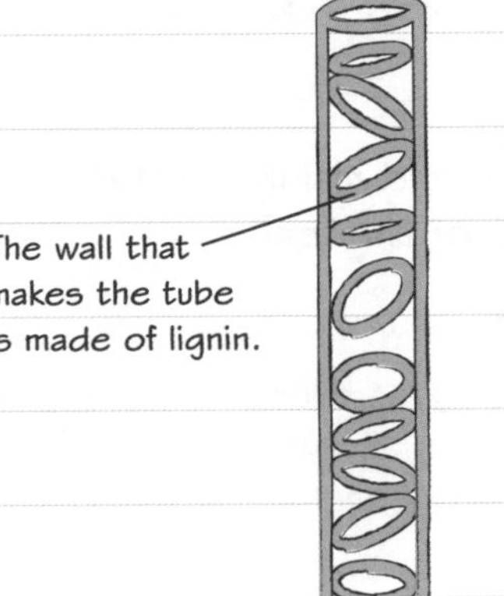

The wall that makes the tube is made of lignin.

Worked example

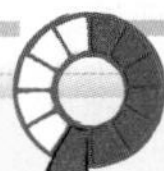

The diagram shows two root hairs on the outside of a root. Describe how these cells are adapted to take up water and mineral ions. **(2 marks)**

Root hair cells have long extensions that stretch out into the soil. This gives them a large surface area where osmosis can take place, which means that more water molecules can cross the cell membrane into the cell at the same time. This also gives a large surface area for mineral ions to enter the root hair cell by diffusion and active transport.

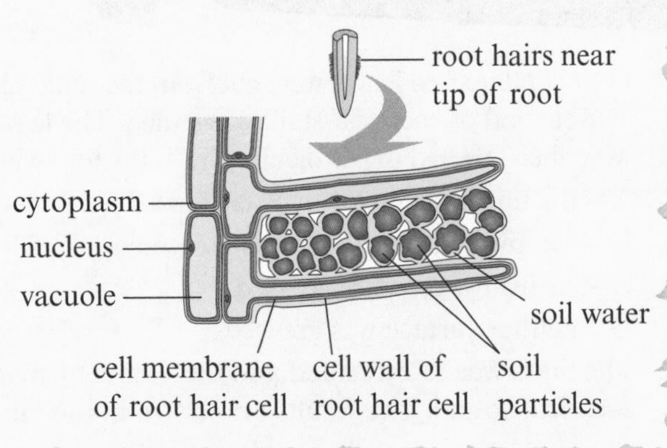

Worked example

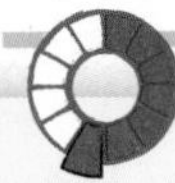

Explain the meaning of the phrase **active transport**. Use minerals entering roots as your example. **(3 marks)**

Mineral salts cannot enter the root cells from soil water by diffusion because there is a higher concentration of mineral salts in the cells than in the soil. So the root cells have to use energy to transport mineral salts into the cells against their concentration gradient.

Now try this

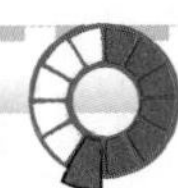

1 Explain how the structure of root hair cells is adapted to support active transport of mineral ions into roots. **(2 marks)**

2 Describe **three** adaptations of xylem vessels and explain how these adapt the cells for transporting water through the plant. **(6 marks)**

Transpiration

Transpiration is the movement of water through a plant from the roots to the leaves. The movement of water from the roots to the leaves is called the **transpiration stream**.

water vapour evaporates from leaves mainly through the stomata

↑

draws water out of the leaf cells and xylem

↑

draws water up the stem through the xylem from the roots

↑

causes water to enter the roots by osmosis

Stomata

Stomata are found mainly on the lower surface of the leaf.

The cell wall is thicker on one side of the cell than on the other.

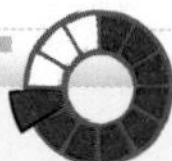

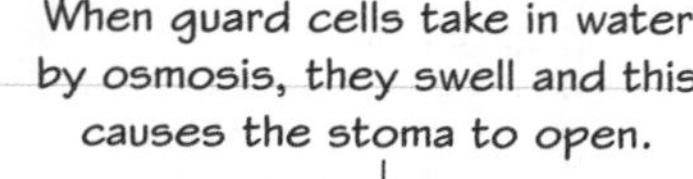

When guard cells take in water by osmosis, they swell and this causes the stoma to open.

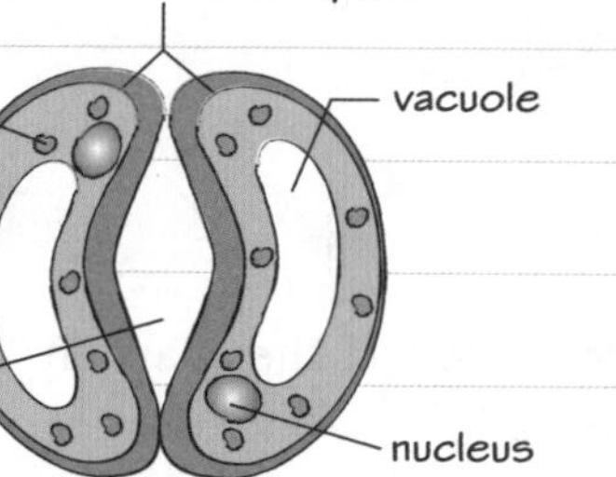

chloroplast
vacuole
cell wall
stoma
nucleus

stoma open

When guard cells lose water, they become flaccid and the stoma closes.

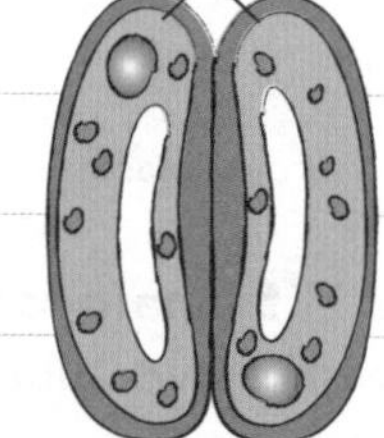

stoma closed

Worked example

Four similar sized leaves were cut from the same plant. The cut end of each leaf-stalk was sealed. The leaves were then covered in petroleum jelly in the following way:

A – the upper surface only was greased

B – the lower surface only was greased

C – both surfaces were greased

D – neither surface was greased.

The mass was re-measured and the % loss of mass of each leaf found. The results are shown in the table.

Leaf	% loss in mass
A	40
B	4
C	2
D	43

Describe and explain these results. **(4 marks)**

Leaves A and D lost the most mass, while B and C lost very little mass. This shows that the leaves that lost the most mass were those that did not have grease on the lower surface. Leaves lose most water through the stomata which causes a loss in mass. Leaves B and C had petroleum jelly covering the stomata so they could not lose water that way. Therefore they lost almost no water.

Do not confuse transpiration with osmosis. Water enters the roots by osmosis, but transpiration is the evaporation of water that 'pulls' water up the plant.

Now try this

1 Define **transpiration**. **(2 marks)**

2 Describe how water moves from the soil into a plant and evaporates from the leaf. **(4 marks)**

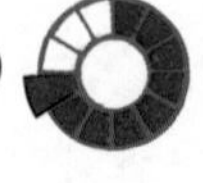

3 Suggest the advantage to the plant of stomata being present mainly on the underside of the leaf. **(2 marks)**

Translocation

Translocation is the transport of **sucrose** around a plant.

Phloem

Dissolved sugars are transported around a plant in phloem.

dissolved sucrose needed for growth in growing regions, e.g. bud

sucrose is produced in leaves from glucose formed during photosynthesis

phloem in plant veins

dissolved sucrose is carried around the plant in phloem

storage organ (e.g. potato)

dissolved sugars converted to starch and stored in storage organs so they can be used later

Plants have two separate transport systems: **xylem** and **phloem**.

Worked example

Carbon dioxide containing radioactive carbon was supplied to a leaf of a plant as shown in the diagram.

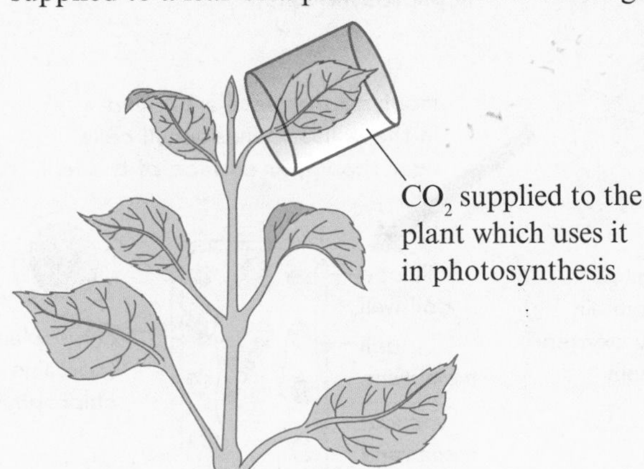

Remember that the phloem transports sugars and organic substances in the plant. See p71 for more information.

(a) Radioactive carbon atoms will be detected in the phloem. Explain why. **(2 marks)**

The carbon dioxide will be used in photosynthesis to make glucose. Some of the glucose will be converted to sucrose which is transported round the plant in the phloem.

(b) Describe how you could use this investigation to show that sucrose can move both up and down the plant. **(2 marks)**

This will be shown if radioactivity can be detected both above and below the leaf being supplied with $^{14}CO_2$.

Now try this

1 An aphid is an insect pest that inserts needle-like mouthparts into the veins of a plant. It feeds on sugars.
Explain which tissue in the veins the aphid feeds from. **(2 marks)**

2 A young potato plant grows rapidly during the spring and summer, but in the autumn develops new potatoes, which are storage organs. Compare the direction of movement of sucrose in the plant at different times of the year. **(3 marks)**

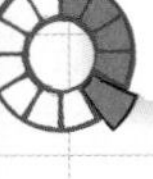

3 Name the **two** transport systems found in plants. **(2 marks)**

Remember that sugars can be transported both upwards and downwards in a plant.

Leaf adaptations

The structure of a leaf is **adapted** for photosynthesis and gas exchange.

Leaf structure adaptations

air surrounds most of the surface of each cell so that gas exchange can take place over most of the surface

epidermis cells are transparent to let light pass through to the photosynthetic cells

waxy cuticle is transparent to let light through

flattened shape of leaf gives large surface area

the mesophyll cells are packed with chloroplasts for maximum photosynthesis

xylem cells bring water for photosynthesis

phloem removes the sugars made in photosynthesis

most chloroplasts are found in the palisade mesophyll cells near the upper surface of the leaf

internal air spaces increase surface area for diffusion of gases

stomata (pores) allow carbon dioxide from air into leaf and allow oxygen from photosynthesis to leave leaf

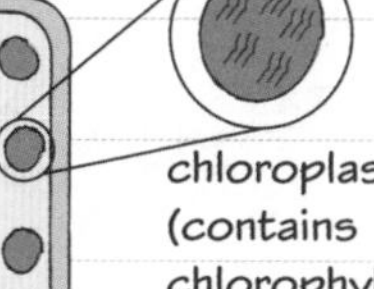

cellulose cell wall

cell membrane

vacuole

vacuole membrane

chloroplast (contains chlorophyll)

nucleus

cytoplasm

Worked example

Explain why the stomata are usually open in the day time and closed at night. **(2 marks)**

In the day time the stomata are open to allow carbon dioxide into the leaf for photosynthesis. At night the stomata are usually closed because photosynthesis does not occur unless there is light available. Closing the stomata reduces water loss.

Remember that it is one stoma but two or more stomata.

Now try this

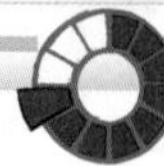

1 Explain why most leaves are a thin, flat shape. **(2 marks)**

2 The leaf is adapted for photosynthesis, but these adaptations mean the leaf can lose water. Explain how. **(2 marks)**

3 Some plants living in hot, dry places have stomata that open at night and close in the daytime. These plants store carbon dioxide at night to be used in the day time. Suggest why their stomata open only at night. **(2 marks)**

Water uptake in plants

Environmental factors can change the rate of water uptake in plants.

Factors that affect transpiration

Factor	Effect on transpiration
light intensity	High light intensity causes the stomata to open. This increases the rate of evaporation of water from the leaf so more water is taken up to replace this.
air movement	Wind blows moist air away from the stomata, keeping the diffusion gradient high. So the more air movement there is, the higher the transpiration rate.
temperature	The higher the temperature, the more energy water molecules have, so they move faster which means a faster rate of transpiration.

Using a potometer

You can measure the **rate** of transpiration using a **potometer**.

1. Note the position of the air bubble on the ruler at the start of the investigation.
2. Note the position of the bubble on the ruler after a known number of minutes.
3. Divide the distance moved by the bubble by the time taken.

Rate of transpiration can be measured as

$$\frac{\text{distance moved}}{\text{time taken}}$$

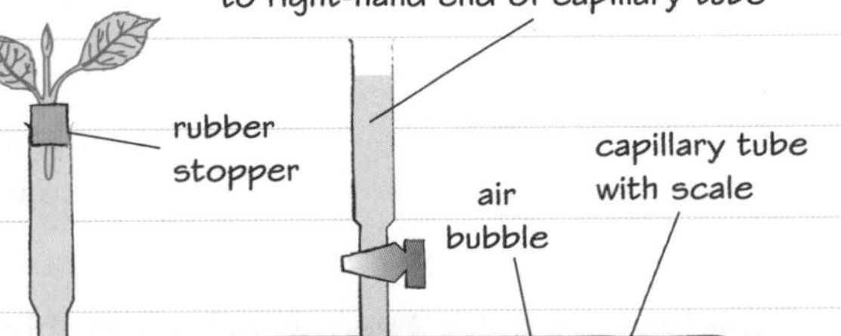

Maths skills You can find the **volume** of water taken up by finding the volume of the capillary tube between the bubble's start and finish points using the formula $\pi r^2 d$ where r = radius of tube, d = distance moved by bubble and $\pi = 3.14$.

Worked example

Three identical potted plants were watered and their mass recorded. Their pots were wrapped and sealed in plastic bags so that only the plant was in the open air. Each plant was then placed in different conditions. After 6 hours, the bags were removed and the mass of the plants was recorded again. The table shows the results.

(a) Calculate the percentage change in mass for plants B and C. **(2 marks)**

Mass in g	Plant A (cool still air)	Plant B (warm still air)	Plant C (warm windy)
at start	436	452	448
at end	412	398	332
% change	5.5	11.9	25.9

(b) Explain the differences in results. **(2 marks)**

The results show that evaporation of water from the plant was faster in warm air than cool air and even faster in windy air than in still air. This is because evaporation from the stomata is faster in hot and windy conditions.

Now try this

(a) A student placed a leafy shoot in a potometer. The radius of the capillary tube was 0.5 mm. The bubble moved 50 mm in 5 minutes. Calculate the rate of transpiration in mm^3/min. **(2 marks)**

(b) Explain how this measurement would be different if you repeated this with the same shoot in warmer conditions.

(2 marks)

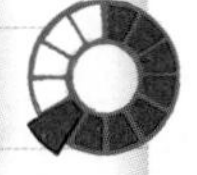

(c) Describe how you would carry out this investigation to make sure the results in the two different conditions could be compared fairly. **(2 marks)**

Plant adaptations

Plants have **adaptations** that allow them to survive in extreme conditions.

Adaptations to dry conditions

In the desert where it is very hot and dry, or sand dunes where it is windy and there is little fresh water because sand does not hold much water, plants such as **marram grass** have developed adaptations to their leaves.

Marram grass lives in windy conditions on sand dunes.

You do not need to know specific examples.

rolled leaf to reduce air movement around stomata

stomata sunk in pits to reduce water loss

leaf hairs to trap moist air round stomata

waxy cuticle to reduce water loss

Adaptations to tropical conditions

Plants that grow on the ground in a tropical rain forest have to be adapted to wet conditions with low light intensity.

Adaptations include:

- large leaves to take in as much light as possible
- stems and leaves that climb up the trees to obtain more light, with the plant's roots still in the ground
- leaves with 'drip tips' so water runs off them.

Adaptations to waterlogged soil

Waterlogged soils have no air spaces so the root cells have difficulty obtaining enough oxygen for respiration. Adaptations include:

- spongy tissue in their roots that stores oxygen
- fine surface roots that take in oxygen at the water surface.

Worked example

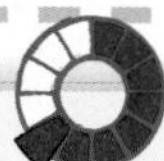

Label the diagram to describe how the listed adaptations help a cactus to survive in a dry environment. **(3 marks)**

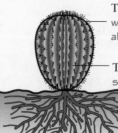

The cactus has no leaves which reduces water loss to air, but its green body still allows photosynthesis to take place.

Thick fleshy body stores water inside for times of drought.

Large root system collects as much water as possible from underground.

Now try this

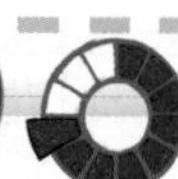

You need to apply what you have learned to a new example.

The creosote bush lives in very hot, dry conditions in Arizona, USA. Explain how the following adaptations help it to survive.

(a) Very small leaves covered with wax. **(2 marks)**

(b) During very dry conditions its leaves fold in half and some of the leaves may drop off the plant. **(2 marks)**

(c) It has a special kind of photosynthesis that means it takes in carbon dioxide at night and stores it to use in photosynthesis by day. **(2 marks)**

Plant hormones

Plant hormones control and coordinate **plant growth** and **development**.

Tropisms

A tropism is a plant's response to a **stimulus** (a change in the environment) by growing. A **positive tropism** is when the plant grows *towards* the stimulus.

- Plant shoots show **positive phototropism** because they grow towards light.
- Plant roots show **positive gravitropism** because they grow downwards – towards the pull of gravity. (Gravitropism is also called **geotropism**.)

Auxins and tropisms

Plant hormones are chemicals that cause changes in plants. **Auxins** are plant hormones that make cells grow longer. Auxins are affected by light and cause phototropism in shoots. In a shoot, where light is coming from one side:

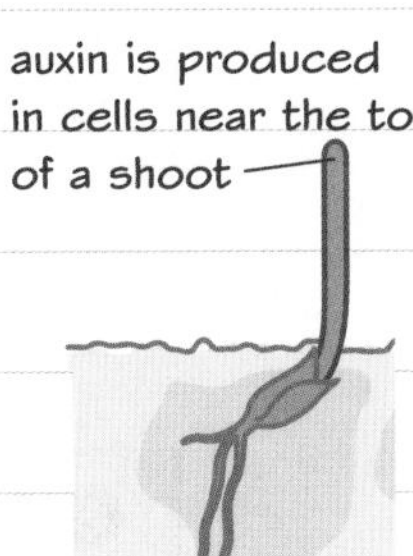

auxins move to shaded part of shoot

light

shaded side of shoot

auxins cause cell elongation

lit side of shoot

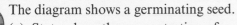

Worked example

The diagram shows a germinating seed.

(a) State where the concentration of auxin is higher, A or B. **(1 mark)**

It is higher at B.

A high concentration of auxin stimulates cell elongation in shoot cells, but inhibits cell elongation in root cells.

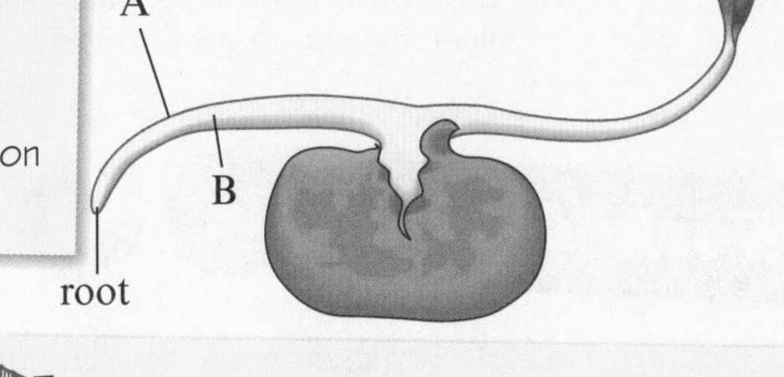

(b) Explain how this has caused the root to grow downwards. **(2 marks)**

In the roots, a higher concentration of auxin inhibits cell elongation. This means that the cells at A elongate more than the cells at B so the root grows downwards.

Tropism is a **growth** response. Do not say it is movement of a plant, as that implies the plant can actually move from place to place.

Make sure you describe the effect of light on auxin, and how this affects cell elongation, do not just link the direction of light to the curvature of the shoot.

Now try this

1 Explain how auxin helps a shoot to grow towards light shining from one side. **(3 marks)**

2 Explain the advantage of gravitropism to plant roots. **(2 marks)**

3 Auxin is produced

☐ **A** on the light side of a plant

☐ **B** on the shaded side of a plant

☐ **C** in the root tip

☐ **D** in the shoot tip **(1 mark)**

Uses of plant hormones

Plant hormones, including **auxins**, **gibberellins** and **ethene**, control the way plants grow and can therefore be used commercially in different ways.

Selective weedkillers

Selective **weedkillers** contain auxins.

Weed plants compete with crop plants for water and minerals from the soil.

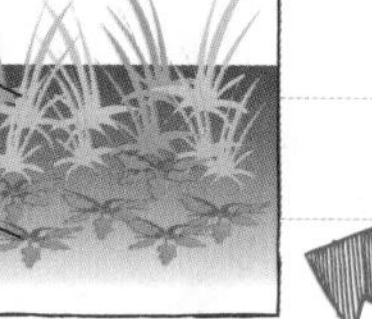

Remember: auxins stimulate the growth of shoots.

Broad-leaved plants absorb more of the auxins than narrow-leaved plants. This causes them to grow too quickly and die.

The crop plants get more water and minerals, and so grow better.

Rooting powder

Gardeners take **cuttings** (small pieces) of plants to grow into new plants. They dip the stalk end of the cutting into **rooting powder**. This contains auxins that cause the stalk to produce roots quickly. This helps the cuttings grow well into fully developed plants.

Gibberellins

Gibberellins stimulate germination of seeds which increases crop yields. They also stimulate flower and fruit production, again increasing the yield. Gibberellins stimulate stem elongation. If this is done on crops like sugar cane, it increases the yield of sugar.

Worked example

Tomatoes are often picked while they are green and unripe, then transported to the distributors. Here, they are exposed to ethene gas.

(a) Suggest why the tomatoes are transported before they are ripe. **(2 marks)**

The fruit is still quite hard at this stage so it is less likely to be damaged. Therefore, most of the tomatoes will be undamaged and the shops can make more profit.

(b) Explain why ethene gas is added to the tomatoes before they are taken to the supermarkets. **(1 mark)**

This causes ripening so that the tomatoes turn from green to red.

Seedless fruit

Gibberellins sprayed on to flowers can stop seeds developing in the fruits. They can also make the fruit grow larger. Many people prefer large seedless fruit, so they are worth more money.

Spraying gibberellins on to flowers increases costs for the grower. This is only worth doing if the resulting crop sells for a higher price.

Now try this

1 Explain why selective weedkillers are useful. **(2 marks)**

2 Ripe bananas give off a gas called ethene. Pears stored next to ripe bananas ripen more quickly than pears stored next to unripe bananas. Explain why. **(2 marks)**

Extended response – Plant structures and functions

There will be one or more 6 mark questions on your exam paper. For these questions, you will need to think scientifically, and structure your answer logically showing how the points you make are related to each other. You can revise the topics for this question, which is about the **effect of environmental factors on transpiration rate**, on pages 74 to 76.

Worked example

A student watered a pot plant and placed it on a sunny windowsill. By the early afternoon the plant had wilted. A few hours later, when the air was cooler, the plant had recovered and was fully upright again.
Explain these observations. **(6 marks)**

wilted plant

recovered plant

Plants absorb water from the soil through their roots and lose it through stomata in their leaves by evaporation in a process called transpiration.

A good start to this answer is to identify the processes that are involved in the question.

The rate of evaporation of water from the leaf surface increases as temperature increases, because water molecules move around faster. When the temperature was high, the rate of evaporation from the leaves was faster than the rate of absorption of water from the soil. This meant there was not enough water in the plant cells to keep them strong and support the upper part of the plant, so the plant wilted.

To answer this question well, you need to explain clearly how changes in temperature affect the rate of evaporation of water from leaves. Remember to link ideas to explanations with words such as **because**, or **this means that**.

When the plant was cooler, the rate of evaporation of water from the leaves decreased. The rate of absorption of water from the soil was then fast enough to fill all cells with water so the stems were strong enough to stand upright and support the leaves.

There are two situations that need to be explained in this answer: when the plant was hot, and when it was cooler. Arranging the explanations in time sequence helps to make the answer clearer.

Now try this

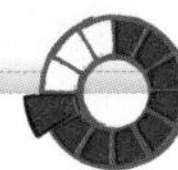

A student was studying a pond on a sunny day. During the morning he noticed bubbles coming from the pondweed. The rate of bubbling increased until early afternoon, and then decreased again towards evening.
Explain these observations. **(6 marks)**

Hormones

Hormones are 'chemical messengers' that target organs in the body.

Production and transport

Hormones are produced by **endocrine glands** and released into the blood. They travel around the body in the blood until they reach their **target organs**. Each hormone causes its target organ(s) to respond, e.g. by releasing another chemical substance.

Different hormones have different target organs and cause different responses.

Hormones and nerves

Nerves and hormones both help you to respond to changes in the environment and in your body. Hormones usually have a long-lived effect while nerves have a short-term effect. Nerve impulses work quickly while hormones take longer to work.

Release of hormones

Different endocrine glands produce different hormones.

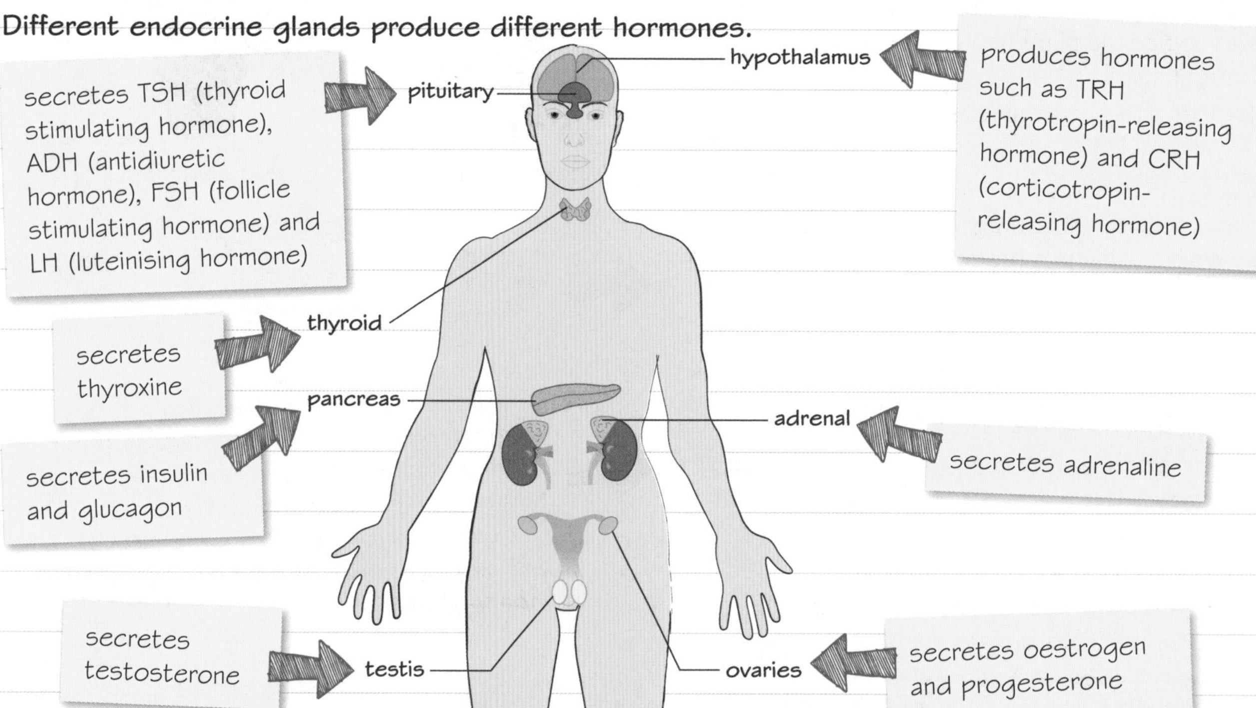
hypothalamus
produces hormones such as TRH (thyrotropin-releasing hormone) and CRH (corticotropin-releasing hormone)
pituitary
secretes TSH (thyroid stimulating hormone), ADH (antidiuretic hormone), FSH (follicle stimulating hormone) and LH (luteinising hormone)
thyroid
secretes thyroxine
pancreas
secretes insulin and glucagon
adrenal
secretes adrenaline
testis
secretes testosterone
ovaries
secretes oestrogen and progesterone

Worked example

Complete the table to show the target organs for each hormone. **(9 marks)**

Hormone	Target organ(s)
TRH and CRH	pituitary gland
TSH	thyroid gland
ADH	kidney
FSH and LH	ovaries
insulin and glucagon	liver, muscle and adipose tissue
adrenaline	various organs, e.g. heart, liver, skin
progesterone	uterus
oestrogen	ovaries, uterus, pituitary gland
testosterone	male reproductive organs

Remember: a target organ is where the hormone **acts**, not where it is produced.

Now try this

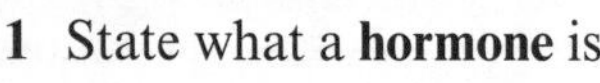

1 State what a **hormone** is. **(2 marks)**

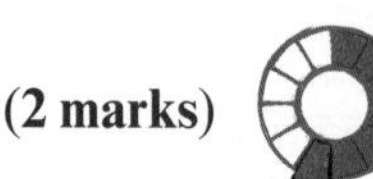

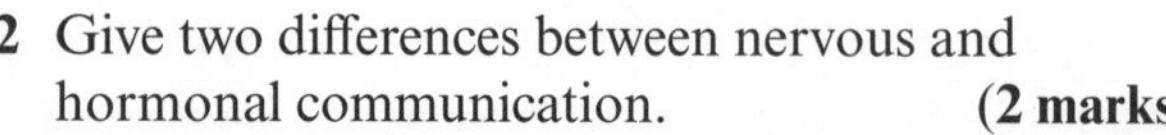

2 Give two differences between nervous and hormonal communication. **(2 marks)**

Adrenalin and thyroxine

Adrenalin and thyroxine are hormones produced in the human body. The production of thyroxine is an example of **negative feedback**.

Negative feedback

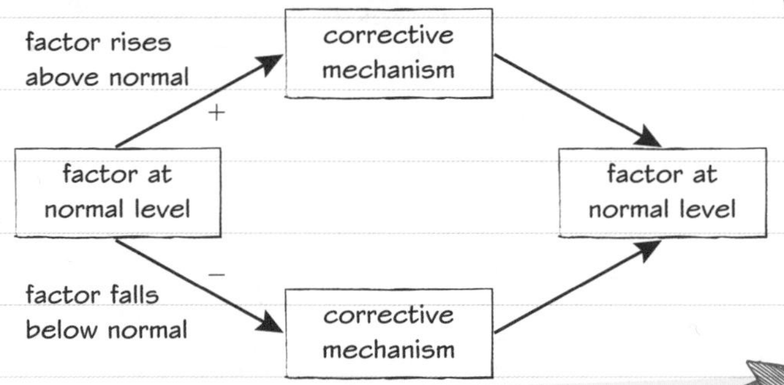

Make sure you can explain negative feedback by describing how a change from the normal level brings about changes to restore the normal level.

Worked example

Explain how the production of thyroxine is controlled by **negative feedback**. **(4 marks)**

When the concentration of thyroxine in the blood is too low, this stimulates a corrective mechanism. The hypothalamus secretes more TRH which causes the pituitary to produce more TSH. As a result, the thyroid produces more thyroxine. If the thyroxine concentration is too high, this inhibits TRH production by the hypothalamus, so less thyroxine is produced.

Adrenalin

Adrenalin is a hormone that is released from the adrenal glands in response to sudden stress. It brings about the **'fight or flight' response**.

Thyroxine

Thyroxine is a hormone that controls **metabolic rate**. This is the rate at which the cells respire. It is measured as the rate of energy transfers in the body.

Effects of adrenalin

Adrenalin has many target organs including the liver, the heart and blood vessels. It:

- increases heart rate
- constricts some blood vessels to make blood pressure higher
- dilates other blood vessels to increase blood flow to muscles
- causes the liver to convert glycogen to glucose, which is released into the blood.

Remember that explain means 'give a reason' – try to use 'because' in your answer.

Remember to name the target and the effect that adrenalin has for both cells or organs.

Worked example

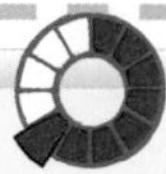

Explain two ways in which adrenalin is useful for preparing skeletal muscles for fight or flight. **(4 marks)**

The heart beating faster means that oxygen is carried round the body faster; because this allows faster respiration in muscle cells, energy is released for cell contraction faster.

The blood glucose concentration also increases, making more glucose available for respiration in muscle cells.

This question could have been answered in other ways, such as increased blood flow to muscles to supply oxygen and nutrients for faster respiration.

Now try this

1 (a) Name two target cells or organs that adrenalin affects. **(1 mark)**

(b) Explain how adrenalin affects them. **(1 mark)**

2 Beta-blockers are drugs that reduce the effect of adrenalin on the heart. Explain why they are prescribed for people with heart disease. **(2 marks)**

This is testing whether you can apply what you know to a specific example.

3 People who produce too much thyroxine tend to eat a lot but generally do not get fat. They also feel very warm most of the time. Explain why. **(3 marks)**

The menstrual cycle

Between puberty and about the age of 50, women have a **menstrual cycle** that occurs about every 28 days. During the cycle, changes take place in the ovaries and the uterus.

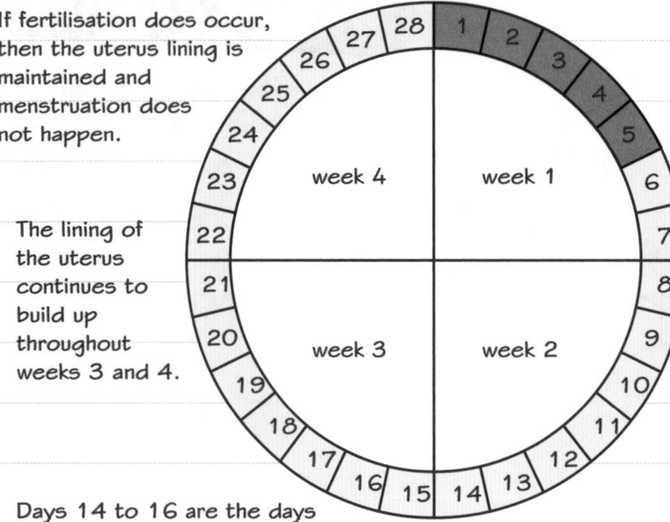

If fertilisation does occur, then the uterus lining is maintained and menstruation does not happen.

Menstruation is the breakdown of the uterus lining. It begins on day 1 of the cycle and usually lasts about 5 days.

The lining of the uterus continues to build up throughout weeks 3 and 4.

Oestrogen and **progesterone** are two of the hormones that control the menstrual cycle.

During the second week, the lining of the **uterus** is gradually built up.

Days 14 to 16 are the days when **fertilisation** is most likely to take place.

Ovulation is the release of an egg from an ovary. This usually takes place around day 14.

If fertilisation occurs, the uterus lining remains thick so that the embryo can embed in the lining and obtain the nutrients it needs.

Contraception

Contraception is the prevention of fertilisation. **Hormonal contraception** includes hormone pills, implants or injections, and works by releasing hormones to prevent ovulation and thicken mucus at the cervix, preventing sperm from passing. **Barrier methods** include male and female condoms, the diaphragm, caps and sponges. These work by stopping the sperm from reaching the egg.

Worked example

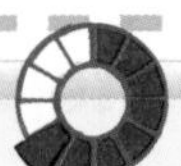

Give one advantage and one disadvantage of hormonal contraceptives compared with condoms. **(2 marks)**

Hormonal contraceptives are more effective than condoms at preventing pregnancy. However, condoms protect against sexually transmitted diseases (STDs) but hormonal contraceptives do not.

Different methods have different success rates at preventing pregnancy when used correctly. Condoms = 98%, diaphragm/cap = 92–96%, hormonal methods = >99%.

Now try this

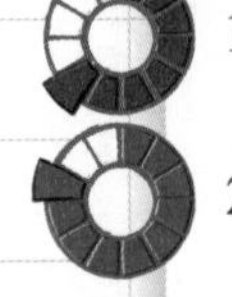

1 Explain why failure to menstruate may be the first sign of pregnancy. **(2 marks)**

2 The box opposite shows some information on the use of the contraceptive pill.
Use the information to evaluate the benefits and problems that may arise from using contraceptive pills to control fertility. **(3 marks)**

Around $\frac{1}{3}$ of UK women of reproductive age take a contraceptive pill. If used properly, the pill is 100% effective against pregnancy. Studies over 40 years show that the pill reduces the risk of many cancers. If the woman smokes heavily or is obese, taking the pill greatly increases the risk of thrombosis (blood clot). The increase in risk of thrombosis for women who do not smoke or are not overweight is very small, and is far less than the risk of thrombosis during pregnancy.

Control of the menstrual cycle

Four hormones control the menstrual cycle: **oestrogen**, **progesterone**, **FSH and LH**.

Changes during the menstrual cycle

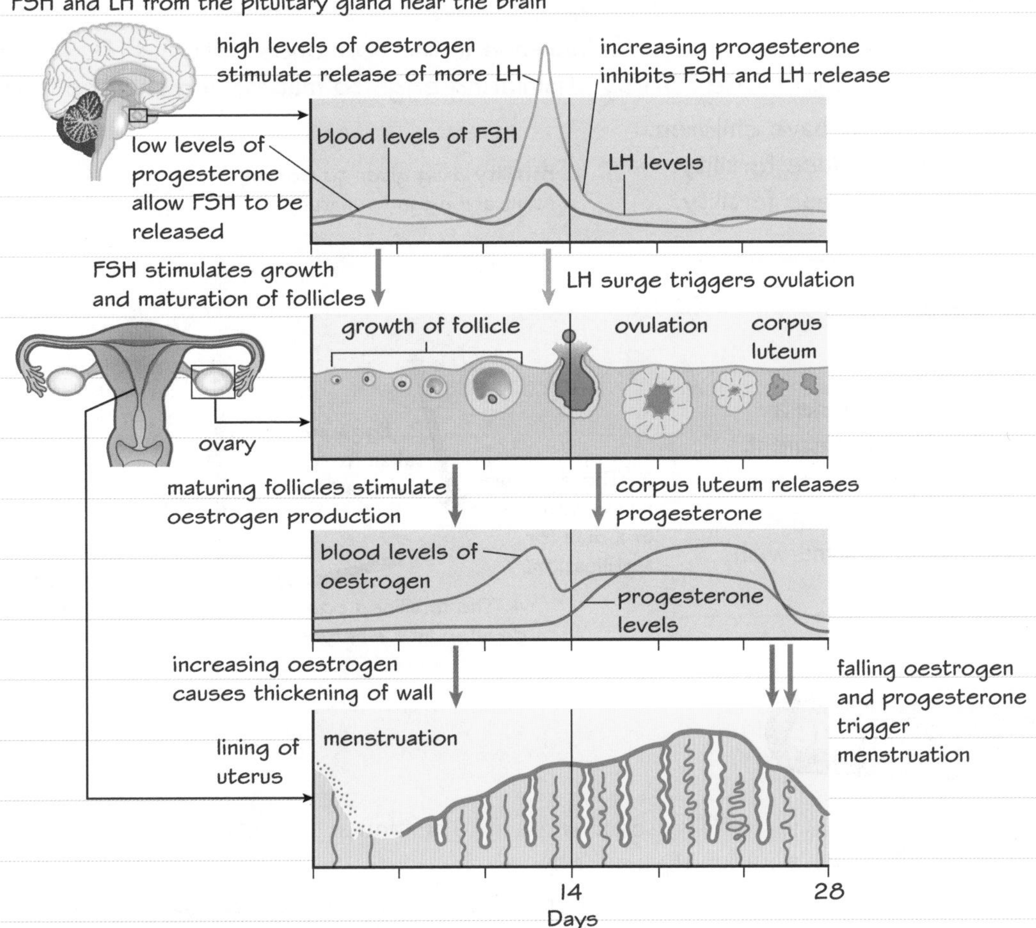
FSH and LH from the pituitary gland near the brain
high levels of oestrogen stimulate release of more LH
increasing progesterone inhibits FSH and LH release
blood levels of FSH
LH levels
low levels of progesterone allow FSH to be released
FSH stimulates growth and maturation of follicles
LH surge triggers ovulation
growth of follicle
ovulation
corpus luteum
ovary
maturing follicles stimulate oestrogen production
corpus luteum releases progesterone
blood levels of oestrogen
progesterone levels
increasing oestrogen causes thickening of wall
falling oestrogen and progesterone trigger menstruation
lining of uterus
menstruation
14
28
Days

Worked example

The question asks you to explain how the hormones interact, so it is important to say how they affect each other

Explain how FSH, LH, oestrogen and progesterone interact to control the menstrual cycle. **(6 marks)**

FSH is secreted from the pituitary gland. This causes a follicle in the ovary to mature. As it matures it secretes oestrogen which inhibits FSH and starts to thicken the lining of the uterus. A high concentration of oestrogen causes a surge in LH from the pituitary gland. This causes ovulation when the egg is released from the follicle. The ruptured follicle becomes a corpus luteum which secretes progesterone and some oestrogen. These cause the uterus lining to thicken even more. Progesterone inhibits FSH and LH. If the egg is not fertilised, the corpus luteum breaks down, and the progesterone concentration falls. This triggers menstruation. FSH is no longer inhibited, so it can be secreted from the pituitary gland again.

Now try this

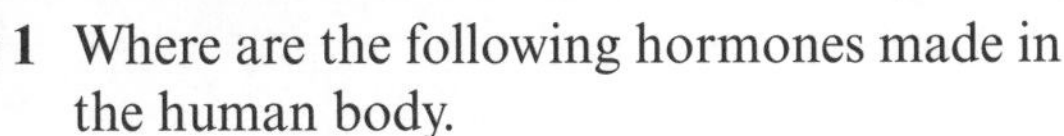

1 Where are the following hormones made in the human body.
(a) oestrogen and progesterone
(b) FSH and LH. **(2 marks)**

2 Describe the hormonal changes that cause menstruation. **(1 mark)**

3 Give the role of the following hormones in the menstrual cycle:
(a) oestrogen
(b) progesterone
(c) FSH
(d) LH. **(4 marks)**

Assisted Reproductive Therapy

Hormones are used in Assisted Reproductive Therapy **(ART)** including **IVF** treatment and **clomifene** therapy.

Fertility drugs

Fertility drugs such as clomifene cause an increase in the hormones FSH and LH. The drugs can help women who produce too little FSH by stimulating eggs to mature and then be released.

Fertility is the ability to have children.

- Contraceptive pills reduce fertility.
- Fertility drugs can increase fertility.

IVF (*in-vitro* fertilisation)

IVF is fertilisation outside a woman's body. This treatment is offered to couples who are having difficulty conceiving a child (i.e. having problems with fertilisation).

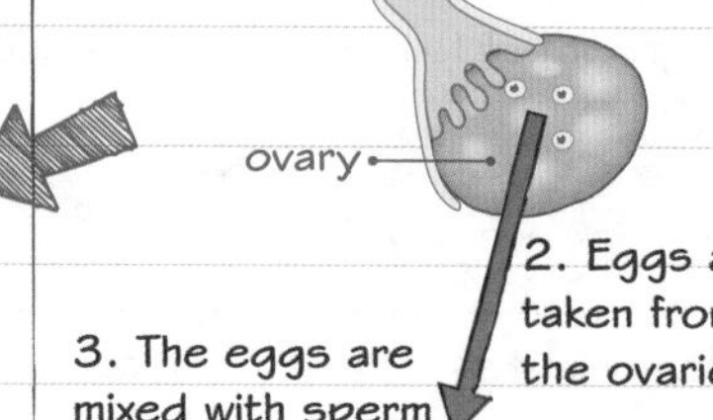

1. Fertility drug given to woman to stimulate eggs to mature.
ovary
uterus (womb)
2. Eggs are taken from the ovaries.
3. The eggs are mixed with sperm in a dish for fertilisation.
4. The fertilised eggs develop into embryos.
5. When the embryos are tiny balls of cells, one or two of them are placed in the mother's womb to develop.

Worked example

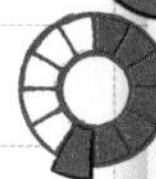

(a) Follicle stimulating hormone (FSH) is used to stimulate ovulation in a woman undergoing IVF treatment, even if she ovulates naturally. Explain why. **(2 marks)**

This is to stimulate the maturation of many eggs. Normally only one egg would mature in a normal cycle.

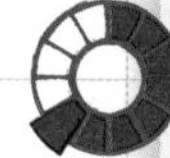

(b) The table shows the proportion of IVF treatments carried out in the UK in 2008 that resulted in a baby for mothers of different ages.

Age of mother	<35	35–37	38–39	>40
proportion of successful treatments	33.1%	27.2%	19.3%	10.7%

Use these data to suggest the advantage of using FSH in IVF treatment. **(3 marks)**

The data show that IVF treatment is not always successful, especially as women get older. Stimulating more eggs to mature means more embryos can be produced. This means that there are enough embryos for the woman to undergo several cycles of IVF if necessary.

Now try this

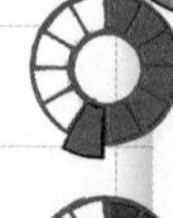

1 Describe how IVF can make it possible for a couple to have a baby when the woman does not normally release matured eggs from her ovaries. **(4 marks)**

2 Explain how clomifene can be used to treat fertility problems. **(3 marks)**

You need to outline all the steps in IVF treatment.

Homeostasis

Homeostasis maintains some conditions inside the body at a more or less constant level, in response to internal and external change. **Negative feedback** mechanisms respond to a change in a condition to help bring the condition back to the normal level.

Osmoregulation

Osmoregulation controls how much water is lost in urine, and so controls the amount of water in the body. This stops animal cells from swelling up or shrinking by osmosis if the water content of the body changes.

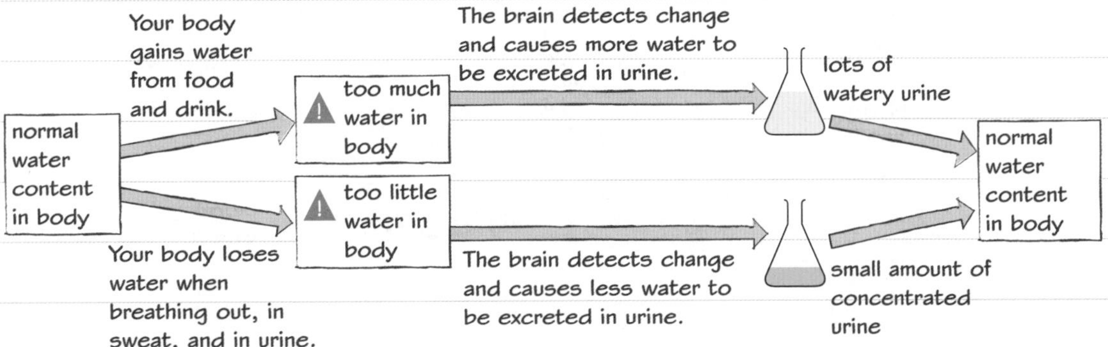
normal water content in body
Your body gains water from food and drink.
too much water in body
The brain detects change and causes more water to be excreted in urine.
lots of watery urine
normal water content in body
Your body loses water when breathing out, in sweat, and in urine.
too little water in body
The brain detects change and causes less water to be excreted in urine.
small amount of concentrated urine

Thermoregulation

Thermoregulation keeps core body temperature steady at around 37 °C. This is controlled by the **hypothalamus**, which triggers changes in the skin and muscles. The **thermoregulatory centre** in the hypothalamus of the brain monitors and controls core body temperature.

Blood vessels **dilate** or **constrict** to change the blood flow near the skin. They **do not** move up and down!

body temperature rises due to hot environment or exercise →	**hypothalamus** in brain detects rise and causes body responses →	• changes triggered in blood flow so more blood flows near skin surface • sweat glands release more sweat onto skin surface to evaporate • sebaceous glands produce oil that helps sweat spread out over skin →	increases transfer of energy to surroundings
body temperature falls due to cold environment →	**hypothalamus** detects fall and causes body responses →	• changes triggered in blood flow so less blood flows near skin surface • sweat glands stop producing sweat • body hairs raised by erector muscles in skin (causing 'goosebumps') →	reduces transfer of energy to surroundings

Worked example

Explain **two** changes that occur in the body if core temperature is too low. **(2 marks)**

1 Blood vessels that supply skin capillaries constrict and get narrower, which reduces blood flow through the capillaries near the skin surface. This means that less heat is transferred to the environment.

2 Muscles quickly contract and relax in succession (causing shivering), releasing energy to warm the body.

Remember it is the blood vessel that leads to the capillaries that constricts or dilates – not the capillary.

Now try this

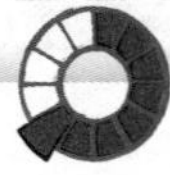

1 Explain why it is important for the enzymes in our bodies that our internal temperature is fairly constant. **(2 marks)**

2 Describe osmoregulation in terms of a negative feedback system. **(3 marks)**

Make sure you can explain how negative feedback works.

Controlling body temperature

It is important to control body temperature because enzymes in the main organs are most active at this temperature. The **skin** plays an important role in thermoregulation.

Skin structure

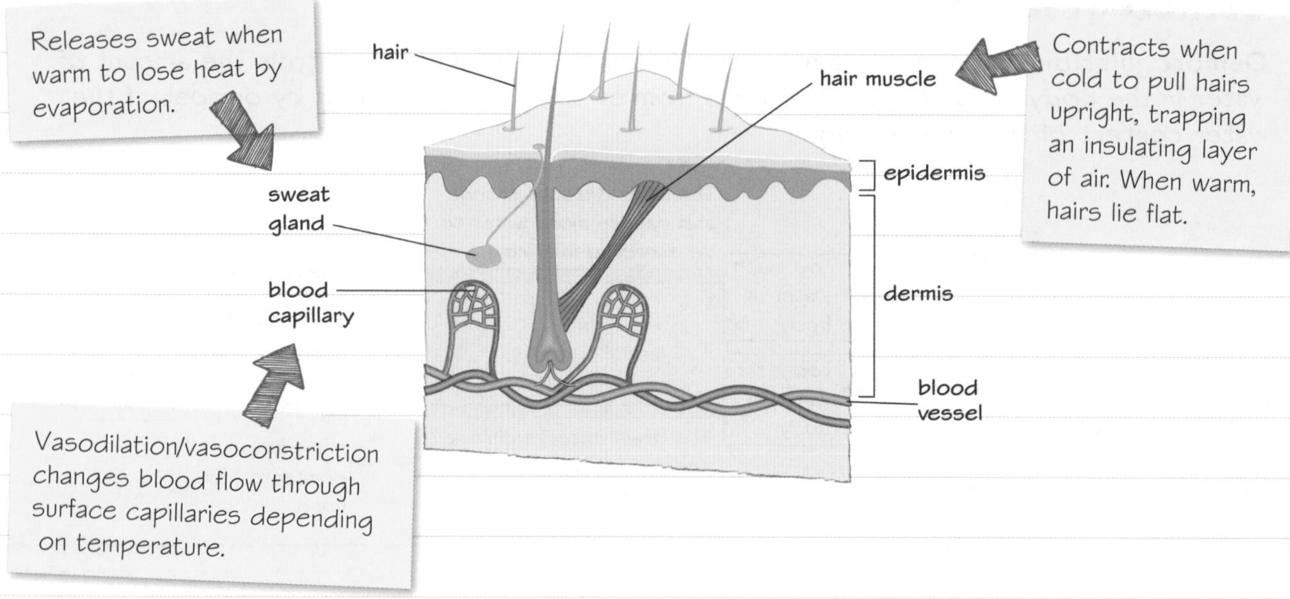

Releases sweat when warm to lose heat by evaporation.
hair
hair muscle
Contracts when cold to pull hairs upright, trapping an insulating layer of air. When warm, hairs lie flat.
sweat gland
epidermis
blood capillary
dermis
blood vessel
Vasodilation/vasoconstriction changes blood flow through surface capillaries depending on temperature.

Vasoconstriction

More blood flows through deep skin blood vessels so less blood flows through surface capillaries.

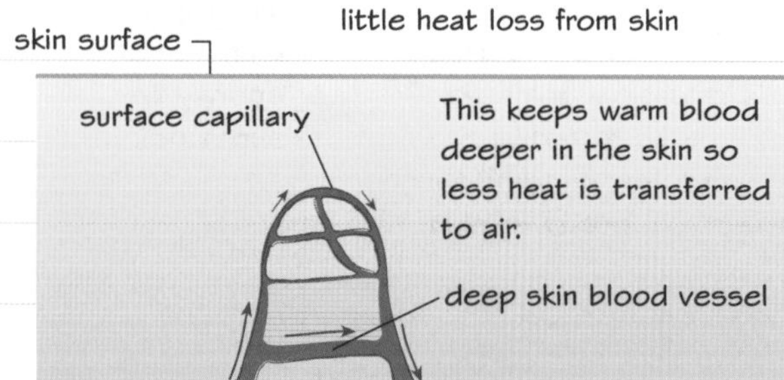

little heat loss from skin

Vasodilation

Less blood flows through deep skin blood vessels and more blood flows through surface capillaries. This increases heat loss by radiation.

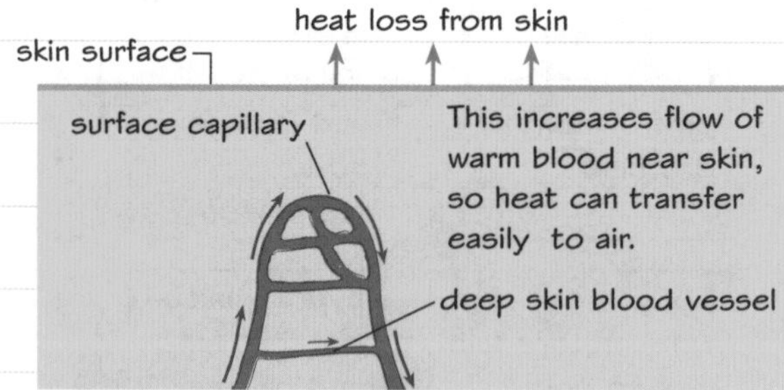

heat loss from skin

This increases flow of warm blood near skin, so heat can transfer easily to air.

Worked example

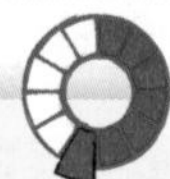

Describe the role of the dermis and epidermis of the skin in cooling the body. **(4 marks)**

Sweat glands in the dermis secrete sweat on to the epidermis. This evaporates, cooling the body down.

Muscles in the dermis relax, allowing hairs in follicles to lie flat. This means there is a thinner layer of insulating air trapped against the epidermis.

There are other answers, e.g. the role of blood vessels in vasodilation.

Now try this

A pale-skinned person may look pink after exercise.

(a) Identify what causes this change. **(1 mark)**

(b) Describe and explain what effect this has on body temperature. **(2 marks)**

Blood glucose regulation

Blood glucose regulation is another example of homeostasis. It is controlled by two hormones: **insulin** and **glucagon**.

Pancreatic control

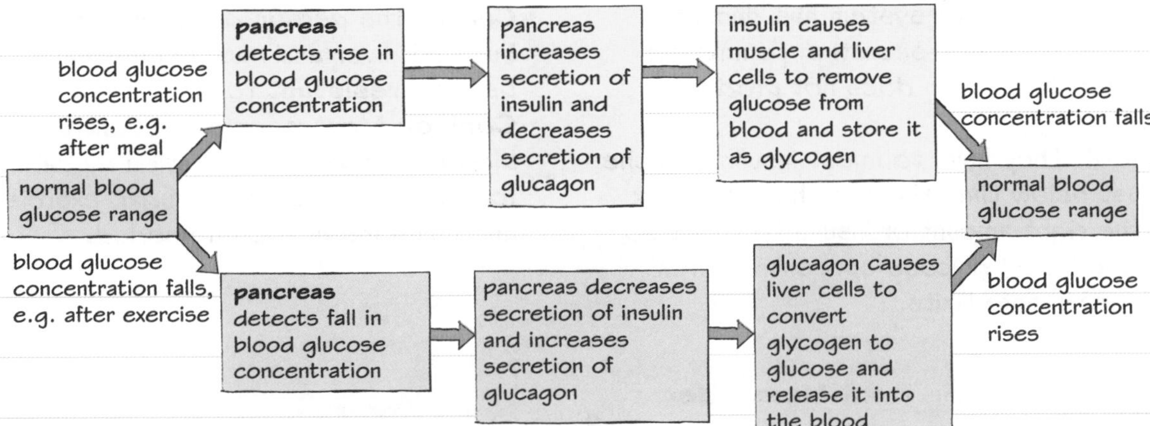

normal blood glucose range
blood glucose concentration rises, e.g. after meal
pancreas detects rise in blood glucose concentration
pancreas increases secretion of insulin and decreases secretion of glucagon
insulin causes muscle and liver cells to remove glucose from blood and store it as glycogen
blood glucose concentration falls
normal blood glucose range
blood glucose concentration falls, e.g. after exercise
pancreas detects fall in blood glucose concentration
pancreas decreases secretion of insulin and increases secretion of glucagon
glucagon causes liver cells to convert glycogen to glucose and release it into the blood
blood glucose concentration rises

Worked example

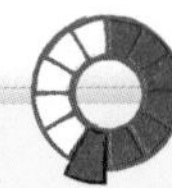

The graph shows the changes in blood glucose concentration of a person who has just had a meal.

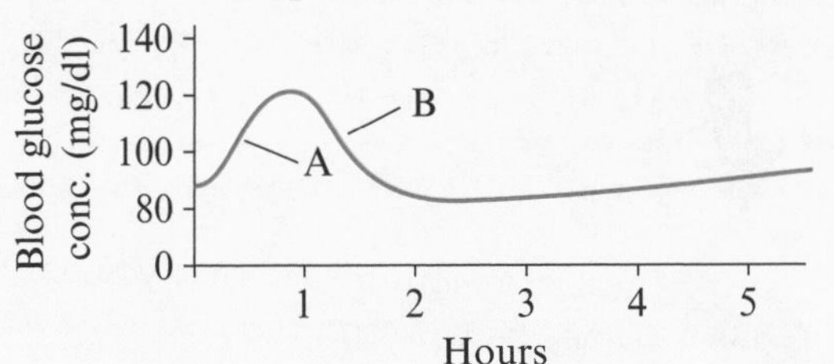

Describe what is happening. **(3 marks)**

Remember to refer to the graph when you answer a question like this.

At A the person has just had a meal, so the carbohydrates are being digested and absorbed into the blood as glucose. This causes the blood glucose concentration to increase.

At B insulin has been secreted from the pancreas which converts glucose to glycogen. Therefore, the blood glucose concentration is falling.

Now try this

1 Name the endocrine gland that secretes glucagon, and the target organ that the hormone affects. **(2 marks)**

2 The control of blood glucose concentration is an example of negative feedback. Explain why. **(2 marks)**

3 Insulin converts glucose to

☐ **A** glycogen
☐ **B** glucagon
☐ **C** galactose
☐ **D** starch **(1 mark)**

It may help to look back at page 80.

Diabetes

A person who cannot control their blood glucose concentration properly has a condition known as **diabetes**. There are two main types of diabetes.

Type 1 diabetes

- **Cause**: The immune system has damaged the person's insulin-secreting pancreatic cells, so the person does not produce **insulin**.
- **Control**: They have to inject insulin into the fat just below the skin. They have to work out the right amount of insulin to inject so that the blood glucose concentration is kept within safe limits.

Type 2 diabetes

- **Cause**: The person does produce insulin but their liver and muscle cells have become **resistant** to it.
- **Control**: Most people can control their blood glucose concentration by eating foods that contain less sugar, exercising and using medication if needed.

A person's **Body Mass Index (BMI)** is calculated using the equation:

$$\text{BMI} = \frac{\text{weight (kg)}}{(\text{height (m)})^2}$$

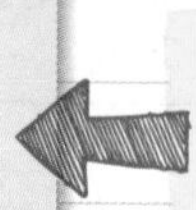

You may be asked to evaluate data on the correlation between Type 2 diabetes and BMI or waist : hip ratio.

There are other factors that are linked to diabetes, apart from obesity. These include ethnic group, type of diet eaten and activity levels. The effect of exercise and diet is covered on page 63.

Worked example

Use the graph to evaluate the correlation between obesity and Type 2 diabetes. **(3 marks)**

'Evaluate' here means that you have to say how strong the link is between these factors, giving reasons.

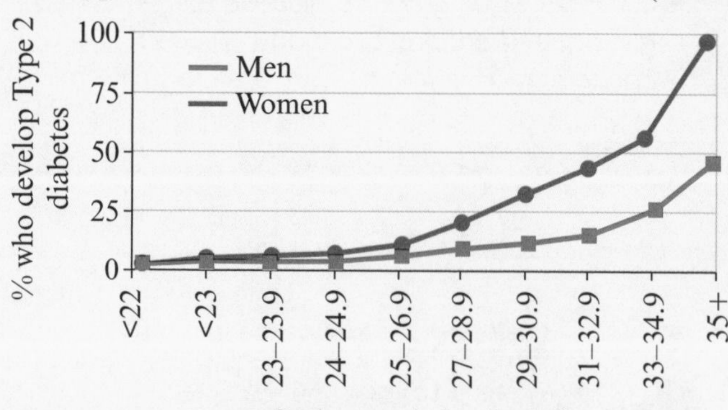

Sample sizes
men: 51 529
women: 114 281

The risk of developing Type 2 diabetes increases as BMI increases. It increases faster for women than for men. The large sample sizes and the smooth curves suggest that this is a strong correlation.

Now try this

1 Explain why the dose of insulin needed by a person with Type 1 diabetes will vary, depending on the food eaten and exercise. **(3 marks)**

2 Many health professionals advise that weight control is needed to prevent a huge increase in cases of diabetes over the next decade or two. Evaluate this advice. **(4 marks)**

You need to give the pros and cons and then come up with your own conclusion. It may help to remember there are 2 types of diabetes with different causes.

The urinary system

The urinary system **maintains water balance**, removes excess substances absorbed from food and **removes waste products** from metabolism such as urea from the breakdown of proteins.

Structure of the urinary system

Make sure you know the difference between urea and urine, and between ureter and urethra.

The **renal veins** carry cleaned blood back to the body.

The **ureters** carry **urine** from the kidneys to the bladder.

The bladder stores urine.

Urine flows through the **urethra** to the outside of the body.

The **renal arteries** carry blood from the body to the kidneys.

The **kidneys** remove substances including urea from the blood and make urine.

A muscle keeps the exit from the bladder closed until we decide to urinate.

Urea is produced from the breakdown of excess amino acids in the **liver**. It is toxic in excess.

Inside the kidney

Each kidney contains around one million tiny tubules called **nephrons**. The nephrons make **urine**.

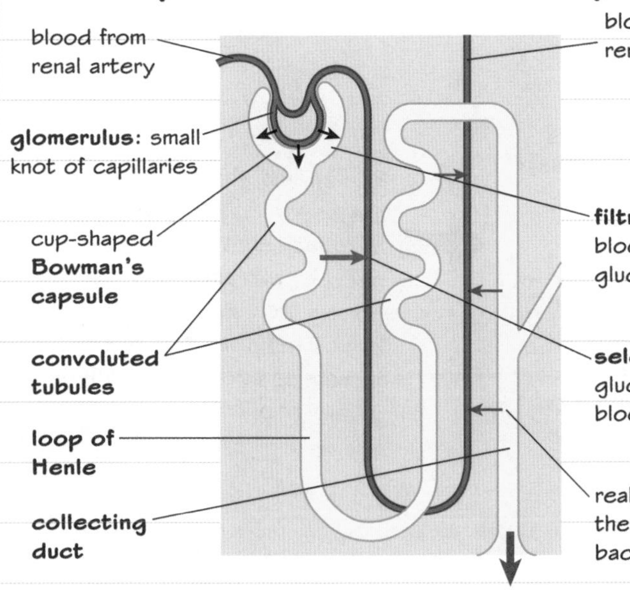

blood to renal vein

Large molecules, such as proteins, usually cannot filter into the nephron and so stay in the blood.

filtration of small molecules from blood into tubule, including water, glucose, salts and urea

↓

selective reabsorption of glucose from tubule back into blood by active transport

↓

reabsorption of water that the body needs from the tubule back into the blood (**osmoregulation**)

urine containing urea and excess water to ureter

'Selective reabsorption' is when useful molecules are absorbed back into the blood. Other molecules are left in the tubule.

Now try this

1 List the structures of the urinary system that urea passes through, in order, starting with blood in the renal artery. **(2 marks)**

2 Explain why a patient will die if they have kidney failure which is not treated. **(2 marks)**

Think about what is needed for 2 marks. What change will happen if a person has kidney failure? Then say why that change would be harmful.

The role of ADH

The amount of water reabsorbed from the nephrons is controlled by a hormone called **ADH** (antidiuretic hormone). This regulates the water content of the blood (**osmoregulation**).

Control of water content

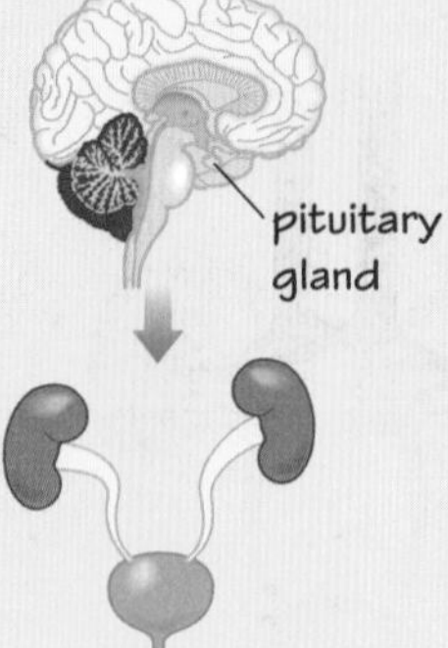

The brain senses there is not enough water in the blood.
pituitary gland
The pituitary gland secretes more ADH.
More ADH makes the collecting ducts more permeable.
So more water is reabsorbed from the kidney tubule back into the blood.
A small volume of concentrated urine is produced.

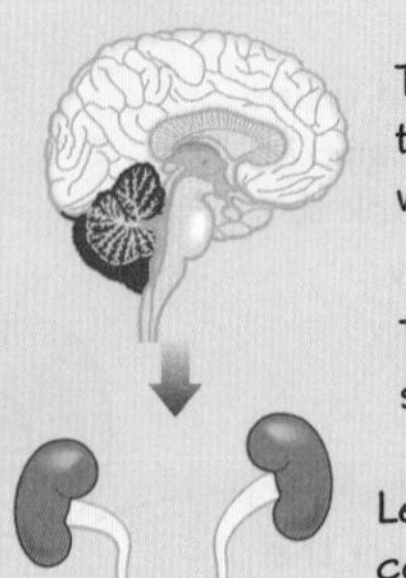

The brain senses there is too much water in the blood.
The pituitary gland secretes less ADH.
Less ADH makes the collecting ducts less permeable.
So less water is reabsorbed from the tubule back into the blood.
A large volume of dilute urine is produced.

ADH increases the **permeability** of the cell membranes in the **collecting duct** of the nephron so that more water is reabsorbed from the urine by osmosis.

Worked example

Explain what is meant by a negative feedback mechanism, using ADH production as an example. **(4 marks)**

An increase in blood water content causes the pituitary gland to secrete less ADH. This causes less water to be reabsorbed by the collecting duct in the kidneys so more water is excreted by the kidneys. A decrease in blood water content causes the pituitary gland to secrete more ADH, which causes less water to be excreted by the kidneys. This is a negative feedback mechanism because a change in blood water content causes an opposite change that restores the 'normal' blood water content.

Remember when you are describing negative feedback systems that you need to explain how the normal level is restored, both when the level increases too far and when it falls too low.

Now try this

1 (a) State where ADH is produced and its target organ. **(2 marks)**
(b) State what is meant by a target organ. **(1 mark)**

2 Blood samples were taken from a person half an hour after they had been exercising and again after they had drunk a large glass of water. Explain which sample contained the most ADH. **(3 marks)**

3 Alcohol inhibits the production of ADH. A man is in his garden mowing the lawn on a hot sunny day. He is feeling thirsty so he drinks a glass of beer. Explain why this is not the best choice of drink. **(2 marks)**

Kidney treatments

Kidney failure is when the kidney stops working properly, so excess water, mineral ions and urea build up in the body. People with kidney failure may be treated with **dialysis**, or by **transplant** of a healthy kidney.

Dialysis

Dialysis must be carried out every 2 or 3 days, usually in a hospital.

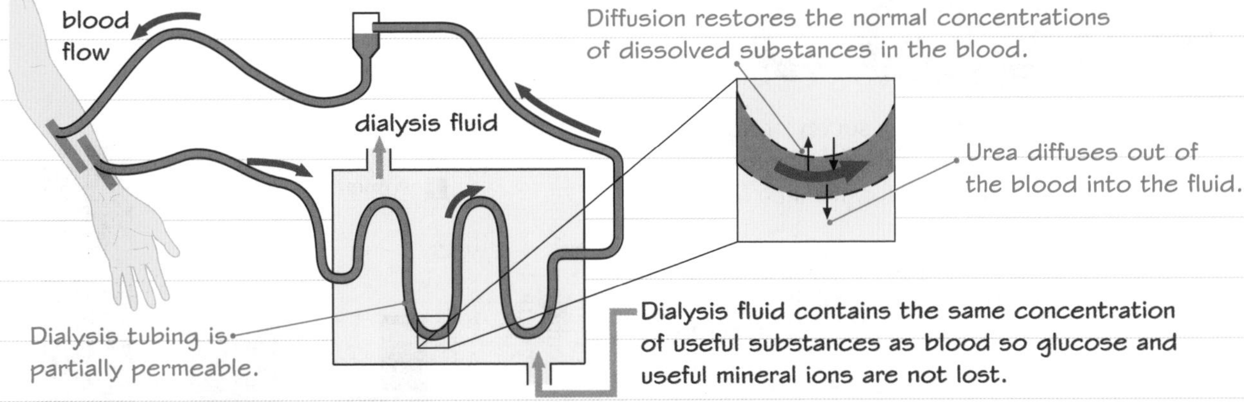

blood flow
dialysis fluid
Diffusion restores the normal concentrations of dissolved substances in the blood.
Urea diffuses out of the blood into the fluid.
Dialysis tubing is partially permeable.
Dialysis fluid contains the same concentration of useful substances as blood so glucose and useful mineral ions are not lost.

Kidney transplant

A healthy organ such as a kidney may be donated by a **donor**, which is **transplanted** into a patient.

A healthy kidney is connected to the blood circulation, to do the work of the diseased kidneys.

Problem: The **antigens** on the transplanted kidney cells are different from antigens on cells in the patient's body.

The **antibodies** in the patient's immune system attack the transplanted kidney and **reject it**.

To prevent rejection:
- the antigens on the transplanted kidney and patient's tissues must be as similar in type as possible
- the patient must be treated for life with drugs to reduce the effects of the immune system.

This means the patient may get more infections than normal.

Antigens are proteins on the surface of cells. They are the same on all cells from one person, but differ from person to person.

Worked example

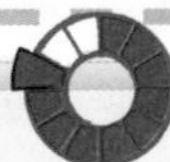

Compare dialysis with the way that a healthy nephron works. **(4 marks)**

Both dialysis and a healthy nephron remove harmful urea from the blood and control the water content of blood. Both also ensure that useful substances such as glucose and mineral ions are not lost unless they are in excess. However, a healthy nephron works all the time so the blood water concentration is controlled all the time, and urea is removed continually as well. Dialysis uses a machine, so this usually happens in a hospital. While dialysis is taking place a person is attached to the machine so cannot do very much.

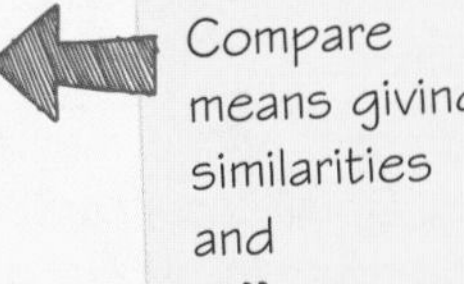

Compare means giving similarities and differences.

Now try this

1 Name **two** ways that kidney failure is treated. **(2 marks)**

2 Describe how dialysis works to make sure that the blood has the right concentration of substances. **(4 marks)**

You need to think about the composition of the dialysis fluid to answer this question.

Extended response – Control and coordination

There will be one or more 6 mark questions on your exam paper. For these questions, you will need to think scientifically, and structure your answer logically showing how the points you make are related to each other. You can revise the topics for this question, which is about the **link between BMI and Type 2 diabetes**, on page 88.

Worked example

The chart shows the results of a survey of adults in the UK who have Type 2 diabetes. The results are grouped by BMI category for men and for women.

Use the chart to explain how controlling weight could affect the occurrence of Type 2 diabetes.

(6 marks)

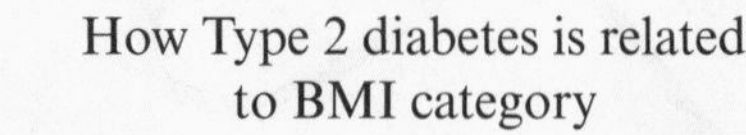

How Type 2 diabetes is related
to BMI category

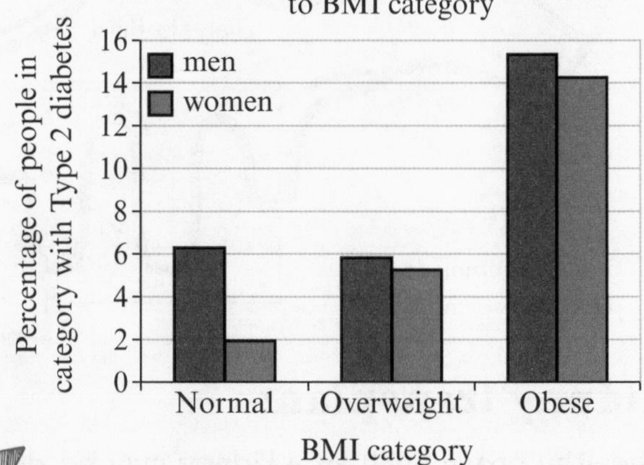

BMI is a measure of body mass (weight) and is calculated by dividing mass by height squared. As the amount of body fat increases, BMI increases. People with a BMI over 30 are said to be obese.

> A good start to answering this question is to show that you understand what terms in the question (BMI and Type 2 diabetes) mean.

People with Type 2 diabetes are not able to control their blood glucose concentration properly because their pancreatic cells do not produce enough insulin, or because their muscle and liver cells do not respond properly to insulin.

The chart shows that the risk of developing Type 2 diabetes increases as BMI increases, both for men and for women. The risk for women increases more rapidly than for men above a BMI of about 27.

> Before directly answering the question, you should explain what the graph shows. As well as describing trends shown by the bars on the graph, make sure you identify differences. Using values from the graph can show how well you understand the graph.

If people control their weight so they do not develop a high BMI, then they should keep their risk of developing Type 2 diabetes low. This beneficial effect will be greater for women than for men.

> As there are two categories on the graph (men and women), you need to explain how they respond differently to controlling weight.

The chart shows men and women in the UK only. So this conclusion may not be the same for people in other countries, or other ethnic groups, or for other variables such as exercise or diet.

> This point evaluates the link, showing why the the conclusion may not apply in different studies.

Now try this

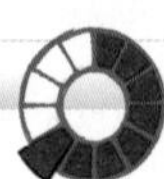

Explain how blood glucose concentration is regulated in a healthy person. **(6 marks)**

Exchanging materials

Substances such as oxygen, carbon dioxide, water, dissolved food molecules, mineral ions and urea need to be **transported** into and out of organisms.

How substances are exchanged

The table below shows different substances that need to be transported, where this happens and why.

More complex organisms

As organisms get **bigger**, their surface area to volume ratio gets **smaller**. This means they cannot rely on diffusion. They need to have specialised **exchange surfaces** and **transport systems**.

Substance	Site of exchange	Reason for exchange
oxygen	alveoli in lungs	needed for respiration
carbon dioxide	alveoli in lungs	waste product of metabolism
water	nephrons in kidney	needed for cells to function properly
dissolved food molecules	small intestine	needed for respiration
mineral ions	small intestine	needed for cells to function properly
urea	nephrons in kidney	waste product of metabolism

Worked example

(a) Complete the table to calculate some measurements relating to cubes of different side lengths. **(3 marks)**

Length of one side of cube (cm)	Surface area of cube (cm^2)	Volume of cube (cm^3)	Surface area : volume ratio
1	6	1	6
2	24	8	3
3	54	27	2
4	96	64	1.5

(b) Describe the pattern shown by these data. **(1 mark)**

As the length of one side of the cube increases, the surface area to volume ratio falls.

Maths skills Do not just talk about the surface area – it is the surface area to volume ratio that is important.

Adaptations for exchange

Special organs are adapted to make exchange efficient. For example, the **lungs** are adapted to exchange gases, and the **small intestine** is adapted to exchange solutes.

Now try this

1 Name **one** human organ that is specially adapted for exchanging substances with the environment. **(1 mark)**

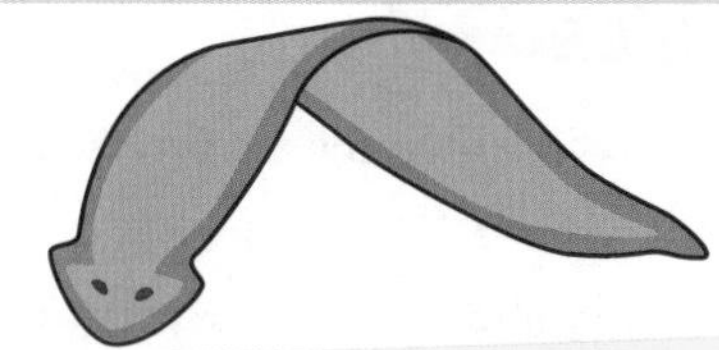

2 The flatworm shown in this diagram is multicellular but it does not have an exchange system or a transport system. Explain why. **(3 marks)**

Look at the shape of the flatworm and think about its surface area to volume ratio.

Alveoli

Alveoli are adapted for **gas exchange** by diffusion between air in the lungs and blood in capillaries.

The lungs

The **lungs** are part of the breathing system. The breathing system takes air into and out of the body. In the lungs:

- oxygen diffuses from the air into the blood
- carbon dioxide diffuses from the blood into the air.

(There is more about diffusion on page 12.)

The lungs are **adapted** for efficient gas exchange.

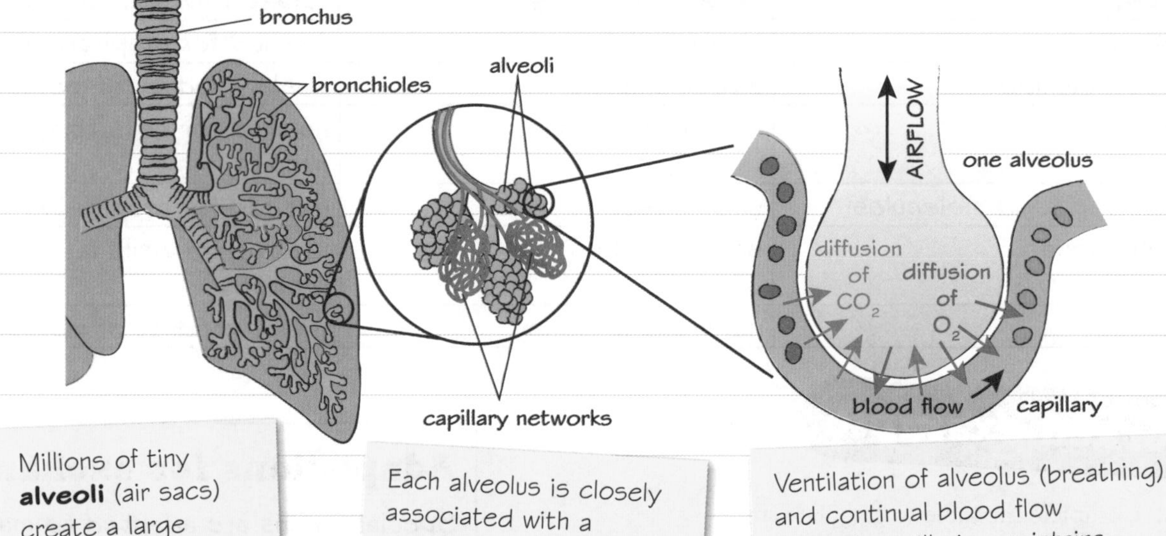

Millions of tiny **alveoli** (air sacs) create a large surface area for **diffusion** of gases.

Each alveolus is closely associated with a **capillary**. Their walls are one cell thick, minimising diffusion distance.

Ventilation of alveolus (breathing) and continual blood flow through capillaries maintains high concentration gradients, to maximise rate of diffusion.

Worked example

In some lung infections, fluid builds up inside the alveoli. Explain why this makes it harder for the person to breathe properly. **(3 marks)**

This reduces the surface area of the alveoli over which diffusion can take place and so decreases the rate of gas exchange.

This question says 'Explain…', so your answer needs to specifically refer to how the function of the lung will be disrupted. You should try to use correct scientific language throughout.

Now try this

1 State **one** way in which the air breathed out is different from the air breathed in. **(1 mark)**

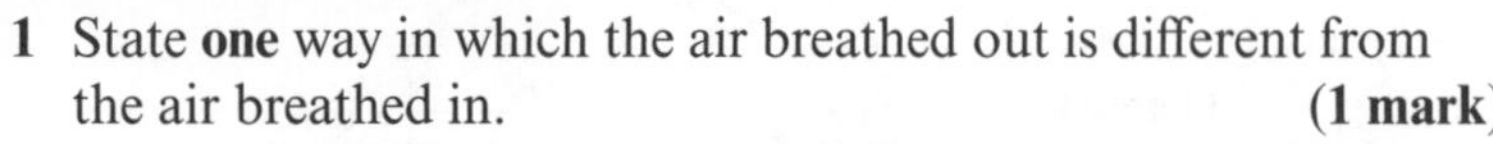

2 Explain why you breathe faster when you exercise. **(2 marks)**

3 Explain the advantage of the alveoli having many capillaries around them. **(2 marks)**

You need to consider both what the body needs to take in and what it needs to lose.

Rate of diffusion

The **rate of diffusion** across an exchange surface is affected by the structure of the surface.

Factors affecting diffusion rate

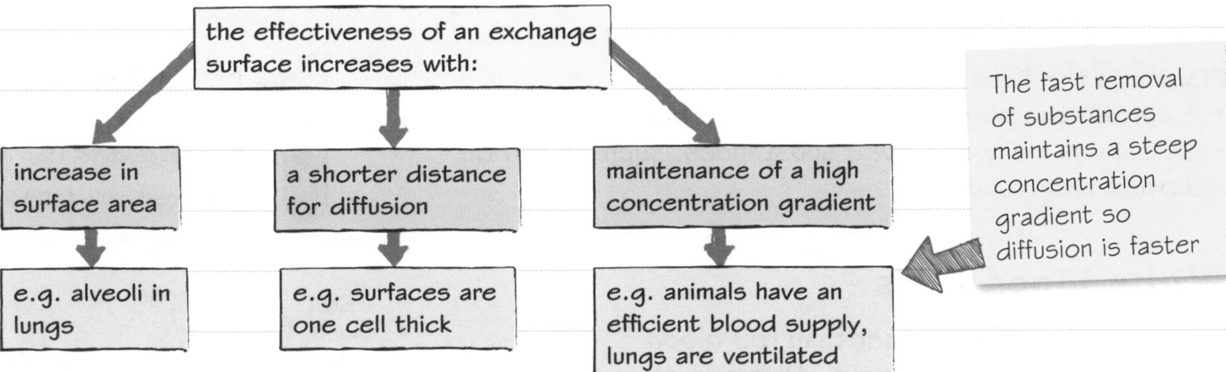
the effectiveness of an exchange surface increases with:
increase in surface area
a shorter distance for diffusion
maintenance of a high concentration gradient
e.g. alveoli in lungs
e.g. surfaces are one cell thick
e.g. animals have an efficient blood supply, lungs are ventilated
The fast removal of substances maintains a steep concentration gradient so diffusion is faster

Fick's law

Fick's law is used to calculate the rate of diffusion.

For this to be as **high** as possible

...these need to be as big as possible

$$\text{rate of diffusion} \propto \frac{\text{surface area} \times \text{concentration difference}}{\text{thickness of membrane}}$$

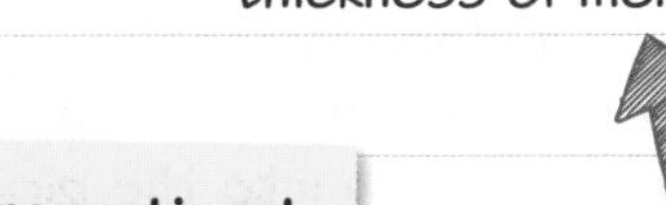

The symbol ∝ means '*proportional to*'. Two variables are **proportional** if a change in one is always accompanied by a change in the other, and the changes are always related by a constant factor.

...and this needs to be as low as possible

Worked example

People who smoke develop a disease in which the walls of the alveoli break down. These people become breathless easily. Explain why. **(3 marks)**

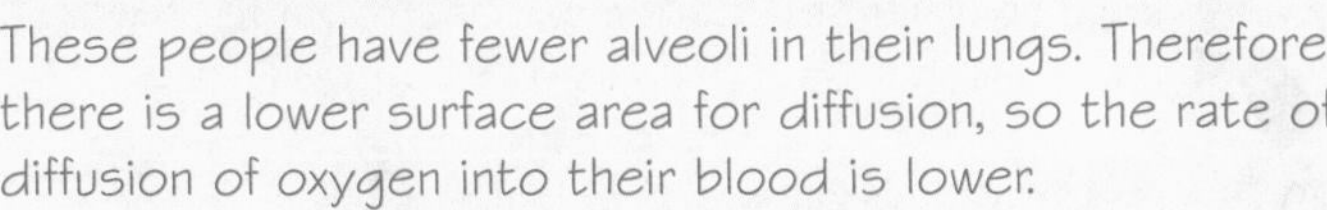

These people have fewer alveoli in their lungs. Therefore there is a lower surface area for diffusion, so the rate of diffusion of oxygen into their blood is lower.

You need to be able to apply the principles of Fick's law to real life situations.

Now try this

1 Explain why an extensive capillary network and ventilation of the lungs helps to maximise the effectiveness of gas exchange. **(4 marks)**

2 Describe what would happen to the rate of diffusion if:
(a) the surface area of an amoeba was halved **(1 mark)**
(b) the concentration difference was increased. **(1 mark)**

You do not need to give actual values, just **describe** the change in the rate of diffusion.

Blood

Blood is made of four main parts: **plasma, red blood cells, white blood cells** and **platelets**. Each part of the blood has a particular **function** (job).

Blood plasma

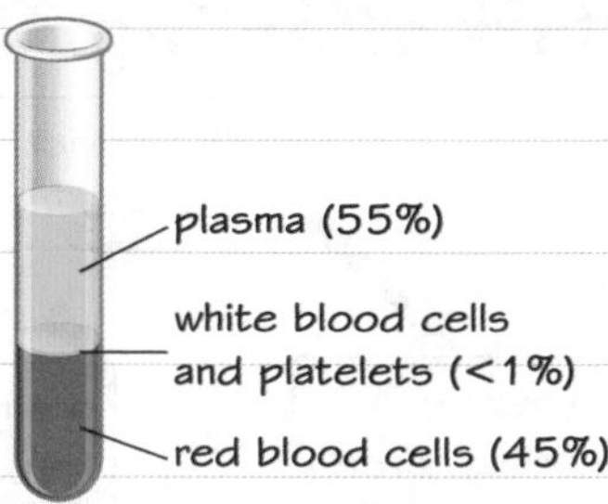

Plasma is the liquid part of blood:
- It carries the blood cells through the blood vessels.
- It contains many dissolved substances, such as carbon dioxide and glucose.

White blood cells

White blood cells are larger than red blood cells, and they have a nucleus. All types of white blood cells are part of the **immune system**, which attacks pathogens in the body.

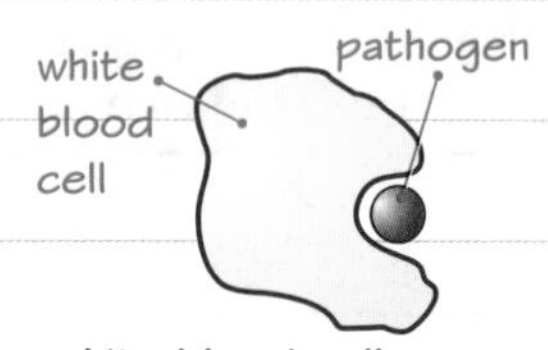

Some white blood cells (**phagocytes**) flow round (**ingest**) pathogens and destroy them.

Platelets

Platelets are fragments of larger cells. They have no nucleus. Their function is to cause blood to clot when a blood vessel has been damaged. The clot blocks the wound and prevents pathogens getting into the blood.

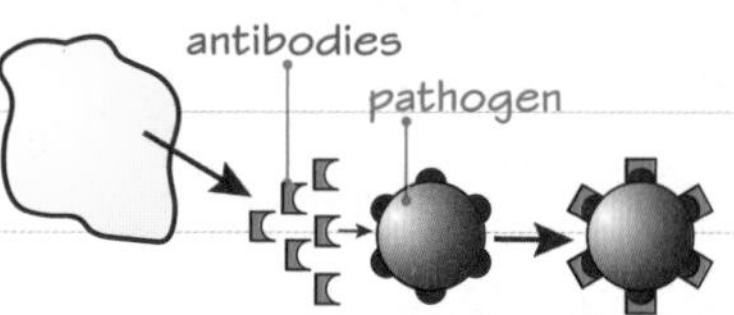

Some white blood cells (**lymphocytes**) produce chemical **antibodies** that attach to pathogens and destroy them.

Worked example

Explain how the structure of a red blood cell (erythrocyte) is related to its function. **(4 marks)**

Red blood cells contain haemoglobin which carries oxygen. The biconcave shape of a red blood cell means it has a large surface area. This means it is easier for oxygen to diffuse into and out of the cell. The cell has no nucleus. This means the cell has room for more haemoglobin to carry more oxygen.

Biconcave means the cell is dimpled on both sides so that it is thinner in the middle than at the edges.

Now try this

1 Respiring cells need oxygen and glucose. State which parts of the blood carry each of these substances. **(2 marks)**

2 Describe two ways in which white blood cells help to protect the body against disease. **(2 marks)**

3 Explain how platelets help to protect the body against infection. **(3 marks)**

Blood vessels

There are three types of **blood vessels** – **arteries**, **veins** and **capillaries**. Their structure is related to their function.

Veins

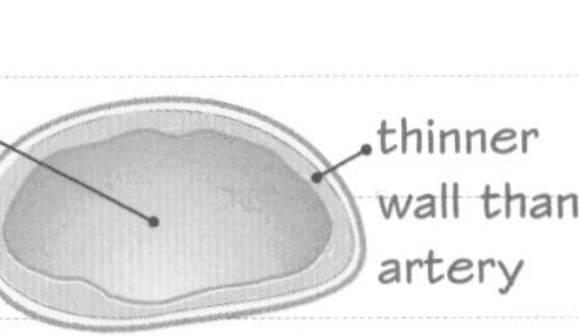

vein (cross-section)

vein (long section)

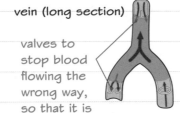

valves to stop blood flowing the wrong way, so that it is returned to the heart

Exchange in capillaries

Substances are exchanged between the body cells and blood in **capillaries**. Capillaries are **adapted** for their function of exchanging substances between the blood and body cells.

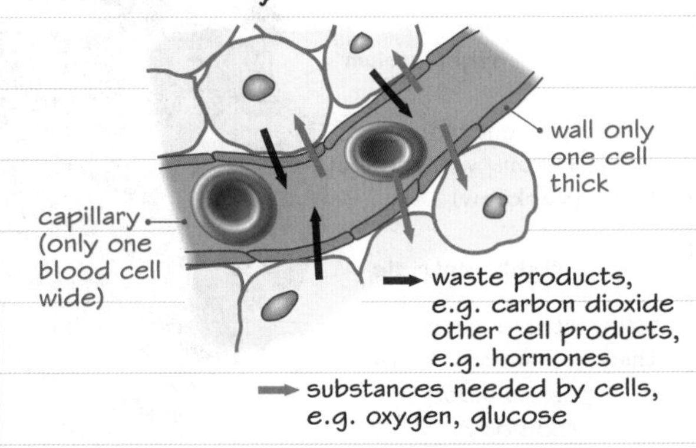

Worked example

Describe the role of arteries, veins and capillaries in the human circulatory system. **(3 marks)**

Arteries carry blood away from the heart – all arteries except the pulmonary arteries carry oxygenated blood to the body. Veins carry blood towards the heart – all veins except the pulmonary veins carry deoxygenated blood from the body back towards the heart. Capillaries exchange materials, such as oxygen, glucose and carbon dioxide, with body tissues.

Remember: a key function of blood is to deliver oxygen and glucose to cells for respiration and to remove the carbon dioxide produced by respiration from cells.

Now try this

Think carefully about the key function of blood, and what body cells need to survive.

1 (a) Which is the narrowest blood vessel?

☐ **A** artery ☐ **B** capillary ☐ **C** heart ☐ **D** vein **(1 mark)**

(b) Which type of blood vessel has the thickest wall?

☐ **A** artery ☐ **B** capillary ☐ **C** vein ☐ **D** all the same **(1 mark)**

2 Explain why almost every body cell is very close to a capillary. **(4 marks)**

The heart

The **heart** pumps blood round the body. The heart and the blood vessels together make up the **circulatory system**, which delivers oxygen and nutrients such as glucose to all parts of the body.

Structure and function of the heart

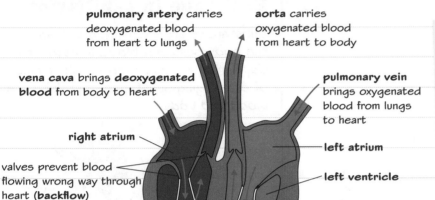

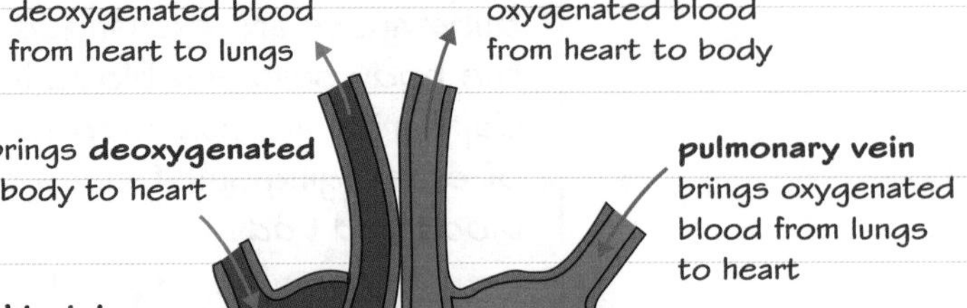

The sides of the heart are labelled left and right as if you were looking at the person. So the left side of the heart is on the right side of the diagram.

Remember - arteries take blood away from the heart, veins bring it back in to the heart.

Blood circulation

Valves in the heart make the blood flow in the right direction.

Blood enters the atria. → The atria contract, forcing blood into the ventricles. → The ventricles contract, forcing blood into the arteries. → Blood flows through arteries to the organs and returns to the heart through veins.

There are two circulation systems: one through the lungs and one through all the other organs.

Worked example

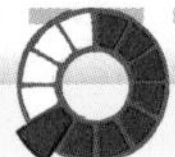

Explain how the structure of the heart adapts it to circulate blood effectively to the lungs and body. **(4 marks)**

Blood returning to the heart from the body is low in oxygen. This enters the right side of the heart and is pumped to the lungs by the right ventricle. It becomes saturated with oxygen in the lungs. The blood then enters the left side of the heart so it does not mix with the blood that is low in oxygen on the other side of the heart.

The left ventricle has a very thick muscular wall to pump the blood all the way round the body. There is a double circulation because blood passes through the heart twice to make a complete circulation round the body, making sure the pressure of the blood never falls too low.

Now try this

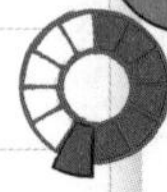

1 Give one reason why there are valves in the heart. **(1 mark)**

2 The muscular wall of the left ventricle of the heart is much thicker than that of the right ventricle. Give a reason for this difference. **(3 marks)**

Aerobic respiration

Cellular respiration is a process that releases energy from glucose for use in cellular activities. The main type of cellular respiration is **aerobic respiration**, which uses oxygen.

Aerobic respiration

Aerobic respiration is a series of chemical reactions that take place mostly inside mitochondria in the cell. This is an **exothermic** process because it releases energy. This happens continuously in living cells. It is the main source of energy for cells.

Make sure you use the phrase 'releases energy' when describing the function of respiration.

glucose + oxygen → carbon dioxide + water

(glucose: broken down; a sugar. oxygen: from air. → : releases energy)

The need for air makes this respiration 'aerobic'.

Use of energy from respiration

In animals:

- for metabolic processes to build larger molecules from smaller ones, e.g. proteins from amino acids, large carbohydrates (e.g. starch, glycogen) from small sugars (e.g. glucose), fats from fatty acids and glycerol
- to enable muscle contraction
- in birds and mammals, also to maintain steady body temperature in colder surroundings.

In plants:

- to build larger molecules from smaller ones, e.g. sugars, nitrates and other nutrients into amino acids, which are then used to make proteins.

Worked example

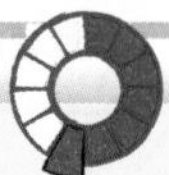

The graph shows the concentration of oxygen and carbon dioxide dissolved in the water of an aquarium that contains only pond weed. Explain the shape of the carbon dioxide curve. **(2 marks)**

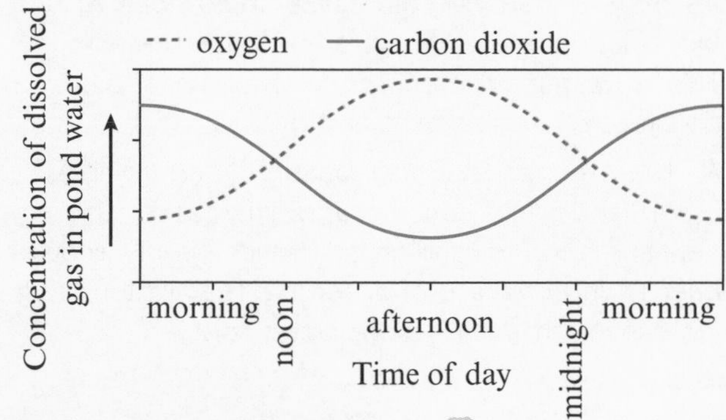

Carbon dioxide concentration increases during the evening and night because it is produced by respiration. Plants need to respire all the time. Carbon dioxide concentration falls during the hours of daylight when carbon dioxide is used in photosynthesis.

This question requires you to use knowledge about photosynthesis and respiration.

Now try this

1 Define the term aerobic respiration. **(2 marks)**

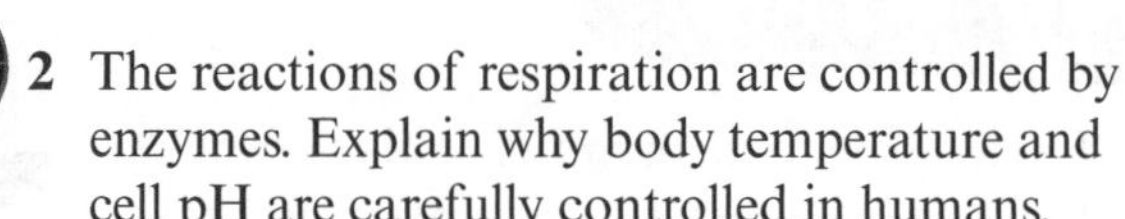

2 The reactions of respiration are controlled by enzymes. Explain why body temperature and cell pH are carefully controlled in humans. **(2 marks)**

Anaerobic respiration

During exercise, energy needed for muscle contraction comes from **aerobic respiration**. If there is not enough oxygen, or aerobic respiration is not possible, **anaerobic respiration** takes place.

How anaerobic respiration works

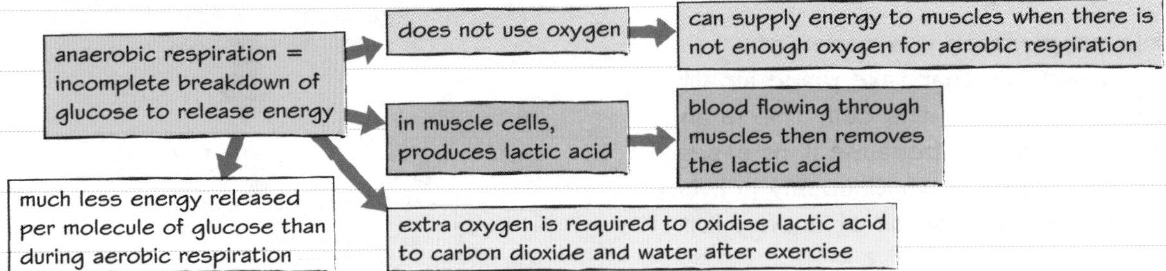

anaerobic respiration = incomplete breakdown of glucose to release energy
does not use oxygen
can supply energy to muscles when there is not enough oxygen for aerobic respiration
in muscle cells, produces lactic acid
blood flowing through muscles then removes the lactic acid
much less energy released per molecule of glucose than during aerobic respiration
extra oxygen is required to oxidise lactic acid to carbon dioxide and water after exercise

In **plants and fungal cells**, there is a different form of anaerobic respiration that produces ethanol. However, like anaerobic respiration in animals:

- it involves breakdown of glucose
- no oxygen is used
- less energy is released per glucose molecule.

Advantages

- Anaerobic respiration is useful for muscle cells because it can release energy to allow muscles to contract when the heart and lungs cannot deliver oxygen and glucose fast enough for aerobic respiration.
- Respiration can continue in organisms that have no, or very limited, oxygen supply.

Disadvantages

- Anaerobic respiration releases much less energy from each molecule of glucose than aerobic respiration.
- Lactic acid is not removed from the body. It builds up in muscle and blood, and must be broken down after exercise.

Worked example

The graph shows how the concentration of lactic acid in the blood varies with level of exercise.

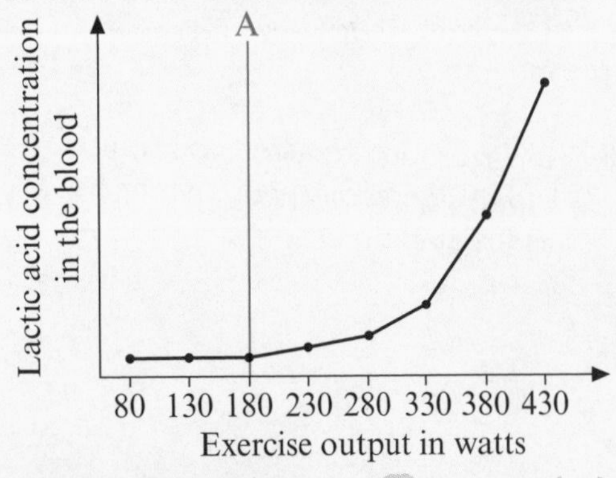

Explain what the graph shows. **(2 marks)**

As the exercise level increases up to point A, blood lactic acid concentration stays the same. This is because the energy for the exercise is coming from aerobic respiration.

As the exercise level increases beyond point A, blood lactic acid concentration increases. This is because aerobic respiration cannot supply enough energy and the rate of anaerobic respiration increases, producing more lactic acid.

Now try this

1 Explain why human muscle cells cannot function on anaerobic respiration alone. **(2 marks)**

2 After vigorous exercise has ended, an athlete will continue to breathe deeply for several minutes longer. Explain why. **(2 marks)**

Rate of respiration

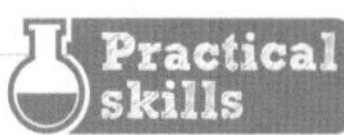

You need to understand how **the rate of respiration in living organisms can be investigated.** This experiment can use small invertebrates (e.g. maggots, woodlice) or germinating peas. See page 99 for more information on respiration.

Worked example

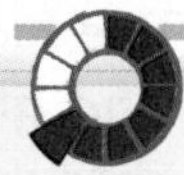

The diagram below shows a **respirometer**, which is used for investigating rates of respiration.

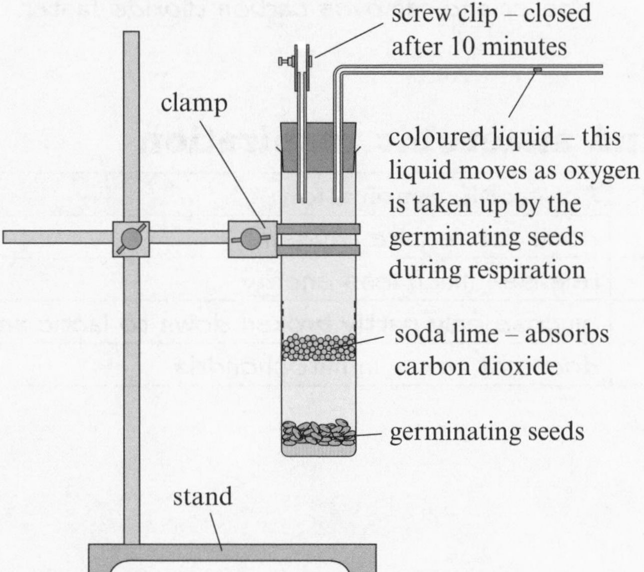

(a) Explain the function of the soda lime in the respirometer. **(2 marks)**

Soda lime absorbs carbon dioxide produced by the seeds during respiration, so that it does not affect the movement of the liquid blob.

(b) Explain why the liquid blob moves during the experiment. **(2 marks)**

Oxygen is absorbed from the surrounding air by the germinating seeds. This reduces the volume of air in the container, so the blob will move towards the container.

(c) Explain how this respirometer could be used to measure rate of respiration of the seeds. **(2 marks)**

The distance that the liquid blob moves over a particular time could be measured, and a rate calculated by dividing distance by time.

Safety and living organisms

You must consider the safe and ethical use of working with living organisms. You should minimise harm to small invertebrates, and return them to their natural environment as soon as possible. You should also wash your hands thoroughly after working with living organisms.

Factors affecting respiration

Remember that respiration is affected by environmental factors, particularly temperature, and that microorganisms also respire. So the investigation will need controls.

Control for temperature – e.g. by keeping respirometers in a water bath during the experiment.

Control for something other than the study organisms affecting the gas volume – e.g. by using the same volume of an inert substance as the organisms, such as glass beads instead of seeds.

$$\text{rate} = \frac{\text{change}}{\text{time}}$$

In this case the change measured could be the amount of oxygen absorbed. In other investigations, you might measure the amount of carbon dioxide produced.

Now try this

The table shows the results of an investigation in which respirometers containing woodlice were kept at different temperatures. The uptake of oxygen in each respirometer was measured at the end of 20 min.

(a) Calculate the rate of oxygen uptake per min for each respirometer. **(2 marks)**

(b) Draw a graph to show rate of oxygen uptake against temperature. **(4 marks)**

(c) Describe the relationship shown by this experiment. **(2 marks)**

Temperature (°C)	Volume of gas absorbed in 20 min (cm^3)
5	0.6
10	1.0
15	1.7
20	2.4

Changes in heart rate

On this page you will revise the formula **cardiac output = stroke volume × heart rate.**

Effects of exercise

When you exercise, your **heart rate** increases. The harder you exercise, the more your heart rate increases. Heart rate can be measured by taking your **pulse** at the wrist. It is usually measured as number of **beats per minute**.

During exercise, muscle cells are respiring faster. This means that they need more oxygen and glucose, and release more carbon dioxide. A faster heart rate means that blood is pumped faster around the body. The blood takes oxygen and glucose to cells faster and removes carbon dioxide faster.

Differences between aerobic and anaerobic respiration

Aerobic respiration	Anaerobic respiration
requires oxygen	does not require oxygen
releases a lot of energy	releases much less energy
glucose broken down completely	glucose only partly broken down to lactic acid
occurs mostly in mitochondria	does not occur in mitochondria

Worked example

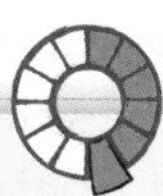

The table shows the stroke volume and heart rate for two people at rest. **(2 marks)**

	Stroke volume (cm^3)	Heart rate (beats per minute)
trained athlete	90	55
untrained person	60	70

Calculate the cardiac output for these two people.

athlete: $90 \times 55 = 4950\,cm^3$ per minute

untrained person: $60 \times 70 = 4200\,cm^3$ per minute

Maths skills cardiac output = stroke volume × heart rate

Stroke volume is the volume of blood pumped by the heart in one beat.

Now try this

1 Describe how heart rate varies with level of exercise. **(2 marks)**

2 A person has a cardiac output of 4500 cm^3 per minute and a resting heart rate of 75 beats per minute. Calculate their stroke volume. **(2 marks)**

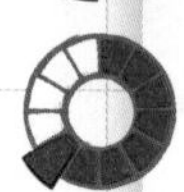

3 Suggest why a trained athlete may have a similar cardiac output to an untrained person but a lower resting heart rate. **(2 marks)**

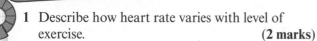

Maths skills Rates are always how often something happens in a particular time period. So heart rate is how many times the heart beats in a minute.

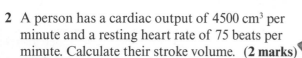

Always show your working. This means the examiner can still give you credit for the right method even if your maths is wrong.

Extended response – Exchange

There will be one or more 6 mark questions on your exam paper. For these questions, you will need to think scientifically, and structure your answer logically showing how the points you make are related to each other. You can revise the topics for this question, which is about **aerobic respiration** and **anaerobic respiration**, on pages 99 and 100.

Worked example

Athletes who run a marathon race usually keep their rate of running within their 'aerobic zone' for most of the race, but sprint anaerobically as they get close to the end of the race. Compare and contrast the use of aerobic and anaerobic respiration in marathon racing. **(6 marks)**

Aerobic respiration and anaerobic respiration both release energy from the break down of glucose. This energy can be transferred to muscle cells so that they can contract. Aerobic respiration requires oxygen from the air and produces carbon dioxide and water. Anaerobic respiration in muscle cells needs no oxygen and produces lactic acid.

In a long race, staying aerobic is important because more energy is released from each glucose molecule than in anaerobic respiration. This means the athlete has more energy for contracting muscle cells.

At the end of the race, aerobic respiration will not be able to supply extra energy for the sprint because there is a limit to how fast the heart and lungs can deliver oxygen to the muscle cells. So anaerobic respiration provides the extra energy needed for the sprint.

Command words: Compare and contrast

The answer to a **compare and contrast** question should identify similarities and differences between all the examples in the question. No conclusion needs to be drawn from the comparison.

This answer is well organised because it starts by identifying how aerobic and anaerobic respiration are similar, and then describes how they are different.

The question describes two stages of running, so the answer needs to describe what happens in both stages.

Remember that it is not a case of **either** aerobic **or** anaerobic respiration in human muscle cells. Aerobic respiration continues as fast as it can with the oxygen available, while anaerobic respiration provides the extra energy needed.

Now try this

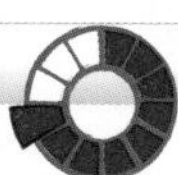

Explain how the lungs are adapted for their role in gas exchange. **(6 marks)**

Ecosystems and abiotic factors

Ecosystems are organised into different levels. At the level of **communities**, both **abiotic** (non-living) and **biotic** (living) factors can have an effect. You will look at abiotic factors on this page, and biotic factors on page 105.

Levels of organisation in an ecosystem

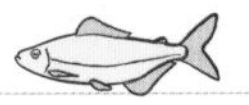

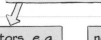

Organism is a single living individual.

Population is all the organisms of the same species in an area.

Community is all the populations in an area.

Ecosystem is all the living organisms (the community) and the non-living components in an area.

All organisms in an ecosystem are **dependent** on other organisms for food, shelter and so on. Remember to think about the impact of this in questions about ecosystems.

Factors that affect distribution

Factors in the environment affect living organisms and their **distribution** (how widely spread they are). Changes in these factors may change their distribution.

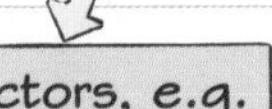

environmental factors

living factors, e.g.
- prey
- competitor
- predator

non-living factors, e.g.
- light
- average temperature
- average rainfall
- oxygen levels in water
- pollution

A change in average temperature or rainfall may change the distribution of organisms in an area.

Oxygen levels are high in unpolluted water and low in polluted water.

A **pollutant** is energy or a chemical substance that has a harmful effect on living organisms.

Changes in non-living factors can be measured using equipment, e.g. oxygen meter, thermometer, rainfall gauge. For example, temperature affects the rates of reactions and light intensity affects the rate of photosynthesis.

Worked example

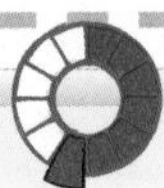

Nettle plants grow taller when they are under a large tree compared with those growing in open ground. Suggest a reason for this difference. **(2 marks)**

Under the tree, the light intensity is lower. Therefore, the plant grows taller so it has more leaves to trap available light.

There are other abiotic factors that you could suggest instead.

Now try this

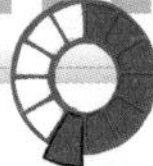

The pygmy shrew is Britain's smallest mammal. It weighs only 2.3 to 5 g and its length (head and body) is only 40–55 mm. It can only live in southern Britain because the rest of the country is too cold. Explain why the pygmy shrew cannot survive in cold places. **(2 marks)**

This question is asking you to apply principles you have learned (for example, about surface area and volume ratios) to an unfamiliar example.

Biotic factors

You have seen how abiotic factors can affect communities. So can **biotic factors**. Biotic factors are factors that involve living organisms, e.g. **competition** and **predation**.

Deterring predators

Many organisms are the food of other organisms. Some animals and plants have special features that deter **predators**.

Some animals advertise that they are poisonous with very bright colours.

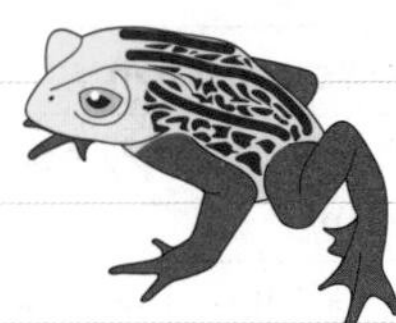

Some animals use colours to make them look more frightening, like these big 'eyes'.

Some plants have big thorns.

Other plants are poisonous.

Competition

Organisms need a supply of materials from their surroundings, and sometimes from other living organisms, so that they can survive and reproduce. This means there is **competition** between organisms for materials that are in limited supply.

... between plants

... between animals

Animals may compete with each other for:

- food
- mates for reproduction
- **territory** (space for feeding, reproduction and rearing young).

Worked example

You will be expected to know the factors that organisms are competing for in a real-life situation

(a) In spring, a male robin will sing loudly. Explain the role of singing in robins in terms of competition. **(2 marks)**

A male robin competes with other male robins for mates (females) and for territory. Singing loudly warns other males to keep out of the robin's territory and attracts females who choose to mate with him.

(b) The ground underneath the trees in a wood is mostly bare. Explain why very few plants can grow here. **(2 marks)**

There is very little light underneath the trees in a wood. Plants are unable to compete with the trees for the sunlight.

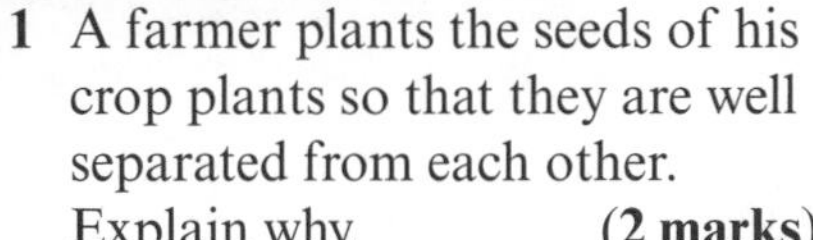

Now try this

1 A farmer plants the seeds of his crop plants so that they are well separated from each other. Explain why. **(2 marks)**

2 Milk snakes are non-poisonous snakes. Coral snakes are highly poisonous. Milk snakes that live in the same area as coral snakes have a bold red and black pattern that is similar to that of the coral snakes. Suggest the advantage to the milk snake of this patterning. **(2 marks)**

Remember to use technical vocabulary in your answer, for example, 'competition'.

Although you may be given an unfamiliar context like this you should be able to apply principles you already know to answer the question.

Parasitism and mutualism

Parasitism and **mutualism** are examples of **interdependence** where the survival of one species is closely linked with another species.

Parasitism

A **parasite** feeds on another organism (the **host**) while they are living together. This harms the host but benefits the parasite.

Parasite	Host	Description
flea (animal)	other animals, including humans	fleas feed by sucking the animal's blood after piercing its skin
head louse (animal)	humans	head lice feed by sucking blood after piercing the skin on the head
tapeworm (animal)	other animals, including humans	tapeworms live in the animal's intestine and absorb nutrients from the digested food in the intestine
mistletoe (plant)	trees, e.g. apple	mistletoe grows roots into the tree to absorb water and nutrients from the host

Mutualism

When two organisms live closely together in a way that benefits them both, they are called **mutualists**.

Remember to explain how **each** organism benefits in a mutualistic relationship.

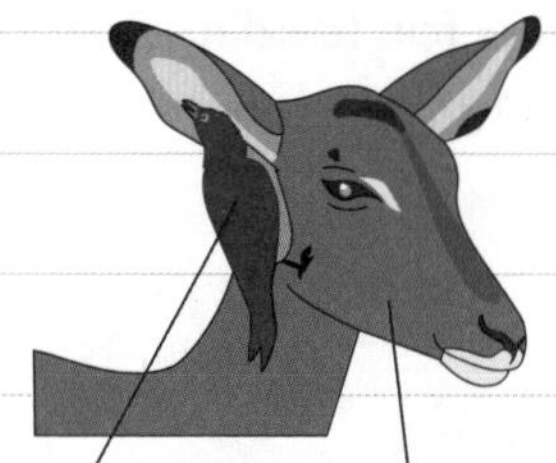

oxpecker bird benefits by getting food

herbivore benefits from loss of skin parasites

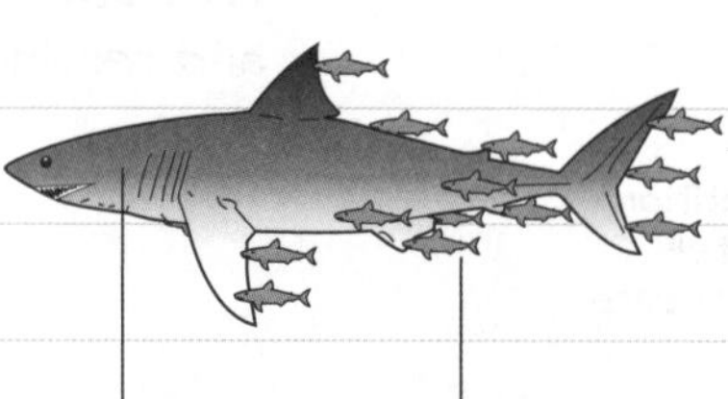

the larger fish benefits from loss of dead skin and parasites

cleaner fish benefit by getting food

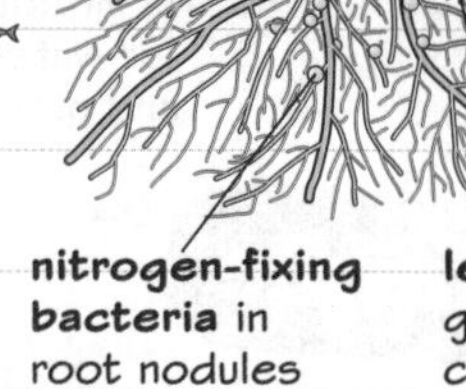

nitrogen-fixing bacteria in root nodules are protected from environment and get food from plant

legume plant gets nitrogen compounds for healthy growth from the bacteria

Worked example

A tapeworm is a parasite that lives in the intestines of mammals. Explain why it is classed as a parasite. **(3 marks)**

The tapeworm depends on the host for its food supply. It absorbs digested food from the host's intestines, so it benefits from the relationship. The host is harmed because it is losing some of the nutrients in the food it eats.

Remember mutualism is a '+ +' relationship as both organisms benefit. Parasitism is a '+ –' relationship because one organism benefits but the other one is harmed.

Now try this

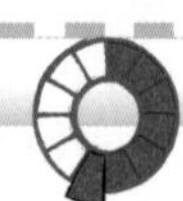

1 Define the term parasite. **(1 mark)**

2 Explain what is meant by mutualism. **(1 mark)**

3 Explain how the relationship between nitrogen-fixing bacteria and legumes is mutualistic. **(2 marks)**

Fieldwork techniques

The number of organisms in an area can be found using **fieldwork** techniques.

Sampling with quadrats

When studying organisms in the field, most areas are too large to count every individual organism. So we take **samples** and use them to draw conclusions about the whole area. Samples are often taken with square frames called **quadrats**.

- Quadrats are placed randomly in the area.
- The number of study organisms is counted in each quadrat.
- The number of organisms in the whole area is estimated using the equation:

number in whole area =

$$\text{mean number of organisms in one quadrat} \times \frac{\text{total area (m}^2\text{)}}{\text{area of one quadrat (m}^2\text{)}}$$

Belt transects

The effect of abiotic and biotic factors on where organisms live (their **distribution**) can be studied using **quadrats** placed along a **belt transect**.

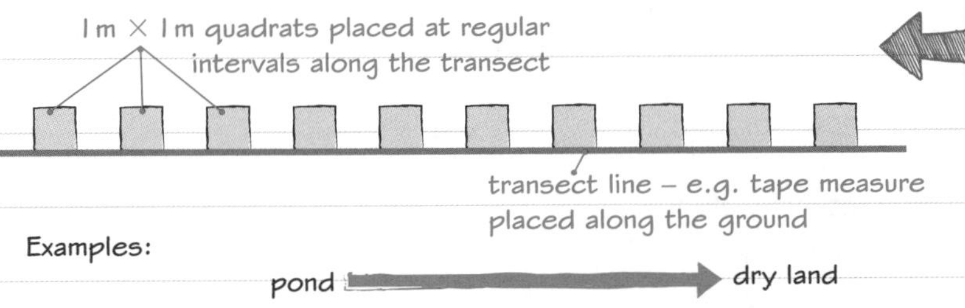

Choosing the number of quadrat samples to take is usually a trade-off – a trade-off between taking more samples (more accurate) and taking fewer samples (quicker).

Changes in **factors** (such as temperature, light intensity, trampling) are also recorded at each quadrat position. This makes it easier to link a change in distribution with a change in physical factor.

Worked example

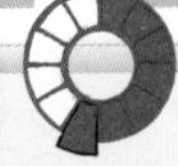

Ten 1 m^2 quadrats were placed randomly on a school field that was 100 m by 200 m. The number of daisies recorded in each quadrat was: 20, 6, 33, 0, 26, 21, 18, 7, 2, and 9. Estimate the total number of daisies on the field. **(3 marks)**

Mean number of plants per quadrat

$$= \frac{\text{total daises sampled}}{\text{number of quadrats}} = 14.2$$

$$\text{Estimated number of daisies} = \text{mean} \times \frac{\text{area of field}}{\text{area of quadrat}}$$

= 14.2 × (20 000/1) = 284 000 daisies

This is an estimate because if the quadrats were placed in different positions, the number sampled might be different.

Quadrats are only useful for sampling plants, or animals that do not move about much.

Maths skills To calculate the mean number of plants for one quadrat, divide the total number of plants by the number of quadrats.

Now try this

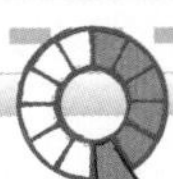

1 State when you would sample randomly with a quadrat. **(1 mark)**

2 Describe the situation in which you would choose to sample along a transect rather than sample randomly. **(1 mark)**

Organisms and their environment

Practical skills You can use **quadrats** and **belt transects** to investigate the relationship between organisms and their environment in the field. See page 107 for more information on these techniques.

Core practical

Aim

To investigate how the change in light intensity from inside a woodland to a nearby open meadow affects where cowslips grow.

Apparatus

- quadrat
- light meter
- long measuring tape

Method

1. Set out a measuring tape from inside the woodland out to the open meadow.
2. Take a quadrat sample at regular intervals.
3. At each quadrat sample, count the number of cowslips, and measure the light intensity.
4. Compare the number of plants with the light intensity along the transect to see how light affects where the plants live.

Random sampling will not help here because you need to sample organisms in relation to how the environmental factor changes.

An alternative to counting plants is estimating percentage coverage of the quadrat (e.g. 10%, 50%) by the species. This is useful if it is difficult to count individual plants, or if some plants are much bigger than others.

Results

The results were recorded in a table.

quadrat number	Q1	Q2	Q3	Q4	Q5
distance from woodland centre (m)	0	10	20	30	40
light intensity (lux)	2.3	2.1	3.5	9.5	13.5
number of cowslips	0	0	1	5	15

The results are displayed in this graph.

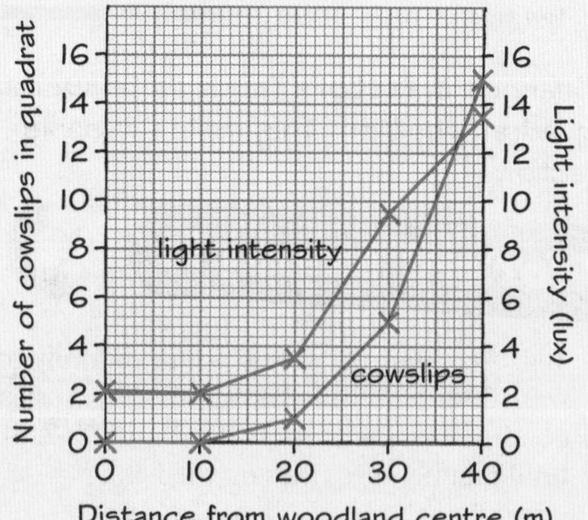

Conclusion

Cowslips seem to grow better in open meadow because the greater the light intensity the greater the number of cowslips.

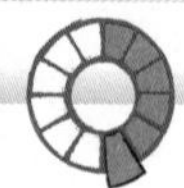

Repeating the transect several times and comparing the results for each transect would help to average out any random variation.

Now try this

In the woodland/meadow transect above, the number of primroses was also counted. The results were: Q1 2; Q2 4; Q3 7; Q4 1; Q5 0.

(a) Display these values, and the light intensity values, on one graph to show how they change over distance along the transect. **(2 marks)**

(b) Describe what your graph shows about the relationship between light intensity and number of primroses. **(2 marks)**

Energy transfer between trophic levels

Energy is stored in the biomass of an organism. This energy is transferred to the next **trophic level** by feeding.

Energy transfers

Not all the energy from one trophic level is stored as biomass in the next level. Some of it is transferred to the environment. Energy that is transferred as heating is less useful to organisms as it cannot be transferred as biomass again.

Trophic levels are the feeding levels in a food chain or food web.

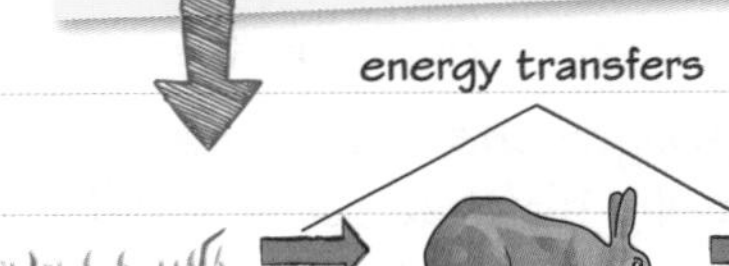

energy transferred to plant by light during photosynthesis

energy from respiration transferred to surroundings by heat

energy stored in new plant biomass which can be transferred to herbivores in their food

energy stored in biomass of food

energy from respiration transferred to surroundings by heat

energy stored in substances in faeces and urine

energy stored as new animal biomass which can be transferred to carnivores in their food

Pyramids of biomass

A **pyramid of biomass** is a diagram that shows the amount of biomass (usually as g/m²) at each trophic level in an ecosystem. The producer level is the bottom bar, and the other bars show the trophic levels in order.

The amount of biomass at each trophic level along the food chain gets smaller. This is because some energy at each level is transferred by heating the environment.

Food chains are usually no more than 4 or 5 trophic levels long because there is not enough biomass in the top level to provide the energy needed by another trophic level.

The food chain for this pyramid is: lettuce → caterpillar → thrush

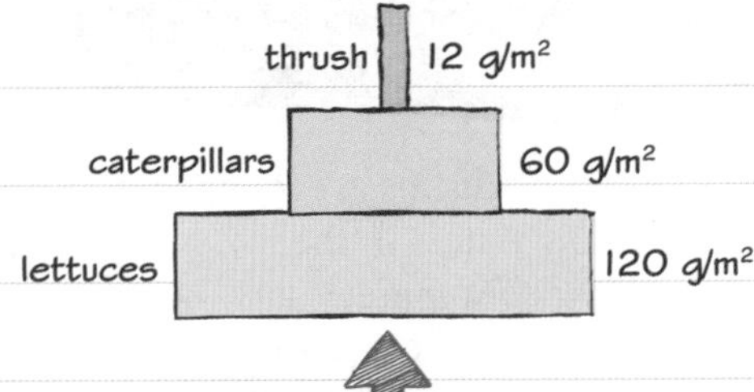

The biomass of an organism is the mass of its body tissue.

Worked example

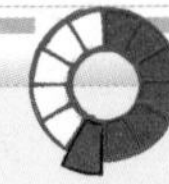

1900 kJ of energy from the Sun's light falls on a hectare of grass in a year. The energy stored in the biomass of the grass is 20 700 kJ. Find the percentage of the energy transferred by light to the plant's biomass as a result of photosynthesis. **(2 marks)**

$\frac{1900}{20700} \times 100 = 9.18\%$

Now try this

1 (a) Identify two ways that energy is transferred from an animal to the environment. **(2 marks)**
(b) Identify one way that energy is transferred to a plant from the environment. **(1 mark)**

2 It has been suggested that food chains in tropical rainforests contain more trophic levels than those in temperate areas (like the UK) because rainforests receive more energy transferred by light from the Sun. Explain the reasoning behind this suggestion. **(3 marks)**

Human effects on ecosystems

Humans have positive and negative effects on **biodiversity** in ecosystems. Biodiversity is the variety of living organisms in an area.

Fish farming

Fish farming involves growing one kind of fish in an area. The fish are fed and the waste they produce is removed from their tanks.

- The waste can pollute the local area, changing conditions so that some local species die out.
- Diseases from the farmed fish (such as lice) can spread to wild fish and kill them.
- Farming fish reduces fishing of wild fish.

Non-indigenous species

Non-indigenous species (organisms that are not found naturally in the area) may be introduced on purpose or accidentally to an area.

- They may reproduce rapidly as they have no natural predators in the new area.
- They may **out-compete** native species for food or other resources.
- They may provide food for native species.

Eutrophication

Fertilisers added to fields for crops may get into streams and rivers. This adds phosphates and nitrates to the water, which is called **eutrophication**. Eutrophication can lead to loss of biodiversity in nearby water.

Eutrophication causes water plants and algae to grow more quickly. → Plants and algae cover the water surface, and block light to deeper water. → Deeper plants cannot get light, so they die. → Bacteria decompose dying plants and take oxygen from the water. → There is not enough oxygen left in the water for fish, so they die.

Worked example

Unionid mussels are found in many waters in the USA. Zebra mussels are small freshwater mussels that are non-indigenous species introduced to this area in 1991. The graph shows the changes in population sizes of both kinds of mussel over a 20-year period in the Hudson River.

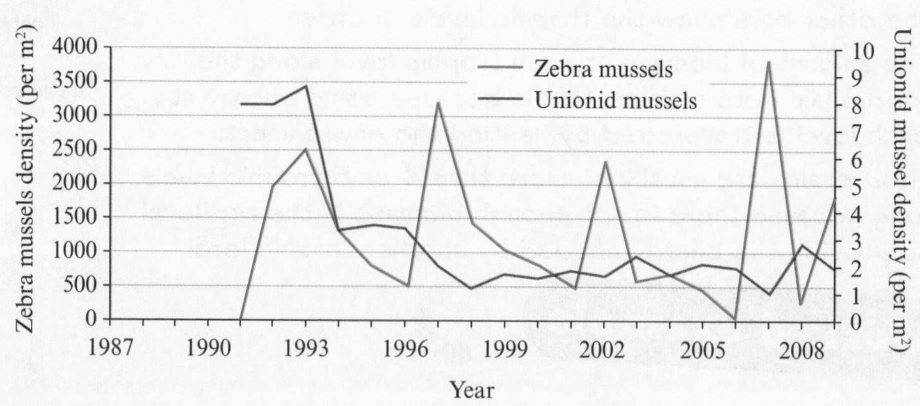

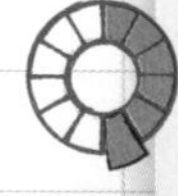

(a) Describe the changes in the unionid mussel population between 1991 and 2009. **(2 marks)**

The population falls rapidly until 1994 then more slowly until 1998. After this the population stays at approximately the same low level.

(b) The zebra mussels do not eat the unionid mussels. Suggest another reason why the zebra mussels have caused this reduction in the unionid mussel population. **(2 marks)**

They may outcompete the unionid mussels for a resource, such as food supply or breeding places.

Now try this

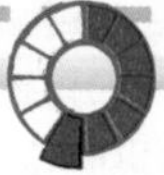

Focus on giving the stages that cause a decrease.

Explain how eutrophication can lead to a decrease in biodiversity. **(3 marks)**

Biodiversity

Maintaining **biodiversity** is very important, at both the **local** and **global** level, because many organisms have important roles in ecosystems and can be useful to humans.

Reasons for maintaining biodiversity

- Moral reasons: Humans should respect other living organisms.
- Aesthetic reasons: People enjoy seeing the variety of living organisms that live in different habitats.
- Ecosystem structure: Some organisms have an important role in ecosystems, such as microorganisms in decay processes and nutrient recycling. If this planet loses species, food chains become more unstable.
- Usefulness: Some species are particularly useful to humans, for example plants that produce life-saving drugs, or wild varieties of plants grown for crops (as a source of genes if the environment changes).

Reforestation

Reforestation is replanting forests where they have been destroyed, for example to create farmland.

Advantages include:

- ✓ Restores habitat for species that are endangered. Restoring rain forest, for example, helps to conserve many species.
- ✓ Reduces the concentration of carbon dioxide in the air as the trees photosynthesise.
- ✓ Tree roots bind the soil together and reduce the effects of soil erosion.
- ✓ Affects local climate, for example reducing the range of temperature variation.

Conservation is important so that we do not lose valuable species. We can conserve organisms by protecting their habitat, preventing poaching, or keeping insurance populations in zoos and seed banks.

Worked example

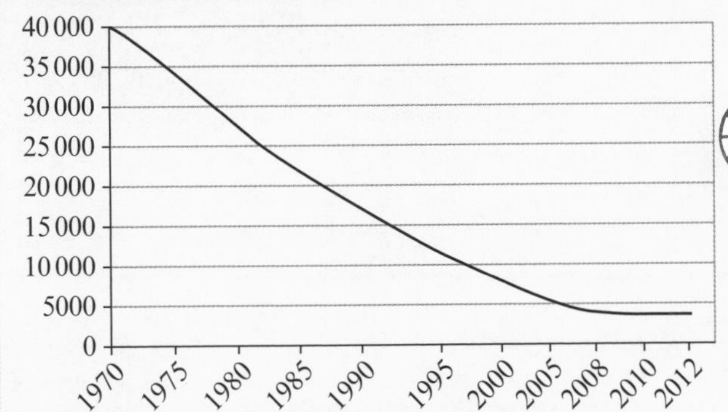

The graph shows the decline in the Asian tiger population.

(a) Calculate the percentage decrease in the population between 1970 and 2008. Show your working. **(2 marks)**

decrease = 40000 − 3500 = 36500

% decrease = (36500 ÷ 40000) × 100

= 91.25%

(b) During this time the human population in tiger regions has increased significantly. Explain how this could be linked to the decrease in tiger population. **(1 mark)**

The tigers' habitat might be being destroyed.

Another suggestion would be hunting by humans.

(c) Suggest why scientists monitor the populations of top predators such as the tiger very closely when they are assessing the biodiversity in an area. **(2 marks)**

If there are plenty of top predators, then there is plenty of energy being transferred through the food web in that ecosystem, which suggests high biodiversity.

Now try this

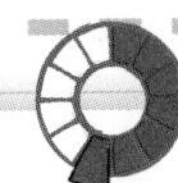

Farmers in the UK are encouraged to keep hedges around their fields. Explain how keeping hedges around fields can help maintain biodiversity. **(2 marks)**

Food security

Increasing human populations need greater **food security**. This means they need to have a reliable and adequate food supply. As people become better off, there is a greater demand for meat and fish.

Effects of increased food demand

Increasing **human population** means more food is needed. → The increasing demand for meat and fish means more land is used for **animal farming** and a greater impact on wild fish populations. → Movement of people and goods introduces new pests and pathogens to areas, damaging local crops and animals. → Increased waste is produced, causing more pollution.

As well as the demand for more food, human activity has had environmental impacts that could reduce the availability of land for food production, e.g. global warming, rising sea levels, increased desertification.

Worked example

Explain the factors that farmers need to consider when using pesticides and fertilisers to increase the yield of their crops. **(2 marks)**

First of all, the farmers need to work out whether the money they get from selling the extra crops will be more than the cost of the fertilisers and pesticides. Secondly, they need to consider whether the fertilisers and pesticides will cause pollution and damage the environment in the long run.

Sustainability means being able to take what you need to live now, without damaging the supply of resources in the future.

Worked example

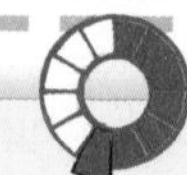

Growing crops to produce biofuels could be a way of reducing the use of fossil fuels and the pollution that this causes. However, some scientists think that growing biofuels is not sustainable. Explain why. **(3 marks)**

Although biofuels are renewable and do not contribute significantly to global warming, they use farmland that is needed to grow crops for food. It is possible that richer people will pay high prices for biofuels, meaning that farmers will grow biofuels instead of food crops. This could mean that poorer people cannot afford to buy food.

Now try this

Bluetongue is a viral disease of sheep and cattle that is spread by insects. It causes a serious illness and many infected animals die. It is usually found in southern Europe but has recently spread to the UK as shown in the map.

(a) Scientists think this may be related to climate change, and farmers are concerned about its impact. Suggest why. **(4 marks)**

(b) Suggest why newly introduced diseases like this are a particular problem. **(1 mark)**

Think about the information you are given here about climate change, the disease being spread by insects, and how the disease has spread. You need to use this information in your answer.

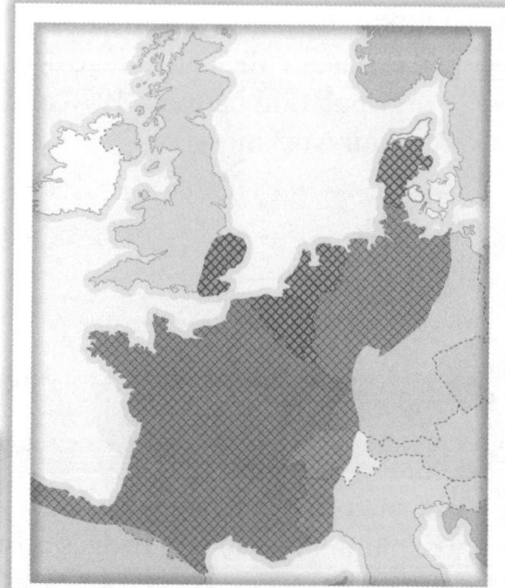

The carbon cycle

Living organisms need substances from the environment. As the amount of these on Earth is limited, they are recycled through both living (**biotic**) and non-living (**abiotic**) parts of the ecosystem. The **carbon cycle** shows how the element carbon passes between the environment and living organisms.

Controls of the carbon cycle

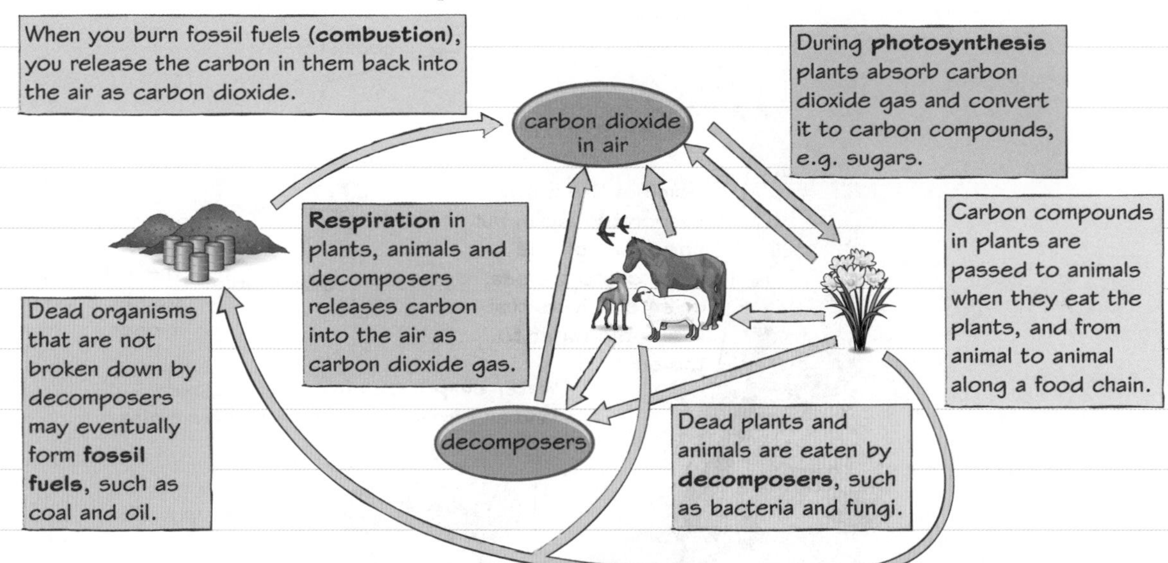

When you burn fossil fuels (**combustion**), you release the carbon in them back into the air as carbon dioxide.
carbon dioxide in air
During **photosynthesis** plants absorb carbon dioxide gas and convert it to carbon compounds, e.g. sugars.
Respiration in plants, animals and decomposers releases carbon into the air as carbon dioxide gas.
Carbon compounds in plants are passed to animals when they eat the plants, and from animal to animal along a food chain.
Dead organisms that are not broken down by decomposers may eventually form **fossil fuels**, such as coal and oil.
decomposers
Dead plants and animals are eaten by **decomposers**, such as bacteria and fungi.

In the air, carbon is part of carbon dioxide gas. In organisms, it is part of complex carbon compounds. The carbon cycle is important because it recycles carbon dioxide released in respiration to be taken in by plants in photosynthesis, to make organic molecules in living organisms.

Worked example

A large forest is cleared by burning. What effects will this have on the amount of carbon dioxide in the air (a) immediately, and (b) over a longer period? **(4 marks)**

(a) Large amounts of carbon dioxide will be released into the air by the burning (combustion) of the trees.

(b) Less carbon dioxide will be removed from the air than before because the trees would have used some for photosynthesis. So the amount of carbon dioxide in the air is likely to remain high.

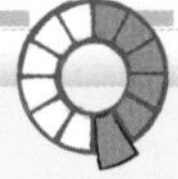

Two key processes in the carbon cycle are **respiration** and **photosynthesis**. These processes are important in maintaining oxygen and carbon dioxide concentrations in the air. Combustion can change this balance.

Remember that plants photosynthesise in the light but, like all other living organisms, they respire all the time.

Now try this

1 Describe the importance of decomposers in the carbon cycle. **(1 mark)**

Decomposers respire using dead plant and animal matter, releasing carbon dioxide into the atmosphere.

2 Explain the effect of respiration, photosynthesis and combustion in the carbon cycle in transferring carbon dioxide to and from the atmosphere. **(3 marks)**

In each case, explain whether these release carbon dioxide into the atmosphere, or remove it.

The water cycle

The **water cycle** describes how water moves between different parts of our planet.

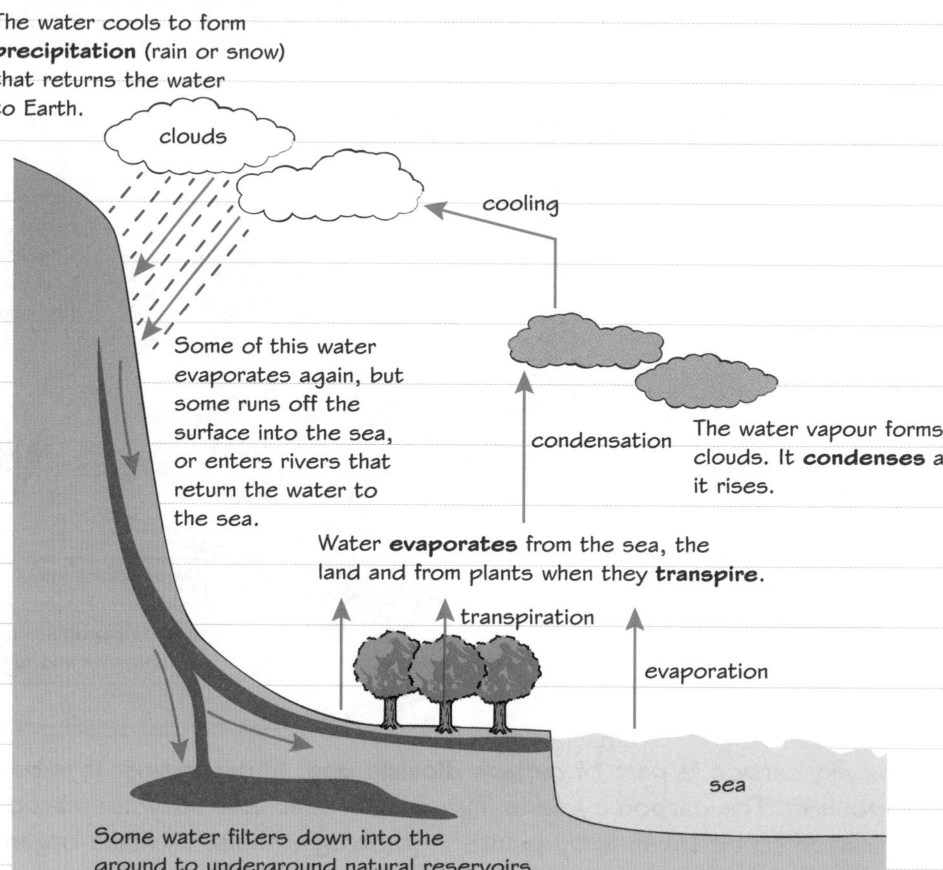

The water cools to form **precipitation** (rain or snow) that returns the water to Earth.
clouds
cooling
Some of this water evaporates again, but some runs off the surface into the sea, or enters rivers that return the water to the sea.
condensation
The water vapour forms clouds. It **condenses** as it rises.
Water **evaporates** from the sea, the land and from plants when they **transpire**.
transpiration
evaporation
sea
Some water filters down into the ground to underground natural reservoirs.

Desalination

Some areas of the world where it is hot and dry suffer **drought**. They do not get enough precipitation to use as their source of **potable** water (that is, fit to drink). If they are close to the sea, they can produce drinking water from salty water by **desalination**. One way to do this is **distillation**.

Worked example

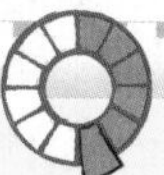

Explain how distillation can be used to produce potable water in a village that is close to the sea. **(4 marks)**

- Salty water is heated until the water evaporates, forming steam.
- The steam is condensed in another container to give pure water.
- The salt and other impurities are left behind in the salty water.
- If renewable energy, such as sunlight, is used this saves electricity costs and avoids pollution.

Now try this

You need to describe each stage in turn.

1 Describe the processes that take place in the water cycle. **(5 marks)**

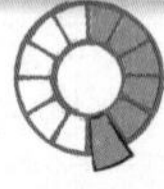

2 Suggest the effect on the water cycle of planting a large number of trees. **(3 marks)**

The nitrogen cycle

Plants need **nitrates** to grow well. They can get nitrates in several different ways, including through the **nitrogen cycle**.

Controls of the nitrogen cycle

A diagram of the **nitrogen cycle** shows how the element nitrogen moves between living organisms and the environment.

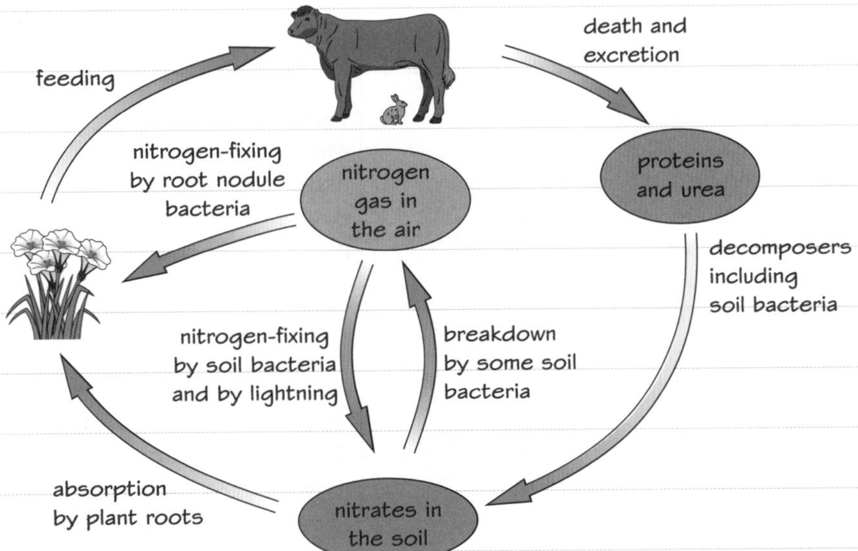

Worked example

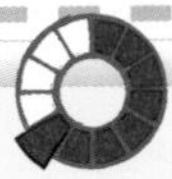

Plants grow well in fertile soil. Explain how bacteria help to keep soil fertile. **(4 marks)**

Plants need nitrogen for making proteins but they can only take in nitrogen in the form of nitrogen compounds such as nitrates. Soil bacteria act as decomposers, releasing ammonia from proteins in dead bodies and from urea. Bacteria in the soil make nitrates. Plants can then use the nitrates to make proteins. Nitrogen-fixing bacteria in the soil and roots of some plants convert nitrogen gas from the air into nitrogen compounds that the plant can use.

In the nitrogen cycle it is important to focus on the role of bacteria.

Fertilisers and crop rotation

Farmers add **nitrates** to crop plants in **fertiliser** to help the plants grow better.

Crop rotation means growing different crops each year, on a rotation basis. This improves soil fertility (the amount of nutrients in the soil) because:

- different crops remove different nutrients from the soil
- plants such as clover have nitrogen-fixing bacteria in their roots, and can be ploughed back into the soil, to add nitrates.

Now try this

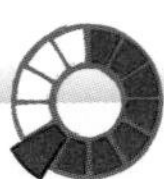

Explain why this could be an advantage to a farmer.

1 Explain why a farmer might decide one year to grow clover plants in a field instead of a crop. **(2 marks)**

2 Farmers plough crop stubble back into the soil after harvesting. Explain how this helps to improve soil fertility. **(4 marks)**

Pollution indicators

Indicator species are used to assess the levels of pollution.

Indicator species

Some species are well adapted to living in polluted conditions. Other species can only live where there is no pollution. The presence or absence of these **indicator species** can show us whether or not there is pollution. Changes in the **abundance** of these species can show changes in the level of pollution.

Indicators of air pollution	Indicators of water pollution
Some species of **lichen** can only grow where there is no pollution. Other species can grow where there is air pollution. So the species of lichen growing on trees can tell you if the air has been polluted. 	**Bloodworms** and **sludgeworms** can live in water that contains little oxygen. So they are found in polluted water. 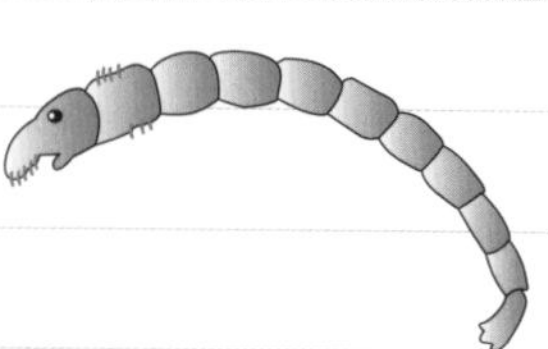
Blackspot is a fungus that infects roses. The fungus is damaged by sulfur dioxide in the air. So where there is air pollution, the roses are clear of the fungus. 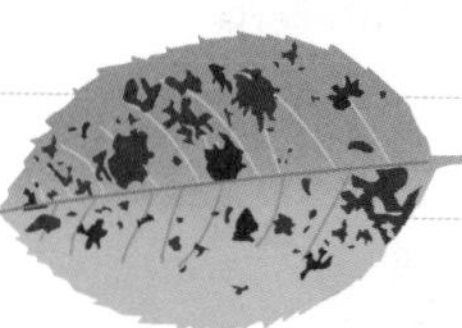	**Stonefly larvae** (young stonefly), some **mayflies** and **caddisflies** can only live in water that contains a lot of oxygen. So they are indicators of unpolluted water.

Worked example

The table shows the results of lichen surveys at the same place in two different years. Use the data in the table to suggest what happened to air quality between 1975 and 2010. **(3 marks)**

The numbers of lichens intolerant of high pollution increased by 2300% between 1975 and 2010, and the numbers of lichens tolerant of high pollution decreased by 37% during this time. These results suggest that the level of air pollution in this place decreased between 1975 and 2010.

Survey year	Number of lichens found on 5 trees	
	Lichens tolerant of high pollution	Lichens intolerant of high pollution
1975	35	1
2010	22	24

You will need to be able to draw a conclusion on the use of indicator species to assess the level of pollution from data.

For an evaluate question you need to give at least one argument 'for' as well as 'against'. Remember that indicator species numbers can change for reasons other than pollution.

Now try this

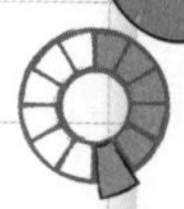

1 Describe how invertebrate animals are used as water pollution indicators. **(2 marks)**

2 Evaluate the use of indicator species as evidence of pollution. **(3 marks)**

Decay

Decay is the break down (digestion) of materials by microorganisms.

Controls of decay rate

The **rate** of decomposition is affected by:

- warm temperatures because this increases enzyme activity in microorganisms
- water content because microorganisms need water for many cell processes to work
- oxygen availability because many microorganisms need oxygen for respiration.

Preventing decay

Refrigerating food makes it last longer because the temperature is too cold for most microorganisms to grow quickly.

Salting food makes it last longer because it causes water to move out of bacterial cells by osmosis, so there is not enough water in the microorganism cells for them to grow.

Packing food in nitrogen makes it last longer because it means there is no oxygen for microorganisms to respire.

Recycling kitchen and garden waste

Garden and kitchen waste can be used to make **compost**, either in the garden or by council schemes. Conditions in the compost should be controlled to encourage the growth of decay microorganisms, which grow and digest faster in conditions that are: moist, warm and aerobic (oxygen present).

Worked example

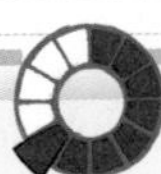

A student investigating decay set up three thermos flasks. One was filled with damp grass clippings, one with dry grass clippings, and one with damp grass clippings and disinfectant. All three thermos flasks were placed in the same room with no lids. The student weighed and recorded the proportion of clippings (in grams) that looked green on day 0 and day 6. The results are given in the table below.

Sample	Green clippings (g)		Rate of decay (g/day)
	Day 0	Day 6	
damp	50	5	7.5
dry	50	22	4.7
disinfectant	50	35	2.5

Complete the table by calculating the rate of decay for each sample. State which grass sample decayed most quickly and explain why. **(3 marks)**

The damp grass clippings decayed most quickly, as there was water and oxygen available, and the flask meant the temperature was warm. The dry clippings did not decay very fast as there was not enough water for microorganisms to grow. The grass with disinfectant did not decompose very much as the disinfectant killed the microorganisms.

There are different ways of measuring rate of decay (how quickly the material breaks down over time). You will be expected to calculate rate of decay from information given to you.

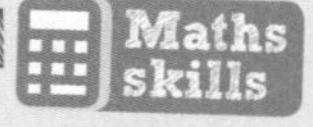

Remember:

$$\text{rate of decay} = \frac{\text{(loss of mass in grams)}}{\text{time in days}}$$

Now try this

1 Explain why compost heaps produce compost most quickly in sunny places. **(1 mark)**

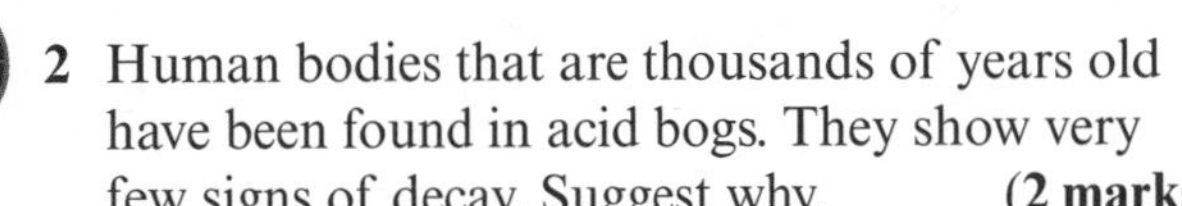

2 Human bodies that are thousands of years old have been found in acid bogs. They show very few signs of decay. Suggest why. **(2 marks)**

Extended response – Ecosystems and material cycles

There will be one or more 6 mark questions on your exam paper. For these questions, you will need to think scientifically, and structure your answer logically showing how the points you make are related to each other. You can revise the topics for this question, which is about **the impact of human interactions on ecosystems** and **plant uptake of nitrates**, on pages 110 and 115.

Worked example

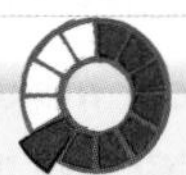

Explain why farmers are advised not to spread fertilisers on their crops when heavy rain is due. **(6 marks)**

Fertilisers contain nitrates and other mineral ions that plants need for healthy growth. Mineral ions in fertilisers dissolve in water, and are absorbed from the soil through plant roots.

If it rains heavily, then the mineral ions could be washed away from the crops and drain into nearby water, such as streams or rivers. This means that there will be fewer mineral ions for the crop plants so they will not grow so well. This will have been a waste of money for the farmer.

Extra mineral ions added to the streams and rivers will cause eutrophication. This will cause rapid growth of algae and water plants. The extra growth blocks light to organisms deeper in the water, meaning these organisms die, and takes oxygen from the water for respiration.

Bacteria that decompose dying plants and animals will also take oxygen from the water. If not enough oxygen is left in the water, fish and other animals may die and biodiversity may be reduced.

Remember the importance of mineral ions in plant growth when discussing fertilisers. This is a good way to start this answer.

Command word: Explain

In **explain** answers, make sure you give reasons for the statements you make. Use linking words like **because** or **this means that** to link cause and effect.

Use appropriate science words, such as eutrophication, in your answers, and make sure it is clear what you mean when you use them.

In questions about the environment, remember to consider how the interdependency of organisms, including microorganisms, can result in changes to biodiversity in the ecosystem.

Remember to consider the **advantages** and the **disadvantages** to ecosystems and biodiversity of fish farming.

Now try this

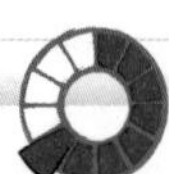

Wild salmon take up to five years to reach adult size. Farmed salmon are kept in conditions so they reach this size in less than two years. Explain the impact of fish farming on ecosystems. **(6 marks)**

Answers

Extended response questions

Answers to 6-mark questions are indicated with a star (*).

In your exam, your answers to 6-mark questions will be marked on how well you present and organise your response, not just on the scientific content. Your responses should contain most or all of the points given in the answers below, but you should also make sure that you show how the points link to each other, and structure your response in a clear and logical way.

1. Plant and animal cells

1 Muscle cells respire more; **(1)**, they need more ATP/energy; **(1)** they carry out (aerobic) respiration/produce ATP. **(1)**

2 The plant is supported by the cell wall around each cell **(1)** and the vacuole in each cell when it is full. **(1)**

3 Not all plant cells photosynthesise, e.g. root hair cells. **(1)** Cells that do not photosynthesise do not need chloroplasts. **(1)**

2. Different kinds of cell

1 Similarity – any one of the following: has cell membrane/cytoplasm/DNA/ribosomes **(1)**

Difference – any one of the following: no nucleus/no nuclear membrane/no mitochondria/has plasmid/has cell wall **(1)**

2 It has a long thin root hair/protrusion, **(1)** which increases the surface area for absorbing water/diffusion. **(1)**

3. Microscopes and magnification

1 magnification = 40 × 10 = ×400 **(1)**

image = 1.2 mm = 1200 μm so actual length of cell = 1200/400 = 3 μm **(1)**

4. Dealing with numbers

1 cell 0.1 millimetres (0.1 mm); chloroplast 2 micrometres (2 μm); protein molecule 10 nanometres (10 nm) all three correct **(2)**; two correct **(1)**

2 (a) 1.3×10^{-4} m **(1)**

(b) 130 micrometres (130 μm) **(1)**

3 approx. 1 μm **(1)**

5. Using a light microscope

1 (a) The description should cover the following points:

- place the lowest power objective below the eyepiece **(1)**
- place the slide on the microscope stage **(1)**
- use the coarse focusing wheel to focus the image **(1)**
- if needed, move a higher power objective into place and focus using the fine focusing wheel. **(1)**

(b) C

6. Drawing labelled diagrams

1 Drawing of one red blood cell and one white blood cell using all rules described **(3)**:

- clean sharp pencil lines
- drawn from photo
- correct relative sizes
- labelled to show nucleus and cytoplasm in white blood cell (no labelling expected on red blood cell)
- labels surrounding drawing with no overlapping label lines
- appropriate title with magnification.

7. Enzymes

1 The part of the enzyme molecule where the substrate binds/bonds/fits; **(1)** where the reaction takes place. **(1)**

2 This means that enzymes are always at their optimum temperature, **(1)** so that reactions occur at the fastest rate. **(1)**

8. pH and enzyme activity

1 (a) rate of reaction = $\frac{1}{80}$ = 0.013 cm^3/min **(1)**

(b) It took the least time for 10 cm^3 oxygen to be released, **(1)** so the rate of reaction was at its fastest. **(1)**

2 The values of pH used are much closer together than in the first experiment, **(1)** so the results should produce a more accurate value for the optimum pH. **(1)**

9. The importance of enzymes

1 The enzyme that digests lipids/lipase has a specific active site; **(1)** only lipids will fit in/proteins will not fit in. **(1)**

2 ribosomes **(1)**

10. Using reagents in food tests

1 The food contains no starch **(1)**, some reducing sugars **(1)**, no protein **(1)** and no fats **(1)**

11. Using calorimetry

1 (a) 500 × 4.2 × 2 = 4200 J **(2)** (1 mark for correct method but arithmetic error)

(b) 4200/200 = 21 J **(1)** (1 mark for incorrect answer from part (a) divided by 200 to give a correct answer)

12. Getting in and out of cells

1 Osmosis is the net movement of water molecules from a region of higher water concentration to a region of lower water concentration **(1)** across a partially permeable membrane. **(1)**

2 (a) Neither diffusion nor osmosis need energy. **(1)**

(b) One from: Diffusion does not need energy but active transport does need energy; **(1)** diffusion takes place down a concentration gradient, active transport takes place against a concentration gradient. **(1)**

3 The cells will still be able to absorb water **(1)** by osmosis because that is a passive process. **(1)** The cells will not be able to absorb mineral ions; **(1)** mineral ions are absorbed by active transport and that needs energy from respiration. **(1)**

13. Osmosis in potatoes

1 (a) Percentage changes in mass correctly calculated:

solution concentration (mol dm^{-3})	percentage change (%)
0.0	+22.0
0.2	−5.0
0.4	−8.0
0.6	−14.9
0.8	−24.1

(a) Four or five correct **(2)**; two or three correct **(1)**

(b) The solute concentration of the potato cells was just less than 0.2 mol dm^{-3}. **(1)** This is because at that concentration there would be no osmosis/net movement of water into or out of the potato cells, and so no gain or loss in mass. **(1)**

14. Extended response – Key concepts

*Answer could include the following points, to 6 marks:

Description of graph:

- As substrate concentration increases the activity of the enzyme increases.
- Reference to values at key points on the graph, e.g. activity fastest between about 75 and 85 mol dm^{-3}.
- Change in activity at different concentrations, as shown by steepness of curve.
- Change in activity is greatest where the graph line is steepest.
- Activity slows at higher substrate concentration.
- Curve flattens after about 125 mol dm^{-3}.

Explanation of graph:

- Starch is the substrate of amylase.
- At lower substrate concentration, there are many free active sites on enzyme molecules.
- At lower substrate concentration, adding more substrate means more substrate molecules can fit into free active sites and be broken down, so activity increases.
- At higher substrate concentration, most active sites of enzyme molecules are filled with substrate molecules.
- At higher substrate concentrations, adding more substrate does not increase activity because substrate molecules must wait till an active site becomes free.

15. Mitosis

1 They will be identical to the parent cell, **(1)** with the same number of chromosomes. **(1)**

16. Cell growth and differentiation

1 It stops mitosis at prophase/before metaphase, **(1)** therefore new cells are not formed. **(1)**

2 a cell that is adapted to carry out a specific function **(1)**

3 It allows cells to become specialised **(1)** so they can carry out a function more effectively. **(1)**

17. Growth and percentile charts

1 Any one from: measure its change in height over time, measure its change in mass over time, measure the change in number and size of leaves over time (or similar). **(1)** *The key point to mention is change over time*. If the measurements increase over time, then the plant is growing. **(1)**

2 A percentile chart compares the growth (or an aspect of growth e.g. length, body mass) of an individual **(1)** against the growth (of the same aspect) of other individuals of the same sex and age. **(1)**

3 The increase in size of a balloon is not a permanent increase in size, **(1)** while the increase in size of a child is a permanent increase in the number of cells in the child's body. **(1)**

18. Stem cells

1 Cutting the top off the shoot removes the meristem, **(1)** so the growing and dividing region is removed. **(1)**

2 Embryos have to be destroyed when the stem cells are removed; **(1)** some people think it is wrong to do this because they believe embryos have a right to life. **(1)**

3 (a) Either: they are easier to extract, or they can produce more different kinds of cell. **(1)**

(b) Adult stem cells from the patient will be recognised **(1)** but embryonic stem cells will not and the body will reject them. **(1)**

19. The brain and spinal cord

1 medulla oblongata; cerebral hemispheres; cerebellum; cerebral hemispheres (2 marks for 4 correct answers, 1 mark for 3 correct answers, 0 marks for 2 or fewer correct answers)

20. Treating damage and disease in the nervous system

1 brain is protected by bone **(1)**

difficult to operate/carry out surgery **(1)**

surgery/radiotherapy removes tumour, but damages healthy cells too **(1)**

blood–brain barrier, difficult for medicines to enter brain **(1)**

21. Neurones

1 Sensory neurones carry electrical impulses from receptor cells to the central nervous system. **(1)**

Motor neurones carry nerve impulses from the central nervous system to effectors. **(1)**

Relay neurones link other neurones together and make up the nervous tissue of the central nervous system. **(1)**

2 The long axon and dendron of the sensory neurone means the cell can collect impulses from receptor cells and carry them through the body to the central nervous system/spinal cord/brain. **(1)**

The myelin sheath insulates the neurone from surrounding neurones and helps the electrical impulse to travel faster. **(1)**

22. Responding to stimuli

1 receptor (in skin) → sensory neurone **(1)** → relay neurone (in spinal cord) **(1)** → motor neurone **(1)** → effector (muscle) **(1)**

2 Only one neurone produces neurotransmitter. **(1)**

There are only receptors for the neurotransmitter on the neurone receiving the impulse. **(1)**

23. The eye

1 (a) B **(1)**

(b) A **(1)**

2 Only rods functioning in dim light/cones cannot work in dim light; **(1)** Rods do not detect colour/only cones detect colour **(1)**.

3 Cornea refracts/bends light/helps to focus light; **(1)** lens focuses light on retina **(1)**.

24. Eye problems

1 all 3 types of cone stimulated equally **(1)**

2 more than one kind of cone stimulated; **(1)** red and green cones stimulated equally (note that second marking point on its own is awarded 2 marks)

3 The lens is less flexible, **(1)** so cannot be pulled thin enough/cannot be rounded enough/cannot focus accurately. **(1)**

25. Extended response – Cells and control

*Answer could include the following points, to 6 marks:

Benefits:

- embryonic stem cells (ESCs) are able to turn into many types of cell
- ESCs could be injected into the heart to develop into new specialised cells, or used to make new specialised cells in the lab before injecting them into the heart

- ESCs good for treating heart damage because several different types of specialised cell may be damaged
- replacing damaged cells will improve health of patient.

Risks:

- ESCs in the body may produce the wrong type of specialised cell in the wrong place
- ethical problems with using ESCs because they involve destruction of embryos
- ESCs may cause cancer if cell division is uncontrolled
- new specialised cells may be rejected by immune system as they are not originally from the body
- to avoid rejection, patient would need to take drugs for life, which is expensive and may produce harmful side effects.

26. Asexual and sexual reproduction

1 B **(1)**

2 At least some are likely to survive if environment changes, **(1)** because offspring show variation. **(1)**

27. Meiosis

1 four cells produced; **(1)** haploid; **(1)** genetically different **(1)**

2 Meiosis reduces the chromosome number to half the diploid number; **(1)** during fertilisation two gametes fuse, so the zygote has the full diploid number; **(1)** if meiosis did not happen before fertilisation, the number of sets of chromosomes in the zygote would double each time. **(1)** *Another possible answer is that mixing of genes is important for variety in offspring.*

3 Haploid = one set of chromosomes; **(1)** diploid = two sets of chromosomes/chromosomes are in pairs **(1)**

4 B **(1)**

28. DNA

1 Any suitable sentences that give appropriate definitions, such as: (a) a gene is a short section of DNA that codes for a specific protein; **(1)** (b) there are four bases in DNA: A, T, C and G. **(1)**

2 GCTA **(1)**; because A pairs with T and C pairs with G **(1)**

3 DNA forms a double helix structure, **(1)** which consists of two strands coiled together **(1)** and held together by the weak hydrogen bonds **(1)** that link the complementary base pairs of A and T or C and G. **(1)**

29. Protein synthesis

1 transcription, **(1)** translation **(1)**

2 (a) mRNA copies the base order from one strand of the DNA. **(1)**

(b) tRNA brings amino acids to the ribosome. **(1)**

3 The order of the bases on the DNA strand is the template for the order of the bases on the mRNA; **(1)** the base order on the mRNA strand determines which tRNA molecules join in and in which order, **(1)** and this fixes the order that the amino acids are joined in the polypeptide. **(1)**

30. Gregor Mendel

1 Nobody knew about DNA and genes at this time. **(1)**

2 To make sure the results were reliable. **(1)**

31. Genetic terms

1 A chromosome is a long strand of DNA. **(1)**
A gene is a small section of a chromosome/DNA that gives the instructions for producing a particular characteristic. **(1)**
An allele is an alternative form of a gene. **(1)**

2 (a) It is heterozygous **(1)** because it has one dominant and one recessive allele. **(1)**

(b) Purple flowers **(1)**, because purple is dominant over white. **(1)** *Remember that phenotype is what it looks like, so writing down the alleles would give you no marks for this question.*

32. Monohybrid inheritance

1 (a) genetic diagram or Punnett square showing this information (any appropriate letter used):

		parent genotype Bb	
	parent gametes	B	b
parent genotype bb	b	Bb brown	bb black
	b	Bb brown	bb black

(1 mark for setting out the parent genotypes and gametes correctly, 1 mark for completing the offspring genotypes and phenotypes correctly)

The predicted outcome of phenotypes is 50% chance of brown and 50% chance of black (could also be presented as a ratio 1 : 1, or probability 1 in 2 for both colours). **(1)**

(b) The actual outcome is different to the predicted outcome because we would expect 2 black and 2 brown baby rabbits but we ended up with all black. **(1)**
This is because at fertilisation it is chance which alleles are inherited. **(1)**

33. Family pedigrees

1 (a) heterozygous/Tt (other letters allowed) **(1)**

(b) genetic diagram or Punnett square showing offspring of Tt × tt; **(1)** 50% or 0.5 **(1)**

34. Sex determination

1 A **(1)**

2 chance is 50%; **(1)** diagram or Punnett square as shown on page 34 (1 mark for parent phenotype, 1 for gametes, 1 for possible outcomes)

3 There is always an X from the mother **(1)** because women are all XX and can only pass on an X chromosome. **(1)**

35. Inherited characteristics

1 Group A is determined by two copies of the I^A allele, or I^A alongside I^O. **(1)** Group B is determined by two copies of the I^B allele or I^B alongside I^O. **(1)** Group AB is determined by both I^A and I^B. **(1)**

36. Variation and mutation

1 Identical twins have the same genes because they come from the same fertilised egg, so characteristics controlled by genes will be the same. **(1)** Any characteristics affected by the environment may be different between the twins because different things may happen to them as they grow up. **(1)**

2 Most body cells will not contain the new allele. **(1)** Most body cells do not divide so they will not produce new cells containing the new allele. **(1)**

37. The Human Genome Project

1 Advantage: person can lead a healthy lifestyle/named precaution e.g. do not smoke to reduce the chances of high blood pressure developing **(1)**

Disadvantage: may depress person since there is no certainty high blood pressure will occur/ person could be discriminated against in some kinds of employment/insurance **(1)**

2 They have the same genes but different alleles, **(1)** therefore a different sequence of bases in their DNA. **(1)**

38. Extended response – Genetics

*Answer could include the following points, to 6 marks:

- it is a sex-linked genetic disorder
- the gene is found on the X chromosome but not on the Y chromosome which is shorter and missing some genes
- a man inherits the faulty allele on the X chromosome from his mother
- as there is no allele to match on the Y chromosome from his father, a man with the faulty allele on his X chromosome will develop the disorder
- the faulty allele is recessive to the healthy allele because heterozygous women do not develop the disorder
- only women who inherit two faulty alleles will develop the disorder
- the chance of a woman inheriting two faulty alleles is much less than a man inheriting one faulty allele
- a woman who is heterozygous for this gene is a carrier for the disorder.

39. Evolution

1 Mutation occurs conferring resistance. **(1)** Lice with mutant allele survives longer/ non-resistant die. **(1)**
(Resistant) Lice pass on allele to offspring. **(1)** Allele frequency of new allele/resistant allele increases. **(1)**

40. Human evolution

1 Any two suitable features for 1 mark each, such as: increase in brain size, increase in height, upright posture and ability to walk over long distances. **(2)**

2 An increase in the complexity of the way the tools are made and in the range of tools produced **(1)** suggests that humans were developing in intelligence/skill OR suggests that humans developed their skills of tool-making as the skills were passed from generation to generation. **(1)**

41. Classification

1 3 domains are: Eubacteria; **(1)** Eukaryota (including plants, animals, fungi, protists); **(1)** Archaea (mainly bacteria living in hot/salty conditions) **(1)**

2 Research on genes/DNA; **(1)**
Shows prokaryotes/bacteria need to be split into 2 groups; **(1)** some bacteria/archaea have genes that work more like eukaryotes. **(1)** (max 2)

42. Selective breeding

1 Advantage: get crop plants/animals with higher yield/more meat/disease resistance etc. **(1)**
Disadvantage: you breed closely related organisms so they show less genetic diversity/may show genetic defects
OR
may inherit a good characteristic but also less desirable characteristics
OR
many offspring do not inherit the desired characteristics **(1)**

2 Natural selection occurs by chance and involves survival of organisms with a more advantageous phenotype. **(1)**
Selective breeding is carried out with a specific aim or result in mind. **(1)**

3 little genetic variation in the population; **(1)** so if a new disease appears, it might spread very easily. **(1)**

43. Genetic engineering

1 transferring a gene from one organism to another/inserting new genes into an organism/modifying the genome of an organism, **(1)** so the desired characteristic is produced in the organism/so that the organism has a new characteristic **(1)**

2 The gene for herbicide resistance is put into some plant cells. **(1)** The cells are treated/grown by tissue culture so they develop into new plants. **(1)**

3 (a) It makes it easier to see which mice have the human disease gene in their cells. **(1)**
(b) The gene for the disease is cut out of a human chromosome and joined to a glow gene from a jellyfish **(1)**. The combined genes are mixed with early mouse embryos so that the genes are taken into the cell nuclei and joined to the chromosomes. **(1)**

44. Tissue culture

1 They all come from the same parent plant. **(1)**
Every cell contains the same DNA. **(1)**

2 Take a small piece of cauliflower and place on agar containing nutrients and plant hormones; **(1)** when plantlets grow put them into compost to grow bigger. **(1)**

45. Stages in genetic engineering

1 Human gene cut out of human DNA using restriction enzymes that leave sticky ends on the gene; **(1)** plasmid removed from bacterium and cut open using same restriction enzymes that produce matching sticky ends; **(1)** human gene and plasmid mixed with DNA ligase enzyme that joins the sticky ends together to make recombinant plasmid; **(1)** recombinant plasmid inserted into another bacterium where it makes the human insulin. **(1)**

2 The bacteria can be grown in ideal conditions in large fermenters **(1)** so that they produce large quantities of insulin quickly and cheaply. **(1)**

3 (a) Mice that glow will also have the disease gene (so scientists can easily tell which mice have the disease gene) **(1)** (b) Breed from glow mice **(1)**; breed from their offspring that glow in blue light **(1)**

46. Insect-resistant plants

1 Seed for the transgenic plants costs more than seed for non-transgenic plants so farmers are less likely to be able to afford it. **(1)**

2 gene for Bt toxin cut out of *Bacillus thuringiensis* bacterium; **(1)** gene inserted into plasmid from *Agrobacterium tumefaciens*; **(1)** plasmid inserted into another *A. tumefaciens*; **(1)** bacterium infects cells in leaf discs from wheat plant; **(1)** sections of the leaf discs are used to grow whole plants in which all cells have the gene for Bt toxin **(1)**

3 Any three from: insect-resistant plants kill only the insects that eat them and not other insects; **(1)** chemical insecticides often kill many species of insect, not just the pest species; **(1)** so there will be fewer predators of insects, such as birds like robins; **(1)** therefore chemical insecticides are more likely to damage food webs, such as reducing the number of birds that eat insects, and could reduce the numbers of predators that feed on the birds. **(1)** *For the last mark, you should give some detail of how the food web may be damaged.*

47. Meeting population needs

1 Advantage: increases crop yield/less bulky to transport than manure **(1)**
Disadvantage: can cause eutrophication/expensive to produce **(1)**

2 uses natural predator/parasite or disease of pest **(1)** which keeps pest population low, **(1)** so less crop lost to pest/increases crop yield **(1)**

48. Extended response – Genetic modification

*Answer could include the following points, to 6 marks:

- extraction of the Bt toxin gene from the bacterium using restriction enzymes
- inserting the Bt toxin gene into a vector that can get it into plant cells
- using the vector to insert the Bt toxin gene into the nucleus of wheat plant cells
- using ligase enzyme to join the Bt toxin gene to the wheat DNA
- making sure that the wheat cells produce the Bt toxin before growing them into plants
- all the cells of the plant will produce the toxin because they all have the gene in their nucleus
- possible use of tissue culture to make many GM wheat plants rapidly.

49. Health and disease

1 non-communicable because it is not caused by a pathogen; **(1)**
blood clots are not spread from one person to another **(1)**

2 spreads rapidly at first because people are susceptible; **(1)** people then develop immunity so fewer susceptible people **(1)**

50. Common infections

1 (a) HIV or Ebola **(1)**
two suitable signs for each, e.g.
(HIV) no signs/symptoms for a long time; flu-like symptoms on first infection; many repeated infections as immune system stops working **(1)**
OR
(Ebola) diarrhoea; muscle pain; severe headache; internal and external bleeding; vomiting; fever **(1)**
(b) malaria **(1)**
two suitable signs, e.g. fever; weakness; sweating and chills **(1)**
(c) Chalara **(1)**
two suitable signs, e.g. leaf loss; bark lesions/damage; dieback from top of tree **(1)**

51. How pathogens spread

1 The mosquito is a vector because it infects the human with the parasite/pathogen. **(1)**
Plasmodium/the protist is the pathogen because this infects the cells and causes the disease/symptoms **(1)**

52. STIs

1 a sexually transmitted infection; **(1)**
spread by contact with sexual fluids/not using a condom during sexual intercourse **(1)**

2 The condom is a barrier between the man's skin and his partner's sexual fluids, **(1)** so pathogens that cause STIs cannot reach the man's skin **(1)**

53. Human defences

1 unbroken skin/mucus in breathing system; **(1)**
lysozyme in mucus/saliva/tears OR hydrochloric acid in stomach **(1)**

2 This stops pathogens infecting the skin. **(1)**
The burn has damaged the outer layer of cells so pathogens can enter the body easily. **(1)**

54. The immune system

1 Three from: The pathogen has an antigen on its surface (that is unique to it); **(1)**
a lymphocyte with an antibody that fits the antigen is activated; **(1)**
this lymphocyte divides repeatedly; **(1)**
and secretes antibodies that destroy the pathogen. **(1)**

55. Immunisation

1 A vaccine contains a dead or harmless form of a pathogen or antigenic material that is used to immunise a person. **(1)** Immunisation means giving a vaccine to cause an immune response in the body. **(1)**

2 Any two from: Infection can only be transmitted from an infected individual to an uninfected individual; **(1)** vaccinated people are immune and so cannot become infected; **(1)** if most people are immune, the chances of an unvaccinated person meeting an infected person are very small. **(1)**

56. Treating infections

1 Antibiotics only kill bacteria/do not destroy viruses. **(1)**

2 antibiotic cannot bind to human ribosomes; **(1)** too big/cannot fit **(1)**

57. Aseptic techniques

1 blown in from the air; **(1)** transferred by touch; **(1)** in the culture media/on the equipment **(1)**

2 The Petri dish and the growth medium must be sterilised before use **(1)**. The inoculating loop must be sterilised by passing it through a flame and allowing it to cool. **(1)** The loop is then dipped into the bacterial culture and used to inoculate the growth medium in the Petri dish, keeping the dish as well covered as possible to reduce contamination. **(1)** After the plant extract is added, the lid of the dish is secured with adhesive tape to prevent contamination from the air. **(1)**

58. Investigating microbial cultures

1 (a) neem 177 mm^2 **(1)**
oregano 227 mm^2 **(1)**
lemongrass 19.6 mm^2 **(1)**
thyme 78.6 mm^2 **(1)**
(b) bar chart showing plant extract on *x* axis against cross-sectional area on *y* axis **(1)** with points plotted correctly **(1)**
(c) In order of effectiveness in killing bacteria, from best to worst, the plant extracts are oregano, neem, thyme, lemongrass. **(1)**

59. New medicines

1 Two from: B may be cheaper; **(1)**
A may have side-effects; **(1)**
patient may be allergic to A; **(1)**
A may not be suitable for pregnant women; **(1)**
A may not be compatible with other drugs the patient is taking **(1)**

2 The benefit of using animals as models is that the drugs can be tested for safety without harming humans. **(1)** A problem with using animals as models for humans is that the drugs may not work in the same way in the animal as they would do in a human. **(1)** *(Other problems may be acceptable, e.g. many people are against the use of animals for testing.)*

60. Monoclonal antibodies

1 Cancer cells carry antigens that are not found on healthy cells; **(1)** monoclonal antibody binds only to this antigen. **(1)**

(Or the opposite – healthy cells do not have this antigen; **(1)** monoclonal antibodies cannot bind. **(1)**)

2 Normally cells that produce antibodies do not divide, so you cannot get large numbers of cells that produce the same antibodies; **(1)** cancer cells do divide but cannot produce antibodies; **(1)** a fusion of the two cells produces hybridoma cells that make the antibodies and that can divide to make more cells that produce the same antibodies. **(1)**

61. Non-communicable diseases

1 (a) So we can compare the different groups, **(1)** as different groups have different numbers of people in them. **(1)**

(b) (Yes) (no mark), two from:

risk of cancer much higher in people with *p16* mutation; **(1)**

use of figures from graph to support answer; **(1)**

but only gives data for two kinds of cancer/may not be true for all cancers **(1)**

62. Alcohol and smoking

1 (a) The more cigarettes smoked, the more likely a person is to die of coronary heart disease; **(1)**

The older a person is the more likely they are to die of coronary heart disease; **(1)**

(b) Smoking causes blood vessels to narrow, **(1)** increasing blood pressure (leading to CHD). **(1)**

63. Malnutrition and obesity

1 The study is a very large study and so the results are valid. **(1)** The study is only of American men, so the conclusion may not apply to other groups of people. **(1)** The conclusion does not distinguish between fit and unfit men who are not overweight, and these two groups may have differences in their risk factors for health that also cause some of the differences between fit and unfit overweight people. **(1)**

2 She has a BMI of 31 **(1)** and is obese. **(1)**

64. Cardiovascular disease

1 Two from:

there is always a risk that the person might not recover after the operation; **(1)**

surgery is expensive; **(1)**

may take time to recover after operation/risk of infection **(1)**

65. Plant defences

1 Two from: thick bark/cuticles which make it hard for pests/ pathogens to penetrate; **(1)** thick cellulose cell walls that are difficult for pathogens to break down; **(1)** spikes/thorns to deter pests from eating them **(1)**

2 Pests and pathogens damage plants; **(1)** if the plant produces chemicals that protect it against attack, then the plants will be able to produce more food and so grow more rapidly. **(1)**

3 C **(1)**

66. Plant diseases

1 soil sample can be tested to see if a soil factor is causing the symptoms; **(1)**

plant material allows scientists to see the symptoms; **(1)**

can examine plant material with microscope (to look for pathogens) **(1)**

67. Extended response – Health and disease

*Answer could include the following points, to 6 marks:

- MMR vaccine protects against infection by the three diseases
- many more children in 2004 than 1996 would not be immune to measles, mumps and rubella
- increased chance of catching the diseases if they come into contact with an infected person
- increased chance of suffering problems/complications or death from the diseases
- increased cost of treatment of children suffering diseases and of treating lifelong complications
- reduced herd immunity
- children who could not be immunised for health reasons would have increased risk of coming into contact with infected person.

68. Photosynthesis

1 Energy is taken in. **(1)**

Energy in the form of light is transferred to energy in the form of chemical (potential) energy in sugars. **(1)**

2 Plants carry out photosynthesis, **(1)** which uses energy transfered by light **(1)** to produce glucose **(1)** which can be converted into other food substances. **(1)**

69. Limiting factors

1 Something that limits the rate of photosynthesis **(1)** when it is at a low level. **(1)**

2 Photosynthesis produces oxygen. **(1)** The more rapidly oxygen is released, the faster the photosynthesis reactions must be happening. **(1)**

70. Light intensity

1 Carbon dioxide is taken in by plants when they photosynthesise. **(1)** Removing carbon dioxide from the solution will increase its pH. **(1)** The rate of change in pH will indicate the rate at which carbon dioxide is removed from the solution. **(1)**

2 Temperature also affects the rate of photosynthesis. **(1)** If temperature is not controlled, then it will change with distance and so confuse the results. **(1)**

3 The tube will act as a control **(1)** as it should show no change in pH as there will be no photosynthesis in the tube **(1)**.

71. Specialised plant cells

1 Two from: contain many mitochondria; **(1)** supply energy from respiration/ATP; **(1)** for active transport (of mineral ions) **(1)**

2 1 mark for feature and 1 mark for explanation, e.g.

Pits in side walls; for sideways movement of water/mineral ions.

No cell contents; so water flow not obstructed.

No end walls; so water flow not obstructed.

Thick walls made of lignin; so cell does not collapse/strength. (max. 6)

72. Transpiration

1 Movement of water through a plant **(1)** from roots to leaves. **(1)**

2 Four from: water enters root hair cell by osmosis; **(1)**
moves through plant via xylem; **(1)**
evaporates from leaf as water vapour; **(1)**
via stomata; **(1)**
draws water out of leaf cells/xylem **(1)**

3 On the surface the stomata could get blocked by water droplets; **(1)** this would reduce /prevent gas exchange/ transpiration. **(1)**

73. Translocation

1 From the phloem, **(1)** because dissolved sugars are transported around the plant in phloem. **(1)**

2 Sucrose is made in the leaves after photosynthesis. **(1)** In the spring and summer most of the sugars will be transported in phloem to the growing parts of the plant, such as the tips of shoots and roots. **(1)** In the autumn, less sucrose will transported to these growing parts and more will be transported to the potatoes for storage. **(1)**

3 xylem; **(1)** phloem **(1)**

74. Leaf adaptations

1 Two from: large surface area to absorb light for photosynthesis; **(1)**
large lower surface of leaf for gas exchange; **(1)**
thin for short diffusion pathway for gas exchange **(1)**

2 large surface area from which water can evaporate; **(1)**
stomata open for gas exchange which allows water to evaporate **(1)**

3 hotter in day/cooler at night; **(1)** this reduces water loss. **(1)**

75. Water uptake in plants

1 (a) $\pi r^2 d = 3.14 \times 0.5^2 \times 50 = 39.25\,mm^3$ **(1)**
Rate = $39.25/5 = 7.85\,mm^3/min$ **(1)**
(b) higher rate/faster, **(1)** because (increased temperature) increases rate of evaporation of water from leaf **(1)**
(c) all conditions kept the same except temperature; **(1)** one example is, e.g. air movement/light intensity **(1)**

76. Plant adaptations

1 (a) smaller surface area for evaporation of water; **(1)**
wax to reduce water loss/make leaf waterproof **(1)**
(b) reduces surface area, **(1)** for evaporation of water **(1)**
(c) stomata open at night/closed by day, **(1)** which reduces water loss **(1)**

77. Plant hormones

1 When a shoot gets light from one side auxin from the tip moves to the shaded side of the shoot. **(1)** This causes cells on the shaded side to grow longer than those on the light side **(1)**, so the shoot will curve as it grows so the tip is pointing to the light. **(1)**

2 Plant roots are positively gravitropic/grow downwards towards gravity. **(1)** Growing downwards increases the chance that the root will reach soil, which provides support, as well as water and nutrients in the soil. **(1)**

3 D **(1)**

78. Uses of plant hormones

1. Selective weedkillers kill weed plants but not the crop plants. **(1)** This means that the crop plants can get more water and minerals from the soil and so grow better/bigger/produce more food for us. **(1)** *It's not enough here to give just the effect of the weedkillers on the different plants. You also need to explain how this benefits the crop.*

2. Ripe bananas release a gas which acts as a ripening hormone on other fruit. **(1)**
Unripe bananas do not release this gas. **(1)**

79. Extended response – Plant structures and functions

*Answer could include the following points, to 6 marks:

- bubbles were of oxygen gas
- oxygen produced by photosynthesis
- rate of photosynthesis affected by temperature because increased temperature indicates molecules moving faster and more likely to react
- rate of photosynthesis affected by light intensity because higher light intensity means more energy is transferred from light to plant molecules so more reactions
- temperature and light intensity both increase during the day as the Sun gets higher in the sky and decrease as the Sun gets lower towards evening
- as temperature and light intensity increase, the rate of photosynthesis increases
- as temperature and light intensity decrease, the rate of photosynthesis decreases.

80. Hormones

1 a substance produced by an endocrine gland; **(1)**
travels in blood and affects target organ/cells **(1)**

2 Two from: Hormones are chemical; nerve impulses are electrical/ionic. **(1)**
Hormones travel in blood to all parts of the body; nerve impulses travel directly to the site of action. **(1)**
Nerve impulses usually only affect one organ; hormones may affect several organs. **(1)**
Nerve impulses short-lived; hormones usually last longer **(1)**

81. Adrenalin and thyroxine

1 (a) Two from the following for one mark: heart/ lungs/ liver/ blood vessels **(1)**
(b) speeds up heart rate/speeds up breathing rate/ increases blood glucose/increases blood pressure/constricts blood vessels **(1)**

2 stops heart rate increasing/keeps heart rate low; **(1)** so reduces stress on heart/reduces blood pressure **(1)**

3 thyroxine stimulates cellular respiration; **(1)**
use up more glucose so eat more; **(1)**
respiration releases heat therefore feel warmer **(1)**

82. The menstrual cycle

1 If the egg is fertilised the uterus lining is maintained; **(1)** so menstruation does not occur **(1)**

2 Contraceptive pills are very effective at preventing pregnancy, so that a couple can decide when they want to have children. **(1)** The pill has some positive side effects, such as reducing the risk of some cancers, and some negative effects, such as increasing the risk of thrombosis/blood clot. **(1)** As long as a woman does not smoke heavily and is not greatly overweight, then the benefit of controlling fertility outweighs the risk of side effects. **(1)**

83. Control of the menstrual cycle

1 (a) in the ovaries **(1)**
(b) in the pituitary gland **(1)**

2 fall in oestrogen and progesterone levels **(1)**

3 (a) thickening of uterus wall and triggering of LH release **(1)**
(b) thickening of uterus wall **(1)**
(c) stimulates growth and development of egg in ovary **(1)**
(d) triggers ovulation **(1)**

84. Assisted Reproductive Therapy

1 The woman is given fertility drugs that contain FSH, which makes eggs mature in her ovaries. **(1)** The drugs also contain LH, which stimulates mature eggs to be released. **(1)** The released eggs are collected and fertilised with sperm outside her body. **(1)** When the embryos have developed into tiny balls

of cells, one or two are placed in the woman's womb to develop until birth. **(1)**

2 clomifene stimulates FSH and LH; **(1)** FSH causes follicles to mature; **(1)** LH stimulates ovulation **(1)**

85. Homeostasis

1 Enzymes work fastest/are most active at a particular temperature. **(1)**
At lower or higher temperatures than this, they are not as active, so chemical reactions are not carried out as quickly as normal and this could cause harm to the body. **(1)**

2 If there is too much water in the body this means that more water is excreted in urine. **(1)** If there is not enough water then less water is excreted in the urine, helping to increase water levels again. **(1)** This is an example of negative feedback because the body works to restore the balance. **(1)**

86. Controlling body temperature

1 (a) They look pink because more blood is flowing near the surface of the skin as a result of vasodilation. **(1)** *Either more blood flowing near skin surface or vasodilation would get this mark, but it's useful to remember the link.*
(b) This increases the rate of transfer of heat energy from the body to the environment **(1)** and so reduces the body temperature. **(1)**

87. Blood glucose regulation

1 gland is pancreas, **(1)** target organ is liver **(1)**

2 A change in blood glucose causes mechanisms to act that bring about the opposite change, **(1)** so that blood glucose concentration is maintained within a small range. **(1)**

3 A **(1)**

88. Diabetes

1 More insulin is needed if a big meal is taken rather than a small meal. **(1)**
More insulin is needed if a meal contains a lot of sugar/carbohydrates. **(1)**
Less insulin is needed if the person is exercising/glucose used up in respiration **(1)**

2 There is evidence to suggest that obesity/being overweight is related to the risk of developing Type 2 diabetes. **(1)** As the number of people who are obese increases this means that the number of people with Type 2 diabetes is also likely to increase. **(1)** Controlling weight may help to prevent this. **(1)** However, it will not affect the number of people who develop Type 1 diabetes. **(1)** *Although there is no evidence that the proportion of people with Type 1 diabetes is changing much.*

89. The urinary system

1 kidney, ureter, bladder, urethra (2 marks for all in correct order, 1 mark for any three in correct order)

2 Body processes make waste products including urea; **(1)** if too much urea builds up in the blood, it becomes toxic, which will damage the body. **(1)**

90. The role of ADH

1 (a) produced in the pituitary gland **(1)** and acts on the kidneys **(1)**
(b) The organ whose function is changed by the hormone. **(1)**

2 after exercise **(1)** because water will have been lost from the body in sweat during exercise **(1)** and more ADH is secreted by the pituitary gland when blood water content is low **(1)**

3 (Beer contains alcohol so it inhibits production of ADH) so less water is reabsorbed by the kidneys; **(1)** more water is lost from the body/he becomes dehydrated/less water for sweat production. **(1)**

91. Kidney treatments

1 dialysis **(1)**, kidney transplant **(1)**

2 The blood flows in a tube with a partially permeable membrane **(1)** through dialysis fluid. **(1)** Dissolved substances in the fluid and the blood are exchanged. **(1)** The substances in the dialysis fluid are at the right concentrations to restore their normal levels in the blood. **(1)**

92. Extended response – Control and coordination

*Answer could include the following points, to 6 marks:

- blood glucose concentration rises after absorbing glucose from a digested meal
- blood glucose concentration falls as glucose is taken from blood by cells for respiration or storage
- as blood glucose concentration rises, cells in pancreas respond by releasing the hormone insulin into the blood
- insulin causes cells to take up more glucose
- liver and muscle cells store extra glucose as glycogen
- when blood glucose concentration falls too low, other cells in pancreas respond by releasing the hormone glucagon into the blood
- glucagon causes liver cells to break down glycogen to glucose and release glucose into blood
- blood glucose concentration kept within limits, which is homeostasis
- control of blood glucose concentration shows negative feedback as a change in one direction causes a change in the opposite direction to happen.

93. Exchanging materials

1 Lungs. **(1)** *There are other possible answers, e.g. small intestine, kidney, but you will be expected to know about the lungs.*

2 (Can rely on diffusion alone because) flatworm is very flat and thin; **(1)**
large surface area to volume ratio; **(1)**
every cell in the flatworm is close to the surface. **(1)**

94. Alveoli

1 Any one from: less oxygen/more carbon dioxide/more water **(1)**

2 more oxygen needed for respiration; **(1)** more carbon dioxide to breathe out **(1)**

3 maintains a concentration gradient; **(1)** larger surface area for exchange **(1)**

95. Rate of diffusion

1 The capillaries deliver blood that has high carbon-dioxide levels and low oxygen levels and take away blood that has high oxygen levels and low carbon-dioxide levels. **(1)** This means that there is always a concentration gradient between the blood and the air in the lungs. **(1)** Ventilation of the lungs replaces air with higher concentration of carbon dioxide and lower concentration of oxygen with air that has a higher concentration of oxygen and lower concentration of carbon dioxide. **(1)** These factors maintain a high concentration gradient between the body and air for the two gases. **(1)**

2 (a) The rate of diffusion would halve/decrease by a factor of 2 **(1)**
(b) The rate of diffusion would increase **(1)**

96. Blood

1 oxygen in red blood cells; **(1)** glucose in plasma **(1)** *You must say which substance is carried by each part of the blood. In an exam, you would not get marks for just saying 'red blood cells and plasma'.*

2 Some white blood cells surround and destroy pathogens. **(1)** Other white blood cells produce antibodies that destroy pathogens. **(1)**

3 Platelets respond to a break/wound in a blood vessel by triggering the blood clotting process. **(1)** The clot blocks the wound. **(1)** This prevents pathogens getting into the body. **(1)**

97. Blood vessels

1 (a) B **(1)**
(b) A **(1)**

2 Every body cell needs oxygen and glucose for respiration, and to get rid of waste products such as carbon dioxide. **(1)** If this does not happen quickly enough then the cell may be damaged. **(1)** Capillaries are the blood vessels that exchange substances with the body cells. **(1)**. A short distance for diffusion between a body cell and a capillary helps to make diffusion rapid. **(1)**

98. The heart

1 They prevent the blood flowing the wrong way in the heart. **(1)**

2 The right ventricle pumps blood to the lungs, which are not far away. **(1)** The left ventricle pumps blood out around the rest of the body, including as far as the toes and fingers. **(1)** So the left ventricle needs to pump with greater force than the right ventricle. **(1)**

99. Aerobic respiration

1 The break down of glucose to release energy **(1)** using oxygen. **(1)**

2 If pH or temperature vary too much, the rate of reaction will slow down or even stop. **(1)** This would rapidly lead to death because respiration provides the energy for essential processes in the body. **(1)**

100. Anaerobic respiration

1 It releases less oxygen per glucose molecule. **(1)**
It does not release enough energy for rapid activity. **(1)**

2 There will be a high concentration of lactic acid in the muscles after the vigorous exercise **(1)**, so more oxygen than normal is needed to oxidise the lactic acid to carbon dioxide and water. **(1)**

101. Rate of respiration

1 (a) Rate of oxygen uptake (cm^3/min) = volume absorbed in 20 min ÷ 20 **(1)**
5 °C: 0.03 cm^3/min
10 °C: 0.05 cm^3/min
15 °C: 0.085 cm^3/min
20 °C: 0.12 cm^3/min **(1)**
(b) suitable scales **(1)**; axes labels with quantity and unit **(1)**; axes points plotted accurately **(1)**; line or curve of best fit drawn **(1)**
(c) As temperature increases, the rate of oxygen uptake of the organisms increases **(1)**, which means that their rate of respiration increases **(1)**.

102. Changes in heart rate

1 As exercise level increases/gets more intense **(1)** the heart rate increases. **(1)** OR As exercise level reduces/gets easier **(1)** the heart rate decreases. **(1)** *It is not enough to say 'heart rate increases'. You need to link how heart rate changes as exercise level changes to get both marks.*

2 4500/75 = 60 cm^3
(2 marks for correct answer; 1 mark for correct method with arithmetic error)

3 Cardiac output is heart rate multiplied by stroke volume. **(1)** A trained athlete will have a similar cardiac output because their stroke volume is much larger. **(1)**

103. Extended response – Exchange

*Answer could include the following points, to 6 marks:

- gases exchanged by diffusion in the lungs
- diffusion of oxygen from the air in the lungs into the blood
- diffusion of carbon dioxide from the blood into air in the lungs
- alveoli create a very large surface area for exchange
- each alveolus closely associated with blood capillary
- rate of diffusion depends on area, so the larger the area the more rapid the exchange of gases
- large number of capillaries means large surface area for exchange
- thin walls of alveolus and blood capillary means short diffusion distance, which increases rate of exchange
- continuous blood flow and ventilation of lungs maintain steep concentration gradient which increases rate of diffusion.

104. Ecosystems and abiotic factors

1 large surface area to volume ratio, **(1)** so loses heat rapidly **(1)**

105. Biotic factors

1 so that the plants do not compete **(1)** for an environmental factor such as light/water/nutrients **(1)**

2 Predators of milk snakes may confuse them with the poisonous coral snakes **(1)** and avoid them because they know that coral snakes are poisonous. **(1)**

106. Parasitism and mutualism

1 A parasite is an organism that feeds on and causes harm to a host organism while living on or in the host. **(1)**

2 when two organisms both benefit from a close relationship **(1)**

3 The bacteria benefit from getting food from the plant and protection from the environment. **(1)** The plant benefits from getting nitrogen compounds/nitrates from the bacteria, which it needs to make proteins for healthy growth. **(1)**

107. Fieldwork techniques

1 to estimate population number/size **(1)**

2 When you want to study the effect of abiotic and biotic factors on where organisms live; **(1)** to link a change in distribution with a change in a physical factor. **(1)**

108. Organisms and their environment

1 (a) graph with axes as for graph shown in Core practical; with primrose data correctly substituted for cowslip data **(2)**
(1 mark for correct axes, 1 for accurately plotted points joined by straight lines)
(b) Primroses are more common where there is some light **(1)**, but not where there is a lot of light in the open meadow **(1)**.

109. Energy transfer between trophic levels

1 (a) as chemical energy in faeces and urine **(1)**
as heat energy from respiration **(1)**
(b) as light energy from sunlight **(1)**

2 If more energy enters the system as light energy converted to chemical energy by plants **(1)** then there will be more energy in every equivalent trophic level of a tropical food chain than in a temperate food chain. **(1)** So there may be enough energy in the tropical trophic level equivalent to the top temperate trophic level to support a higher trophic level, producing a longer food chain. **(1)**

110. Human effects on ecosystems

1 (growth of surface plants) blocks light so plants die; **(1)** increase in bacteria uses up oxygen; **(1)** fish and other animals die **(1)**

111. Biodiversity

1 One mark for a suitable effect of hedges on the environment, e.g. provides food/shelter/nesting places **(1)**; one mark for sensible consequence of this effect, e.g. more species of animals supported/more food chains possible/different species can reproduce **(1)**

112. Food security

1 (a) getting warmer; **(1)** insect can survive overwinter in UK/ insect breeds faster in warm weather; **(1)** more outbreaks of disease; **(1)** greater impact on food supply **(1)**

(b) animals have no immunity/resistance **(1)**

113. The carbon cycle

1 Decomposers release carbon back into the air as carbon dioxide from respiration. **(1)**

2 Respiration releases carbon from compounds in living organisms as carbon-dioxide gas into the air. **(1)** Photosynthesis takes carbon-dioxide gas from the air and converts it into carbon compounds in plants. **(1)** Combustion releases carbon from compounds in fossil fuels as carbon-dioxide gas into the air. **(1)**

114. The water cycle

1 water evaporates;
forms clouds;
condenses into precipitation/rain;
runs off land in rivers;
is taken up by plants;
filters through ground (max. 4);
then more evaporation and the cycle continues **(1)**

2 less water available in rivers; **(1)**
less precipitation; **(1)**
less water in rivers/aquifers/drier soil. **(1)**

115. The nitrogen cycle

1 clover roots contain nitrogen-fixing bacteria which means fewer nitrates removed from soil; **(1)**
adds nutrients to the soil when clover plants ploughed in. **(1)**

2 The stubble contains proteins. **(1)** Decomposers break down these proteins and release the nitrogen compounds as ammonia into the soil. **(1)** This makes the ammonia available to nitrifying bacteria, which convert it to nitrates. **(1)** Plants that grow in this soil later will be able to take in the nitrates and use them to make proteins, which they need for healthy growth. **(1)**

116. Pollution indicators

1 Some species of invertebrates are only found in unpolluted water and others only in highly polluted water. **(1)** So by looking at what species are in the water you can see how polluted it is. **(1)**

2 They are sensitive to pollution so useful indicators of unpolluted areas. **(1)**
If they are absent from an area there might be another reason. **(1)**
Measuring numbers over time can indicate changes in pollution. **(1)**

117. Decay

1 Warmth from the Sun will increase the rate of growth of microorganisms in the heap; **(1)** so they break down the materials in the heap faster. **(1)**

2 waterlogged so no oxygen available; **(1)**
acidic so enzymes/bacteria/microorganisms not active **(1)**

118. Extended response – Ecosystems and material cycles

*Answer could include the following points, to 6 marks:

- farmed fish specially bred for rapid growth
- farmed fish treated with antibiotics and other medicines to keep them healthy
- farmed fish supplied with plenty of food
- some of the food and medicines given to farmed fish get out into the environment
- mineral ions from food will encourage growth of water plants nearby which could change the environment
- medicines that kill organisms (e.g. parasites) could reduce biodiversity in the environment
- growing farmed fish reduces impact of fishing wild salmon so maintains biodiversity
- growing salmon provides food for growing human population.

Your own notes

Your own notes

Your own notes

Your own notes

Your own notes

Published by Pearson Education Limited, 80 Strand, London, WC2R 0RL.

www.pearsonschoolsandfecolleges.co.uk

Copies of official specifications for all Pearson qualifications may be found on the website: qualifications.pearson.com

Typeset and produced by Phoenix Photosetting
Illustrated by Phoenix Photosetting
Cover illustration by Miriam Sturdee

First published 2016

19
10 9 8 7 6

British Library Cataloguing in Publication Data
A catalogue record for this book is available from the British Library

ISBN 978 1 292 13171 9

Printed in Great Britain by Bell and Bain Ltd, Glasgow

Acknowledgements

The publishers are grateful to Nigel Saunders for his help and advice with this book.

The authors and publisher would like to thank the following individuals and organisations for permission to reproduce copyright material:

Photographs:
(Key: b-bottom; c-centre; l-left; r-right; t-top)

Bridgeman Art Library Ltd: Musee de Picardie, Amiens, France 40l, Musee des Antiquities Nationales, St. Germain-en-laye, France 40r; **Fotolia.com:** joris17 48; **Science Photo Library Ltd:** Herve Conge, ISM 6l, Steve Gschmeissner 6br

All other images © Pearson Education

Figures
Figure on page 62 from The incidence of liver disease and the mean ethanol consumption per person per year for different countries. Copyright © 2009 Molecular Diversity Preservation International, Basel, Switzerland. Relationship between Dietary Beef, Fat, and Pork and Alcoholic Cirrhosis by Francis Stephen Bridges; Figure on page 94 from Adult BMI graph, *Health Survey for England*: HSE 2013: Vol 1 Chapter 10: Adult Anthropomorphic Measures, Overweight and Obesity, NHS Digital; Figure on page 110 from Native Unionid and Zebra mussels, Cary Institute of Ecosystem Studies. Original material available at http://www.caryinstitute.org/discover-ecology Graph on page 67 is based on data from NHS Immunisation Statistics England 2013–14/ Figure 5: MMR coverage at 24 months; Source: COVER, Health and Social Care information Centre.

Notes from the publisher

1. In order to ensure that this resource offers high-quality support for the associated Pearson qualification, it has been through a review process by the awarding body. This process confirms that this resource fully covers the teaching and learning content of the specification or part of a specification at which it is aimed. It also confirms that it demonstrates an appropriate balance between the development of subject skills, knowledge and understanding, in addition to preparation for assessment.

Endorsement does not cover any guidance on assessment activities or processes (e.g. practice questions or advice on how to answer assessment questions), included in the resource nor does it prescribe any particular approach to the teaching or delivery of a related course.

While the publishers have made every attempt to ensure that advice on the qualification and its assessment is accurate, the official specification and associated assessment guidance materials are the only authoritative source of information and should always be referred to for definitive guidance.

Pearson examiners have not contributed to any sections in this resource relevant to examination papers for which they have responsibility.

Examiners will not use endorsed resources as a source of material for any assessment set by Pearson.

Endorsement of a resource does not mean that the resource is required to achieve this Pearson qualification, nor does it mean that it is the only suitable material available to support the qualification, and any resource lists produced by the awarding body shall include this and other appropriate resources.

2. Pearson has robust editorial processes, including answer and fact checks, to ensure the accuracy of the content in this publication, and every effort is made to ensure this publication is free of errors. We are, however, only human, and occasionally errors do occur. Pearson is not liable for any misunderstandings that arise as a result of errors in this publication, but it is our priority to ensure that the content is accurate. If you spot an error, please do contact us at resourcescorrections@pearson.com so we can make sure it is corrected.